John Montagu of Beaulieu

"A Southern Scott" — *Spy cartoon of John Montagu.*

JOHN MONTAGU OF BEAULIEU

1866-1929

Motoring Pioneer and Prophet

by Paul Tritton

With a Foreword by
HRH Prince Michael of Kent

Golden Eagle / George Hart
73 New Bond Street · London

ISBN 0 901482 32 3

Printed and bound in Great Britain for
Golden Eagle/George Hart
73 New Bond Street, London W1Y 9DD
by Biddles Ltd, Guildford and King's Lynn

Jacket design by Alan Downs

Contents

Foreword

by H.R.H. Prince Michael of Kent

In 1980 I took part in the RAC London-Brighton Run in a 1900 6hp Daimler. It was the most awkward and difficult car I have ever driven. Its least endearing characteristic was that one of the two spark plugs frequently oiled up, so that instead of 6hp, I was down to three. That is not enough to propel a car weighing one and a half tons, with four passengers, up even a gentle slope. So, at one point, I asked my passengers to alight when an uphill gradient presented itself. The car, now much lighter, accelerated up the hill, while my three hapless guests were forced to run along behind. I dared not stop to take them on board again.

That car had been ordered by my great-grandfather, King Edward VII, for use on the Sandringham estate, and is mentioned on page 57 (not the beaters' car — the other one).

John Montagu was instrumental in firing the King's enthusiasm in motoring and drawing his attention to the potential of motor cars to alter radically man's ability to get about and cover long distances rapidly. The account of their friendship has been well described.

The years 1903/4 were crucial in the development of the then Automobile Club, later to become the Royal Automobile Club, of which I am President today.

A leading part was played by John Montagu in forging the Club's future and the graphic account of his triumphs and disappointments in those years show just how entrenched were the views of the people involved, and how much the early cars were held in suspicion even by their so-called protagonists.

The subject of this book lived at a fascinating time in history and took advantage of every opportunity — a true pioneer who lived his life to the full. I have enjoyed reading about John Montagu immensely.

Michael

1

Mamma's Little Tory

John Walter Edward Montagu-Douglas-Scott was born in London on 10 June 1866 at his parents' home, 3 Tilney Street, Mayfair, a few minutes' walk from Hyde Park. He was the first son of Lord and Lady Henry Scott. His grandparents were the Duke and Duchess of Buccleuch and Lord and Lady Wharncliffe.

The child, who was eventually to pioneer travel on land, sea and in the air, would have woken to the rattling clatter of horse-drawn carriages, hansom cabs and trundling omnibuses, threading their way in and out of the bustling traffic. This was London during the heyday of the Victorian era when Britain was the workshop of the world and her material prosperity and her constitution were the envy of the lesser nations with whom she traded. Lord Derby was prime minister and Benjamin Disraeli was leader of the House of Commons; reform was in the air and those who demanded a widening of the franchise were breaching the railings along Park Lane, clambering over the gates and rallying in Hyde Park, six weeks after John's birth. It was a time of economic, political and technological progress when the nation was thrusting forward with immense verve and determination.

The crowded city was congested and dirty, frequently filled with fog and whirlwinds of dust. Every day thousands of tons of horse droppings splattered onto the roads and pavements, to be shovelled up by men and small boys, but change was on the way, for London was being reshaped and cleaned up. Work had already begun on building the Albert and Victoria embankments and in 1866 the Duke of Northumberland was doing his best to prevent the avenue that bears his name from sweeping through his land between Trafalgar Square and the Thames. On the very day that John was christened in Westminster Abbey, polluted water created a cholera epidemic which claimed 6000 lives before the year was out, thus forcing public-health officials to take action.

All the big cities were linked with London by railway lines which penetrated almost to the hub of the metropolis. Victoria Station had been built and work on St Pancras was about to start. The first section of the underground had been running for three years and £20,000 had just been authorized to research the possibility of building twin Channel tunnels to carry the South Eastern line from Folkestone to France.

The coming of the railways had made the long-distance stage-coach but a memory and the great turnpike roads which had been built for this romantic, if uncomfortable, mode of travel were sadly neglected. But in 1866 Aveling and Porter built their first steamroller and Britain's first concrete road had been laid. London streets were still paved with cobbles and wooden blocks but asphalt was to appear before long.

Countryside roads carried very little traffic but the first self-propelled road vehicles had been built, although the infamous Locomotives on Highways Act of 1865, known as the Red Flag Act, had stifled their development.

Steam driven vehicles of various kinds had been around since the 1850s when some of the shortcomings of earlier designs were overcome and there was a revival of interest in 'road steamers'. The promised renaissance was, however, sharply throttled back by the Red Flag Act, which set a road speed limit of 4 mph in open country and 2 mph in the towns. What is more it required all road locomotives to be attended by at least three people, one of whom had to walk not less than 60 yards ahead of the engine, bearing 'a red flag constantly displayed' by day and a red lantern at night. All this had the effect of killing any incentives in Britain for developing small steam vehicles and proper road transport. The roads remained dominated by hoof and hide for another generation and the railways continued to enjoy a monopoly in moving goods and people *en masse*. 'Speed and the Spirit of Progress', to quote from an ode to the road that John wrote 40 years later, went abroad; the first motor cars were built by Britain's new industrial competitors. The opportunity of pioneering yet another step forward in science and technology was missed and the names that became associated with the advent of 'automobilism' were Etienne Lenoir of Paris, who built the first car to have an internal combustion engine; Nicholas Otto, inventor of the four-stroke engine; and Gottlieb Daimler and Karl Benz, who first applied Otto's principles to the motor car and built the first successful petrol-driven cars. Britain was out of the race for the next ten years.

Progress in other branches of technology was less hampered. The telegram had for twenty years been the means of sending urgent messages between the major cities, and in the summer of 1866 the system went intercontinental when Brunel's huge paddle steamer the *Great Eastern*, newly converted as a cable ship, laid the first permanent telegraph link between Britain and North America. Whilst transatlantic telegraphy was revolutionizing the transmission and publication of news, Mahlon Loomis was flying kites in the Blue Ridge Mountains of Virginia. In July 1866 he published his ideas for sending and receiving radio messages.

Sailing ships still outnumbered steam ships by more than four to one but it was already recognized that steam would inevitably supersede sail. P & O was operating ten steamers powered by two-cylinder engines which needed 40 per cent less coal than earlier models and, in 1866, the triple expansion steam engine with three cylinders instead of two, was newly patented. More ominously the torpedo was also invented that year.

In the air, travel was still entirely at the whim of the wind. Occasionally Londoners might see a balloon drifting high overhead, the intrepid balloonist peering out from the rim of his basket, to see where he was being blown. But knowledge of air currents and cloud formations was growing and in 1866, John Glaisher, Superintendent of Meteorology at the Royal Observatory, made a series of ascents during which he reached a height of seven miles and learnt much about thermal currents and wind drift. In the same year, Wenham published his scientific paper *Aerial Locomotion* which inspired much of the research that eventually made sustained, controlled flight a reality. Only 17 days after John was born a group of pioneers met at the London home of the Duke of Argyll and formed the Aeronautical Society of Great Britain.

Such then was the travel scene on land, at sea and in the air when Lord and Lady Henry Scott were receiving the congratulations of their friends and family on the birth of their son and heir. There was unrestricted movement by rail to all the big cities; deserted and deteriorating highways; choked and soiled urban streets; the age of the motor car postponed in Britain but about to emerge on the Continent; sail giving way to steam, and aeronautics in its infancy.

It was a time of expansion and extravagance. Wages had been rising for ten years and the price of many commodities had fallen. A new urban middle class was being created and trade was flourishing. Queen Victoria's wayward eldest son, the Prince of Wales, married for just three years, had an annual income of £100,000. But the Duke of Buccleuch, owner of many estates in England and Scotland, received £500,000 a year. He obtained more in rents alone from his estates than everything that came the Prince's way from investments, estate revenues and grants.

One of the Buccleuch estates was the ancient Manor of Beaulieu which occupied nearly 10,000 acres in the south-east corner of the New Forest. In 1866 the Duke gave this estate to his second son Lord Henry on the occasion of his marriage to Lady Cecily Stuart-Wortley. Here John and later his brothers Robert and James Francis (who died at the age of thirteen months) and sister Rachel, enjoyed a happy and conventional childhood, in which their mother took a close and personal interest. The practice, common enough in Victorian times, of aristocratic mothers enduring their offspring's presence with feigned delight for an hour in the early evening, whilst leaving them out of sight and mind in their nanny's care for the rest of the day, was not part of Lord and Lady Henry's way of life. She went so far as to keep

John's parents, Lord and Lady Henry Scott.

John (far right) with (from L. to R.) his brother Robert, sister Rachel, father and mother.

detailed records of their health and progress which reveal that John was a strong, energetic baby, intelligent, observant but slow in learning to talk.

His mother, it appears, was more assertive and dominant than Lord Henry. 'A woman of strong personality and intellectual vigour' is how one friend of the family described her; traits inherited in no small measure by her son John. She also seems to have been the driving force behind Lord Henry's political activities. At the time of John's birth, he was Conservative Member of Parliament for Selkirk, the Buccleuch family borough, but two years later he began a sixteen year stint as the Member for South Hampshire, in which Beaulieu was situated. During this time Lady Henry played an active role in constituency affairs and became one of the organizers of the Primrose League, which was formed to spread Conservative principles and support 'the maintenance of religion, the estates of the realm and the imperial ascendancy of Great Britain'.

Portraits of Lord Henry suggest that he was a shy and introspective man and this is borne out by the impression held by the older tenants of Beaulieu Manor, several of whom remember their parents talking of him as a kind but rather aloof figure. He certainly lacked the bonhomie that was to be a characteristic of his son. Lord Henry served the Tory party loyally for many years but it is difficult to imagine him giving a scintillating performance on the hustings or attracting and creating the controversy that John was to generate and enjoy. John was to become Lord Henry's political heir, in addition to inheriting his estates and property, but he developed into a more democratic and progressive Conservative than his father. The political path he was expected to tread was laid out before him at a very early age, when Lady Henry taught him to call himself 'Mamma's Little Tory'. When he was only nine years of age she sent him this letter:

> My own dear little boy. How pleased you will have been to hear ... that Papa has won a great victory over the Radicals. Nine hundred and thirty-five more people voted for Papa than for the other candidate.

At this period of his life John could have taken only a polite and passing interest in his parents' political outlook and aspirations. He was happier learning to shoot, fish and sail at Beaulieu. Here acres of unspoilt countryside, a private, winding river and miles of marshy Solent shore were his to explore.

His first chance to obtain a real taste of travel by sea came in 1877, when his family was invited to join HMS *Hawk* at Hythe, near Southampton, for a cruise in the English Channel. Lady Henry and Robert left the ship at Yarmouth, on the Isle of Wight, but 11-year-old John remained on board with his father, who wanted to inspect the coastguards in the West Country. They endured a night passage down the English Channel during a gale that left them both seasick, but recovered by the time they landed at Plymouth, where they swam, fished and played cricket at Mount Edgcumbe, over-looking the Sound. Their cruise was completed by a visit to the Scilly Isles, after which they disembarked at Penzance and took a train home to Beaulieu.

Initially John taught himself to sail by sitting in a rowing boat holding a coachman's umbrella to catch the wind; he soon became sufficiently proficient to have a sailing boat of his own. When he was fifteen, he caused a hue and cry by climbing, unseen, from a window at Palace House and disappearing into the dawn with his friend John Crouch, the gamekeeper's son. Clutching packets of sandwiches, they made their way to Buckler's Hard on the Beaulieu River where John kept his boat, for they were intent on circum-navigating the Isle of Wight. It was eleven o'clock that night before they completed their seventy mile voyage. The adventure was a foolish one, in the sense that today not even the most experienced yachtsman sets off without telling someone where he is going, but successful because John had carefully studied the winds and tides when planning the adventure. His reason for not telling his parents of his intentions was probably that they would have forbidden him to attempt the voyage. His interest in sailing predated that which he later took in other forms of transport, and the reason for this is not difficult to understand. He also enjoyed steam trains and exulted in his journeys to London and to Scotland during family holidays on the Buccleuch's border estates.

Although he suffered few, if any, serious illnesses whilst a baby, John developed bronchial asthma in childhood and this was to plague him periodically for most of his life. His asthma attacks seldom deterred him from pursuing whatever particular venture he happened to be engaged in at the time, but when he first began to experience them they were distressing enough to persuade his parents to abandon his education at a local preparatory school. Instead, private tutors were engaged at Palace House until John was 14 when, by now more capable of coping with his illness, he went to Eton.

John was not a distinguished scholar but his tutor at Eton, Mr Marindin, recognized that he had other qualities which were to be as useful as academic achievements. Many years later, Marindin remembered him as a boy who was 'always straightforward, frank and rather bluff in manner; cheerful, and I should think generally popular'. He was, his teacher added, 'always well up in his regular work ... a useful and valued member of his house and an excellent captain of it, organizing and controlling others and encouraging a good and manly tone'.

During his five years at Eton, John became President of 'Pop' as well as captain of his house, and it is evident from his letters to his father that he found Eton's sporting and social life entirely congenial. He was able to remain in direct touch with his family, too; his grandmother, the Duchess of Buccleuch, lived at Ditton Park, only a few miles away, and he and his friend Lord Ennismore (the future Earl of Listowel) often went there for Sunday tea, hurrying back to Eton in time for evening chapel.

When writing home John proudly told his father of his prowess at rowing and shooting. He had, he wrote in early 1884, been wet-bobbing several times and hoped to win some cups; and during the winter he had shot 34 more wildfowl than in the previous year, though his tally of pheasants and rabbits had decreased because of a general shortage of game. John's marksmanship earned him the captaincy of the Eton Shooting Eight for three successive years. Military affairs also started to appeal to him at this time; he joined the Eton College Volunteers (the 2nd Bucks) in October 1881, became a colour sergeant, and in 1884 passed an efficiency test at the Grenadier Guards depot in Windsor. A year after he left Eton he received a commission in the 4th Battalion of the Hampshire Volunteers.

Whilst John was at Eton in the 1880s, bicycles began to make an appearance in large numbers; at the time they attracted the vilification that was later to be directed towards the first motorists.

For some ten years 'penny farthing' bicycles had been objects of ridicule and curiosity and a considerable hazard both to their riders and those who witnessed their erratic progress, but in the early 1880s the first 'safety bicycles' became available. Those who adopted them attempted prodigious long-distance journeys. John was one of the first members of his generation to appreciate the range, freedom and healthy exercise that this new form of conveyance afforded — though it was on a tricycle, as distinct from a two-wheeler, that he first joined the 'cads on castors' or 'ironmongery riders' as they were derisively called. Forty-five years later he recalled a journey he made in 1883:

> Delighting in the speed of those days I rode a tricycle from my tutor's house in Eton up to my father's house in London. I took about two and a half hours to cover the distance, via Staines and Hounslow, and over the rough macadam roads of those days the time taken was not unreasonable. Later on I used to average 10 to 12 mph on a pedal bicycle when the roads were dry and there was not a strong head wind.

Roads were to become as serious a study for John as the machines that travelled on them, and he made them the subject of an essay entitled 'Our Roads' written towards the end of his five years at Eton. Rudyard Kipling, who was a year younger than John, had not yet penned the line that John was to quote so frequently many years later — 'transportation *is* civilization' — but, as the following extracts indicate, by the age of 18 John had already marshalled his thoughts on the subject:

> The prosperity and civilization of a country may be estimated in a hundred different ways. Some measure it by the population, some by the quantity of money in circulation. Why may we not also draw an inference of the civilization of a country from the condition of its roads?
>
> Where there are no roads, or but few, we may take it for granted that there are few or no books; few or no manufacturers. Whoever has travelled in Europe must have seen with his own eyes the truth of this doctrine. England has more roads and canals than all the rest of Europe put together — therefore more civilization.
>
> Straight roads and symmetrical cities betray a despotic power, caring little or nothing for the rights of property. Who does not discern in the interminable straight roads of France and Poland the arbitrary hand which must have made them so? On the contrary, in England, that ancient land of liberty, the streets are crooked and most of the cities are mere heaps of habitations built without a plan, as necessity or caprice dictated.
>
> Throughout this island the King, his ministers, the Members of Parliament, the gentry and the businessman are all in perpetual motion . . . and by means of this constant coming and going, comfort, wealth and new inventions are diffused equally over the whole surface of the country.

In 1885 John left Eton and went up to Oxford. It was an important year for him in other respects as well for his name changed from Montagu-Douglas-Scott to the Honourable John Douglas-Scott-Montagu, for Queen Victoria had created his father the first Baron Montagu of Beaulieu.

2

The Montagu Dynasty

John Douglas-Scott-Montagu, as he had now become, was ninth in descent from Charles II and could therefore number Mary Queen of Scots and the Stuarts, James I and Charles I, among his undisputed ancestors.

In 1663 James, Duke of Monmouth, married Anne Scott, second Countess of Buccleuch. She was only 12 years old and as a direct descendant of Sir Richard le Scot, one of the richest landowners in thirteenth century Scotland, she was destined to become 'the greatest heiress and finest woman of her time'.

The first scion of the Scott family to bear the title Buccleuch had been Anne's great grandfather, Sir Walter Scott, who became Lord Scott of Buccleuch in 1606. Lord Scott's son, Walter and his grandson, Francis, were the first and second Earls of Buccleuch but from Francis the Scott line passed to a daughter, Mary, after descending from father to son for 400 years. Mary Scott died at the age of 13 — leaving a widower of 16 — and her honours and lands were inherited by her sister Anne.

When he married Anne Scott, Monmouth took her family name and was made Duke of Buccleuch, with Anne as his duchess. His honours were forfeited when he was beheaded in 1685 after the rout at Sedgemoor but Anne's titles and lands survived. Their grandson, Francis Scott, 2nd Duke of Buccleuch, married Lady Jane Douglas, daughter and heiress of the 2nd Duke of Queensberry.

The connection between the Scott and Douglas families and the Montagus was forged when Henry Scott, 3rd Duke of Buccleuch, the grandson of Francis Scott and Lady Anne, married Elizabeth, daughter and heiress of the last Duke of Montagu, a member of an English dynasty that can be traced back to medieval times.

Attempts have been made, without success, to establish that one of the duke's ancestors was Drogo de Monte Acuto, a Norman lord who came to England at the time of the Conquest and who may have founded the Montacute (or Montagu) family of Montacute in Somerset. William Montagu, grandson of Simon, Lord Montagu (the first English Montagu of any importance) was the first Earl of Salisbury and held many high offices during the Age of Chivalry, including those of Governor of the Channel Isles and Constable of the Tower of London. He died in 1344 after being injured whilst tilting at Windsor. His wife, Catherine, is the central figure in one version of the story of the incident that led to the founding of the Order of the Garter. Legend has it that when she dropped her garter at a court festival it was picked up by Edward III, who tied it to his knee and made the celebrated comment: *Honi soit qui mal y pense* (Evil to him who evil thinks). Another variation of the tale suggests that Princess Joan of Kent was the lady in question.

The Earls of Salisbury became extinct in the 15th century but a hundred years later a descendant of the first earl's third son became Chief Justice to Henry VIII. He was Sir Edward Montagu of Boughton, from whom descended the Earls of Sandwich, the Dukes of Manchester, and the Baron Montagus of Boughton. Edward Montagu, the second baron, married Anne, daughter and heiress of Sir Ralph Winwood of Ditton, Principal Secretary of State to James I. Through this marriage, Ditton Park became one of the Montagu estates.

Their son Ralph, the third baron, was one of the promoters of the Glorious Revolution, a role that earned him promotion to the rank of Earl of Montagu early in the reign of William and Mary. Queen Anne made him Duke of Montagu. As her ambassador to the Court of France, Ralph developed expensive tastes, exemplified by his house at Boughton, near Kettering, which he extended in the style of the Palace of Versailles. He married twice and through both marriages added immeasurably to the riches of the generations that succeeded him.

Ralph's first wife was Lady Elizabeth Wriothesley, the youngest of the three daughters of the 4th Earl of Southampton, Lord High Treasurer of England in 1660. The male line of the Southamptons ended when the fourth earl died and his daughters drew lots to decide which of his estates each of them should receive. Lady Elizabeth won the Manor of Beaulieu in the New Forest, which had been purchased after the Dissolution of the Monasteries for £1350.6s.8d. by the 1st Earl of Southampton, Thomas Wriothesley, who became Lord Chancellor to Henry VIII and an Executor of his Will. So thanks to Lady Elizabeth's luck, Beaulieu became a country seat of the Montagus.

Clitheroe, another of the family's estates, was also deftly acquired by Ralph Montagu. These 70,000 acres of Lancashire, later to become even more valuable when coal was discovered there, belonged to Elizabeth Cavendish, wealthy widow of the 2nd Duke of Albemarle. Montagu's first wife died after bearing him three sons and he married Elizabeth Cavendish after a decidedly crazy courtship. She was an eccentric, not to say mad, lady who had declared that her next husband would have to be not a mere duke but a reigning sovereign. The wily Ralph, 'as arrant a rogue as any of his time', according to Jonathan Swift, visited the duchess dressed as the Emperor of China, attended by a retinue of oriental servants. He laid his bogus crown at her feet, proposed marriage, and was accepted. The deception paid off handsomely. Her Grace lived happily ever after, believing until the day she died that she was an Empress. She even instructed her servants to approach her on their bended knees. His Grace lived extravagantly ever after, making the most of her money.

John, the third son of Ralph Montagu and Elizabeth Wriothesley, became the 2nd Duke of Montagu and married Mary, fourth daughter of the great military commander John Churchill, 1st Duke of Marlborough. Their three sons died within their father's lifetime and the Montagu descendancy now depended on the daughters of the family. Only one of them, also named Mary, bore children. She had married George Brudenell, 4th Earl of Cardigan, for whom the title Duke of Montagu was revived. The title Baron Montagu of Boughton was re-created for their son, John, but he died before his father and so his sister Elizabeth inherited the Montagu properties. It was she who married Henry Scott, 3rd Duke of Buccleuch and 5th of Queensberry, and brought the Montagu, Douglas and Scott families and fortunes together.

Henry Scott and Elizabeth Montagu begat a new dynasty, whose power and influence had been handed down for four generations by the time John Walter Edward Montagu-Douglas-Scott was born. No family history is straightforward and that of the Montagus was further complicated by Lord Henry Scott's marriage to Lord Wharncliffe's daughter, Cecily, since the Wharncliffe forebears included Lady Mary Wortley-Montagu, daughter of the 1st Duke of Kingston on Hull. Lady Mary became famous for her literary duel with Alexander Pope and for introducing smallpox inoculation into England. As her husband's ancestors were members of the Sandwich branch of the Montagu family, the subject of this book's parents were distant cousins.

These, briefly, are the facts about the Montagus. But legends, too, abound in the family. One of these concerns John Montagu's grandfather, the 5th Duke of Buccleuch. Tradition maintains that he discovered a certificate proving that Prince Charles and Lucy Walters were married. Had the legitimacy of their son James, Duke of Monmouth, been proven the fifth duke could have had a claim to the throne — though undoubtedly this would immediately have been rejected because of the Act of Settlement of 1701, which established the Hanoverians as the legal line. Buccleuch, so the story goes, presented the certificate to Queen Victoria. She burned it. No more was said about the matter.

Perhaps Queen Victoria was silently grateful. For she was happy to award a peerage to Lord Henry Scott in circumstances which seem unusual compared to the way in which such titles are conferred today.

It was Lord Henry's mother, the Dowager Duchess of Buccleuch, who initiated matters by the most direct course of action available to her. She thought her son deserved a peerage, so on 24 October 1885 she wrote to Queen Victoria and asked for one:

> I trust your Majesty will pardon me if I venture to approach your Majesty with a petition, which would confer a very great favour, should your Majesty be disposed to give it favourable consideration.

> My petition is that your Majesty may be graciously pleased to grant a peerage to our second son Henry. My dear husband has left him a sufficient income to keep up that position and though I know he would never have asked this favour, I know that it would have gratified him much had it been offered to him for his son. My son has been obliged to relinquish his duties as a Member of the House of Commons from his health not being sufficiently strong for the present arduous duties imposed upon a Member of Parliament, but he could still serve your Majesty and her country, if it might please your Majesty, in the House of Lords. He has much energy and zeal and would not be an idle member of that house. If I have done wrong in bringing this matter before your Majesty myself I just crave your Majesty's indulgence and forgiveness.

Next day the Duchess seems to have wondered whether she had done the right thing in writing to the Queen without having first consulted the Prime Minister, Lord Salisbury, to whom she then wrote this explanation:

> I am anxious to tell you what I have done in asking a great favour of the Queen, as I do not wish you to hear of it from anyone else but myself, for I feel that you would consider it not only discourteous but unfriendly of me not to do so, and we have been friends for so many years that I would not do anything that you could consider otherwise. The Queen has always been so kind and affectionate to me and had a most sincere and deep regard for my dear husband. I therefore preferred to make my petition to her instead of through you, that our son Henry should be granted a peerage.

> As you know he has relinquished his seat in Parliament from not having health sufficiently strong for the present arduous duties of a member of the House but he would, as you may feel sure, be an active and zealous member of the House of Lords. It is not for me to say how much my dear husband did for the Conservative cause for that is known to you and to everyone.

> In writing to the Queen I made no allusion of course to politics but only mentioned that although I know my dear husband would never have asked for this favour, yet I know he would have been much gratified had it been

offered to him for his son. You may have heard that owing to his father's Will, Henry will be able to keep up the position of a peer.

No harm had been done, no offence taken. Salisbury supported the Duchess's petition and the Queen replied:

I am anxious to announce to you myself that with Lord Salisbury's entire concurrence I shall confer the Baronry of Montagu on your son Henry. It gives me great pleasure to do this and I am sure you will be glad that the name so long borne by your dear husband's uncle should be revived again.

Thus on 29 December 1885 Lord Henry Montagu-Douglas-Scott became Henry Douglas-Scott-Montagu, 1st Baron Montagu of Beaulieu and thus his eldest son John became the Honourable John Douglas-Scott-Montagu. As this was rather a mouthful, most of his friends and tutors at New College Oxford knew him as John Scott-Montagu.

In 1886 New College was on its way to becoming one of the pre-eminent colleges of Oxford University. It had been a small, closed society of scholars until the 1870s, when new buildings designed by Gilbert Scott were opened, allowing the number of undergraduates to be expanded. The Warden at the time of John's arrival — and, it seemed then, since time immemorial, for he had held the post for 26 years — was the remarkable J. E. Sewell, then 75 years old and fit for another 17. The Dean of the college was the equally illustrious Reverend W. A. Spooner, famous for announcing the hymn in chapel as 'Kinquering Congs their titles take' and for dismissing an under-graduate with the dry comment: 'You have deliberately tasted two worms and you can leave Oxford by the town drain.'

As Marindin, his Eton tutor, had observed, John was no scholar. The only examination he passed at New College was the 1886 equivalent of the modern Classical Moderations. At Oxford, as at Eton, he took greater advantage of sporting and social opportunities than those provided for his academic benefit. The reason, there can be no doubt, was that by now — as his cycling activities at Eton and his essay on 'Our Roads' reveal — he was keenly interested in mechanical transport and travel; and although he had been able to study mechanics at Eton, which had a special department for this subject, there was nowhere at New College for him to develop his elementary knowledge of what made the wheels of transport turn.

One of the college's dons, Mr Matheson, summed up John the under-graduate, in this way:

He was too restless a spirit to fit into the ordinary life of a college and comply with its necessary rules and regulations, although he enjoyed to the full the purely human side of it; the activities of the river and the meeting and talking with all sorts of men. He knew everybody in the college and had no class prejudices, and helped to bring people of different groups together. Unfortunately in those days there was no school of engineering and the history school for which he was supposed to be reading involved more steady and methodical work than his many distractions allowed him to give to it.

The 'wet bob' from Eton had arrived at a time when enthusiasm for rowing was reaching a peak at New College. For twenty years, from 1885 onwards, the college consistently took one of the first three places in the Oxford 'Eights' and John quickly became one of the college's most enthusiastic oarsmen. He rowed in the winning trial eight at Oxford, was No. 2 in the Oxford and Eton crew in the final of the Grand Challenge at Henley and in 1887 he stroked the New College boat to the head of the river.

John (seated centre) with fellow oarsmen at Oxford in 1887.

John Galsworthy, the novelist and dramatist, was an undergraduate at New College at the same time as John Montagu and 40 years later he penned these recollections of his fellow student:

> He was perhaps the most energetic, lively and genial member of New College. He was what you could call the 'life and soul' of the party ... He was a bright-cheeked fellow and wore hand-knitted silk ties of a cheerful hue (the first I ever saw) through a gold ring, very natty, and often light and rather shaggy tweeds ... he was always chock full of beans and very popular. There can rarely have been a more vital undergrad ... he was 'one of the best' and one of the easiest to conjure up from among the ghosts of my youth.

Montagu and Galsworthy were two of the leading lights in amateur dramatics at Oxford in the late 1880s and among the productions in which they performed was *Guddyraw*, a parody on Gilbert and Sullivan's latest comic opera *Ruddigore*, in which impersonations of the college's dons appeared as the Family Portraits. Montagu wrote part of the libretto and

The cast of Guddyraw.
Back row, left to right: Ian Malcolm, M.F.Davies, Robert Montagu, C.H.St J.Hornby, H.A.Pitman. Front row, seated: B.R.S.Pemberton, John Galsworthy, the Earl of Ancram, John Montagu, A.J.Tassell, Hon. L.J.Bathurst. Front: R.L.Dundas.

played one of the mortals, Dame Joannah. 'He looked very charming, if somewhat brawny in the arms', recalled Galsworthy, who played Sir Spooner Purgatroyd.

Montagu also took part in the Oxford University Dramatic Society's summer shows, one of these being *The Alcestis of Euripides* in the original Greek, and he contributed towards improvements to Oxford's New Theatre by donating a blue plush curtain, embroidered with gold, which first rose in April 1889 on a performance of *Julius Caesar*.

As Galsworthy notes, John was clearly a colourful personality and he was inevitably the subject of several tales that became part of New College folklore. As steward of the Junior Common Room he had the opportunity to install electric light for the annual Commem Ball — the first time that this event had enjoyed the benefit of what was still a novel form of illumination. Current for the lights, so the story continues, was derived from the battery of Montagu's car; patently impossible, since there were no cars in England whilst Montagu was at Oxford, nor would there be for nearly ten years. The circumstances surrounding his premature departure from New College have also been embellished. He left, it is said, after one of the traditional 'funerals' that are organized for errant undergrads. That some such celebration was held may well be true, although there is nothing in the college records to confirm the family legend that he was 'sent down', either for being caught with a girl in his room or for blocking the doorways to the dons' quarters with gigantic snowballs. The college's register merely states that John 'took his name off in Easter Term 1889 after having spent some months in travelling around the world'.

He had proved to be 'in every way a most unusual undergraduate', to quote Herbert Fisher, a young don at New College during John's terms there and later the college's warden. 'He kept a valet and a private secretary,' wrote Fisher. 'He belonged to every society and appeared to me to indulge in every kind of activity. I do not imagine he had much time to devote to his academic work, for he was in a perfect turmoil of miscellaneous activities, but I remember that he never spoke as if he was bored with his work. It was an interest to him, but only one of his many interests. For some reason he never took a degree, though of course he had the wits to do very well. In later years I met him occasionally and found him just as fresh and delightful as ever, preserving, despite all the stress and strain of a busy life, that fund of boyish enthusiasm which was so infectious and so irresistible.'

It was obviously John's restless nature that prevented him from applying himself to the discipline of taking a degree; as Matheson's and Fisher's observations indicate, the hard slog of studying for difficult examinations were simply not part of John's make-up. Long before Easter 1889, when he officially left New College, he startled his father — who hoped he might join the Grenadier Guards — by telling him that he intended to become a mechanic in the London & South Western Railway workshops at Nine Elms, near London's Waterloo Station. After that, he said, he wanted to become an engine driver.

In the 1880s the sons of lords simply did not do that sort of thing, any more than they do today, but John's decision may not have been entirely unexpected. Nearly four years earlier Lord Henry (as he then was) had arranged for John to fulfil his wish to travel to Waterloo on the footplate of an LSWR loco. George Chapman, the driver of the engine on that occasion, recalled it vividly 35 years later:

It was on a Sunday evening in the summer of 1885. I was at Southampton on the locomotive of which I was the driver, with a train that was about to leave for London, when two gentlemen — apparently father and son — came up to the engine and the elder gentleman handed me a letter, asking that I would please read it. I did so and found it was from the chief superintendent of the line, with a note authorizing any driver to permit the Hon. John Montagu to ride on the footplate in order to learn the working of the engine. I therefore invited the young man to step on the footplate. This he did, and his father travelled in the train.

The journey was a slow one, the train stopping at all stations, so that we were about three hours on the journey. My unexpected pupil said very little but evidently watched most intently the working of the engine. On arrival at Waterloo, however, he had much to say and I was surprised to find how observant he had been. He asked me to explain several things that were not clear to him and he was evidently greatly pleased by what he had seen on the journey. I congratulated him on his powers of observation and on his wisdom in not conversing during the journey. He frankly replied that he had felt inclined to talk but had been advised by the superintendent not to do so whilst travelling.

Subsequently the Hon. John Montagu made many journeys on the footplate, sometimes on my engine and sometimes on others. He quickly acquired a practical knowledge of the working and then, under strict supervision, he was allowed to take control of the engine. After some time he asked me one day how I thought he was getting on. I replied that he was doing fairly well but was not beginning at the right place. I advised that he should learn how the engine was prepared at the home station and not only take charge when it was all ready. He saw the point at once, with the result that on the next occasion he came to the locomotive depot to see the process of preparation of the engine.

I remember telling him that he was not sufficiently observant on the road and that he needed to take strict notice of the road in case of foggy weather or of dark nights, during which such knowledge would be useful. He became quite proficient in a comparatively short time.

In 1888, probably during the university summer vacation or perhaps as a truant, John went to work at Nine Elms. Calling himself 'Mr Douglas' he temporarily severed his aristocratic connections and found lodgings in Vauxhall Bridge Road, to be close to his place of work and also, perhaps, to save his parents the embarrassment of having a grimy workman leaving and entering the front door of their Mayfair town house. John worked a 48 hour week, for which he was paid 11s. 6d. like everybody else and he spent many enjoyable and useful hours gaining the first hand experience of locomotive maintenance that George Chapman had advised him to acquire.

This period of workshop experience was followed by further tuition in the art of driving main line locomotives, an activity that John indulged in from time to time until a few years before he died. He was to develop a love-hate attitude towards the railways. He remained fascinated by, and full of admiration for, steam locomotives and the men who built them and drove them, even though from about 1900 onwards he regarded roads and motor vehicles as the transport of the future, and railways as having only a limited value.

When, in 1902, John launched his weekly magazine called *The Car Illustrated – A Journal of Transport by Land, Sea and Air*, he commissioned another railway enthusiast in the family, George Montagu MP (the future Earl of Sandwich) to write regular feature articles on railway practice and performance and it was George Montagu who heard, and handed down, what became known as 'the tale of the needy kinsman'.

The kinsman was John's younger brother Robert, who died young and during his short life acquired a reputation for drinking, womanizing and other habits of the kind that caused the downfall of many a young aristocrat in the Gay Nineties and Edwardian times. Robert Montagu had, at the time the 'needy kinsman' story originated, recently borrowed £100 from John — not the first loan of its kind, nor apparently the last. A week or two later John Montagu, railwayman, was on the footplate of a 'special' that had been hired to take a yachting party from Waterloo to Southampton Docks. After the train pulled in, John glanced out of the cab and saw his brother, resplendent in evening dress, leave the train arm-in-arm with the glamorous Lillie Langtry. Robert Montagu paused in his progress along the platform to hand a guinea each to the guard and driver, whereupon John, weary and masked with coaldust after firing the boiler for two hours, butted in with the question: 'Got nothing for me, brother Robert?' Pocketing the coin rather reluctantly proffered, John commented: 'Now you owe me only 99'.

During John's 1887 summer vacation the family's home at Palace House, Beaulieu, had been the scene of a week of celebrations to mark his coming-of-age. His 21st birthday, 10 June, fell during the months in which Queen

Victoria's Jubilee celebrations reached their peak and no doubt many senior members of the Scott and Stuart-Wortley families had other functions to attend, and other duties to attend to, that month. This would have been one of the reasons why the celebrations in John's honour were postponed until the second week of August, when he became the central figure in a hectic programme of parties, dinners and other festivities.

Guests at John Montagu's coming-of-age party at which John (seated third from left, front row) and Lady Cecil Victoria Kerr (on his left) fell in love.

They began on Tuesday 9 August with a garden party at Palace House for close relations and friends, a military and naval presence being added to the proceedings by the arrival of the officers of the 4th Battalion of the Hampshire Volunteers and the Rifle Brigade from Winchester, the Commandant of Hurst Castle, and the captain and officers of the Royal yachts *Osborne* and *Albert & Victoria*, and HMS *Valorous*. The party was followed by boating on the Beaulieu river, a 'naval review' commanded by 'Admiral' Lady Frances Fortescue and a dance in Palace House — the grounds of which were illuminated with Chinese lanterns and fairy lamps.

The celebrations resumed next day with a 21 gun salute followed by a dinner for the Beaulieu Manor's 200 tenants and employees. Afterwards the Vicar of Beaulieu, the Reverend Robert Powles, presented John with a silver inkstand and four silver candlesticks — a gift from the 'tenants, mechanics and workmen' of the manor. This was accompanied by a loyal address:

> It is with great pride that we recall that since your earliest childhood you have always shown such pleasure in spending your holidays and leisure time among us, enlivening us by your genial and kindly presence. We trust that a good Providence will preserve you in manhood as it has done in youth and enable you worthily to follow in the footsteps of your father and grandfather, and in the future to perform the duties belonging to your station, now rendered more than in past times difficult and responsible by the depressed condition of agricultural interests.

These words, probably written with the help of the Reverend Mr Powles, have a forelock-tugging feudal tone when read nearly a hundred years later but the reference to John's 'genial and kindly presence' accurately conveys one of the dominant aspects of his personality. His kindness is one of the main attributes recalled by those relatives, friends and acquaintances whom I've met, who knew John Montagu personally; another is his refreshing lack of class prejudice, as noted by Mr Matheson. The 'depressed condition of agricultural interests' mentioned by Mr Powles is also significant: trade was bad, prices were low, farmers had no incentive to become more efficient, and employment prospects were bleak in many areas. During the agricultural depression of the 1880s several farming families moved from Scotland to Beaulieu, encouraged by the Buccleuchs, and eventually they managed to earn a reasonable living from the farms dotted among Beaulieu's heaths and forests. Descendants of those farmers still live and farm in the area. But the poor quality of the farmland, the consequent low rents and the high cost of maintaining the farms — especially the land drains — were to be constant problems for John when, 18 years after his 21st birthday, he inherited Beaulieu Manor. This was another reason why he did not enjoy the same measure of affluence as his forebears, and had to supplement his income as a landowner with earnings from writing and publishing.

In his reply to Mr Powles' address John revealed his thoughts and feelings about the manor he would eventually inherit, and the abbey around which it had grown many centuries earlier.

> When you look at this place and see that these old walls have been built since 1204 ... and think of the faces that must have looked upon these buildings, it is indeed a proud moment for me to think that I have such a near interest and connection with memories and associations which really are so greatly to be venerated.

I know what hard times these are now for many of you. When I am out shooting I see the fields; I know every field and hedge and gap in this place pretty nearly; I am fond of every tree and everything in this place, and I have seen it ever since I can remember anything.

There was a firework display that evening, a county ball on the Thursday and a tenants' ball on the Friday. On Saturday the house guests said their farewells. Among those who sadly took their leave was Lady Cecil Victoria Kerr, a daughter of the 9th Marquis of Lothian, Secretary of State for Scotland. John and Lady Cecil would soon meet again, for during the celebrations at Beaulieu they had fallen in love. Their relationship during the next 20 years would be turbulent, and fail to live up to the promise of happiness they saw before them under the Chinese lanterns and fairy lamps that had cast their soft glow over the lawns of Palace House at dusk during the fiftieth August of Queen Victoria's reign.

3

'I Love Cis Very Much'

Affection between John and Cis, as Lady Cecil Kerr was known in the family, blossomed and sometime during 1888 John disconcerted his parents by informing them that he and Cis wished to get married. The news was not initially popular because, as well as being childhood friends and near neighbours in Mayfair, John and Cis were first cousins, Lady Lothian being Lord Montagu's sister (their parents had also been distant cousins). Whilst there was no legal impediment to the marriage of first cousins, both parents reacted to the prospect with mixed emotions, for marriage between such close relatives was frowned upon.

It was suggested to them that they were too young to be married since they were both only 22; they were advised to postpone their formal engagement for a few months and John was persuaded to travel around the world in the company of his old Etonian friend, Lord Ennismore, and young Lord Ancram, Cis's brother. No doubt it was hoped that, separated for a time, John and Cis would widen their field of acquaintances, enjoy other distractions and lose interest in each other. But in one of his first letters home John told his father, 'I love Cis very much,' and Ancram's presence ensured that the romance was never far from John's mind.

Six days and two hours after leaving Liverpool, John and his friends arrived in New York — a fast passage for 1888. The roads of New York, he noted, were worse than those he had ever seen in a famous city. However the terrain of Canada was more to his liking. At Montreal the three youthful aristocrats boarded a train on the new Canadian Pacific Railway and after enduring the fierce heat of the prairies for several days they cooled off in the Rocky Mountains, setting forth with ponies, packhorses and an Indian guide on a three-week shooting expedition.

Their Canadian adventures ended in Vancouver, whence they travelled to Japan, where they immediately adopted such national customs as eating live fish, pickled chrysanthemums and swallows' nest soup. Thence to China, where they found that a man and his family could live on $5\frac{1}{2}$d. a week and that a convicted murderer could, for £10, buy a man to be executed in his stead.

Christmas week was spent aboard the P & O liner SS *Clyde*, heading for Colombo. After exploring Ceylon for ten days John sailed for India. The small pocket diary he carried during this part of his journey is one of the few personal documents to have survived from this period of his life, and the brief and often desultory entries reveal that he became ill with fever and asthma on several occasions during his six weeks in India. 'Felt rather unwell', he noted in a shaky hand on 14 February—Cis's 23rd birthday. 'Got a letter from C' he had noted the previous day. Despite his afflictions he accepted numerous invitations to sporting and social functions. 'Went to Volunteers' Ball. Moderate', reads another entry, followed a few days later by 'Up early. Went pig sticking. Got one small one after good gallop. Rode Arab stallion, noble animal. Tumbled 20 ft down a nullah. None the worse'.

After a tour that took in Calcutta, Darjeeling, Benares, Lucknow, Delhi and several other cities, John made his way to Bombay, sailing for Egypt in March. His health improved almost immediately. 'Weak but less feverish', he wrote when 270 miles out into the Arabian Sea. By Sunday he was 'much better'.

In Egypt, John visited Cairo and the Pyramids before sailing from Alexandria for Naples, where he boarded a train for Paris. He arrived home during the second week of April and soon dispelled any hopes or expectations that he would now have second thoughts about marrying Cis by announcing their engagement on 30 April.

Five weeks later, on 4 June 1889, John Douglas-Scott-Montagu married Lady Cecil Kerr at St George's, Hanover Square. It was one of the most fashionable weddings of the year, the Prime Minister, Lord Salisbury, being one of the guests. The couple spent their honeymoon at Blickling Hall in Norfolk, which belonged to Lord Lothian, and then they went to The Lodge, a large house on the Beaulieu estate which was to be their home for the next sixteen years.

John and Cis had sharply contrasting personalities. He was the complete extrovert, gregarious, high spirited, highly strung, restless and passionately fond of outdoor sports, whereas she was sensitive and artistic by nature, happiest when reading, playing the piano or composing hymn tunes on the organ. She had a keen sense of humour but was altogether a much gentler, quieter person than he was. Nor was she as robust as her husband, who could draw on tremendous reserves of nervous energy to take him through a busy day at those times when, to quote one of his favourite expressions, he 'felt seedy'.

The outdoor interests that John pursued so enthusiastically and vigorously at weekends — especially his shooting parties — did not appeal to Cis. Shooting was a sport she deplored. Elizabeth, John and Cis's younger daughter, recalls this aspect of her mother's nature very clearly. 'She hated

Cis, John's bride.

John and Cis in later life at Beaulieu.

The Montagus' 1906 Thornycroft outside Palace House.

killing things. She detested dripping wet woods and seeing dead furry creatures laying on the ground.' But John and his friends enjoyed nothing more than bagging a few furry or winged creatures in the wet woods of Beaulieu and bringing them back to The Lodge, where in rapid high-pitched tones John would give his cook very precise instructions as to how long each bird or rabbit should be cooked, and the correct temperature for the oven.

Cis, though coming from a family background similar to that of her husband, had until her marriage led a sheltered life; as one of five sisters, she had not been obliged to take an interest in the leisure pursuits of exuberant young men. Indeed, she was probably ill-prepared for marriage. In Victorian times embarrassed mothers would go to their daughters on the eve of their wedding day and say things like: 'Darling, I think I ought to tell you something about marriage. I can only ask you to remember that whatever happens tomorrow night, I know your husband will always be a perfect gentleman.' That, Elizabeth Montagu recalls, is all that one of her aunts was told before she married and it is likely that Cis was given similar — or even less — 'advice'. She was probably at a decided disadvantage in more ways than one when she left the peace and seclusion of life with the Lothians at

Monteviot and tried to adapt her outlook and ideas to her ebullient new husband.

Nevertheless, adapt she did, so far as she was able. For the first few years John and Cis were happy; the Beaulieu countryside was entirely to her liking and she made many friends. Their first daughter, Helen, was born in March 1890 and their only cause for concern about the future at this time was that Cis was told by her doctor that she could have no more children. Nineteen years later the doctor was proved wrong, but in the meantime it is likely that the prospect of not being able to have a son and heir contributed to a gradual change in Montagu's feelings towards his wife. That, and his irritation that her delicate constitution deterred her from participating to the full in his sporting and social activities.

Their daughter Helen was to become as unconventional, in her way, as her father was in his. Very much a 'good time girl' she decided that she wanted to be an actress — which, to John and Cis, may have been as surprising as John's intention to become a railway mechanic had been to his parents. John tried to help Helen by sending her to RADA but she tended to fall asleep during lessons and it soon became evident that her real ambition was to be a chorus girl. In an attempt to deter her, John helped finance a production of *Trilby* in return for a minor role in the play for Helen, but one evening she absconded and was eventually discovered in the chorus line at a music hall.

Enough was enough. Her father stopped her regular allowance and instead paid her 2s. 6d. a day subsistence — which she had to collect from his London office at 62 Pall Mall. Later Helen went to New York where, as her sister Elizabeth recalls, she became 'utterly and completely broke'. Montagu refused to send her any money and on this and many subsequent occasions, her mother came to her aid, raising money for Helen by selling some jewellery. Later, Helen's fortunes improved to some extent and she joined the Ziegfeld Follies, but she was always a cause of concern to her parents.

Helen's rebellious behaviour may have stemmed from a somewhat unstable family background caused by John and Cis's basic incompatibility; on the other hand, their differences may have been aggravated by Helen's behaviour. Certainly, their relationship became a complex one. To their surprise they did have another child — Elizabeth, who was born in 1909, when Cis was 43. But John was disappointed. He wanted a son. When Elizabeth was born, in a house the Montagus had rented near Hyde Park Square, Montagu left home and stayed at the Ritz Hotel in Piccadilly for several days. His behaviour caused his wife much distress but eventually a close bond developed between Montagu and his young daughter, whom he alluded to as 'my little feller'.

Elizabeth, a perceptive child, remembers some 'very unhappy scenes' between her parents. On one occasion Cis buried some venison which she considered far too 'high' to eat, only to be told by John to dig it up and cook it. After another contretemps Cis had to auction some of her possessions in order to honour a debt that John refused to pay. Incidents like these contrast sharply with his undisputed kindness to most people with whom he came in contact.

In 1889, at the age of 23, John Montagu was as educated — in the formal sense — as he would ever be; a skilled engine driver; an experienced traveller; an authority on shooting and fishing; a subaltern in the Hampshire Volunteers; and a married man. He was also now helping his father supervise the management of Beaulieu Manor. All this, though, hardly amounted to a plan for his future and whilst many young noblemen quite happily made being the son and heir of a peer a full-time occupation, filling their diaries with social engagements and vague and not especially arduous business appointments, John was far too restless a character to enjoy such an aimless existence. He needed a vocation and about a year after his marriage 'Mamma's little Tory' of some 15 years earlier embarked on a career in politics, aided and encouraged by a friend and neighbour Evelyn Ashley of Broadlands, near Romsey, a nephew of Lord Palmerston.

In 1890, towards the end of Lord Salisbury's second administration, a vacancy occurred for a Conservative candidate to represent the New Forest Division. As the son of the MP who had served the old South Hampshire constituency for 16 years, John Montagu was an obvious choice and soon Ashley was introducing him to the right people as 'our Conservative card'. But things were not quite as they had been in his father's day. Parliamentary reforms had extended the vote to thousands more working class men, and candidates now had to appeal to a wider social order than the original property owning voters. However the lack of class prejudice that John's teachers at Oxford had noted proved a great benefit, especially among the many railwaymen living in the division — who already knew him from his engine driving exploits. John was adopted as the Tory candidate for the New Forest and, in the general election of 1892, he had his first chance to stand.

A major issue of that campaign was Gladstone's long-cherished ambition to grant self government to Ireland — an issue which had split the Liberal party since 1886 and had been opposed by the Tories for 20 years. It was, on the face of it, a rather remote issue to the electors of the New Forest but even in this sleepy corner of rural England the Irish question intruded into what was, by and large, a courteous contest between Montagu and his Liberal opponent, Joseph King, a London barrister who supported Home Rule for Ireland.

First there was what would today be called a 'smear campaign'. Word was put around that John had not paid for a dinner that he had given to the

Hampshire Volunteers at the Swan Inn, Totton, two years earlier. The staunchly Tory *Hampshire Advertiser* commented indignantly: 'Nothing was left undone to damage Mr Montagu in the eyes of the electors, and to catch votes, any amount of untruths being circulated'. To quash the rumour Mr Phillips, mine host at the Swan at the time of the dinner, travelled all the way from Reading to Totton to vote for Montagu and affirm that he had paid for the dinner. 'Mr Phillips', reported the *Advertiser*, 'has asked us to give the most emphatic denial to such a scandalous and unfounded statement. We mention this as a sample of the slanders and *vile* untruths with which our member was assailed by his opponents.'

Alone among the division's principal towns — which included Bournemouth, Christchurch, Lymington, Romsey, Lyndhurst and Hythe — Totton was something of a political powder keg during the campaign. After John's eve of poll meeting there, and on polling day itself, 'disgraceful scenes' (to quote the *Advertiser*) broke out. A gang of 'Radical roughs' paraded through the streets, breaking windows (and a man's finger), splashing bystanders with mud and making it necessary for citizens to seek the protection of the rather small force of policemen that had been summoned to quell the disturbance. The *Advertiser's* reporter wrote it all down:

> The roughs were preceded by a well-known local character blowing the most discordant sounds from a cow's horn and they hooted and yelled at every Conservative. It seems they were indulged in a bread and cheese lunch, with beer, in the morning and had sundry libations of 'fourpenny' served out during the day, but we are quite sure that all right-minded and well-behaved citizens — even Gladstonians — must have been disgusted with the behaviour of this noisy band of nobodies.

The *Advertiser's* leader writer was almost apoplectic. The 'organized rowdyism', he wrote, 'was very little short of a riot. We hope that such disgraceful scenes will never be witnessed in the village again. It is very well known to whom the honour is due for this rowdy organization but it is surprising that any Radical, whose boast is enlightenment and freedom, should lend himself to countenance and encourage such mean and contemptible conduct. It shows to what length Radicals will go in order to gain their ends.'

Down at Lymington Town Hall, where the result of the poll was due to be announced, affairs were being conducted in a more gentlemanly manner. And in a leisurely manner, too, since the returning officer's staff did not start counting the votes until 10 o'clock the next morning. Less than two hours later the result was announced. Mr Montagu: 4481 votes. Mr King: 3726. Tory majority: 755. 'A thrashing for the Radicals, which they thoroughly and heartily deserve' were the *Advertiser's* final words on the campaign. John and Cis made a triumphant appearance on the balcony of the Angel Hotel. As they boarded their carriage in Lymington High Street to return to Beaulieu, the horses were released from the shafts so that John's more ardent and energetic supporters could haul him and his entourage through the town.

Nationally, however, the Tory campaign had not been a success. The 'thrashing' of the Radicals was confined to fewer seats than the Tories had wished. The Liberals won the election, although only by a precarious majority. John, maybe unexpectedly, found himself on the Opposition benches in the House of Commons, from where he made his maiden speech during Gladstone's last bid to push through his controversial Home Rule Bill.

Irish self-determination was a strange topic for John to choose for his parliamentary debut but in April 1893, when the Commons debated the Government of Ireland Bill, he had yet to adopt the cause with which he was to become so closely associated a few years later. Road transport was not yet a political issue. The only banner that was being carried for it was the Red Flag of 1865, which in some places was still impeding progress on Britain's highways and byways. So on 19 April 1893 the fledgling MP for the New Forest caught the Speaker's eye and rose to give what he considered to be 'a view of the Irish question I have not heard set forth in the course of the debate'.

Staunch Unionist though he was, John recognized the trend towards decentralization in the administration of Ireland. The Government's supporters, he freely admitted, had many arguments in their favour. They rightly pointed to the disturbances that were occurring in Ireland and to the fact that that country had not prospered like other parts of the British Empire. The Bill, though, was 'a leap in the dark', declared John, and 'a dangerous experiment' that would lead to 'a still more terrible state of things than that which now exists'. The Government, he said, was proposing to confer upon Ireland a wider measure of self control than England or Scotland possessed and would be treated like a colony — 'yet Ireland is too near to us to be safely trusted in that position'. Ireland had no right to Home Rule until the alternative — a wider scheme of local government — had been tried.

John's moderate line ruffled a few feathers among the diehard Unionists in his constituency, who regarded even local government for Ireland as a step too far in the wrong direction. Arthur Balfour, who had been Chief Secretary for Ireland in Salisbury's cabinet, was also, so it was said, upset by the new backbencher's remarks. John found himself in a position familiar to all politicians — of being misheard, misunderstood, and quoted out of context. He soon clarified his views to his fellow MPs and his more vexed constituents and during the short life of Gladstone's fourth and last administration he developed into a competent debater. As for the Home Rule Bill, it was passed by the Commons but rejected by the House of Lords. The Liberals remained divided between those who wanted sweeping reforms and those who advocated cautious progress, and in June 1895 the Conservatives were returned to power with an overwhelming majority. This time there were no unseemly scenes in the New Forest. John was returned unopposed. His interest in Irish affairs soon waned when two developments — one at home, the other abroad — attracted his interest.

4

Adventures in Matabeleland

By 1890 Cecil Rhodes, that most ambitious of British Empire builders, was at
the height of his political and commercial powers. A multi-millionaire, he had
made his fortune from the diamonds of Kimberley and the gold of Witwaters-
rand, and then become Prime Minister of Cape Colony. His British South
Africa Company, under the charter granted to it by Queen Victoria, enjoyed
sweeping powers in the 400,000 square miles of tribal territories once known
as Mashonaland and Matabeleland, later called Rhodesia and now Zimbabwe.

John's father had visited South Africa some years before and had invested
money in various companies there, and in Rhodesia; in 1892 John went to see
these places for himself and was most impressed by all that Cecil Rhodes had
achieved. On his return to England he began to champion Rhodes in his
regular contributions to the weekly newspaper *The Western Gazette*, whose
circulation area included his New Forest constituency. This was his first
serious venture into journalism, albeit one in which, initially at least, his
position as an MP rather than his skill as a writer ensured that his every word
found its way into print. He was no doubt also helped by his father being a
director of the paper.

In the autumn of 1893 controversy reigned in the Commons over an
allegedly brutal attack by a British officer on a group of natives in Matabeleland. Sydney Buxton, Under-Secretary for the Colonies, condemned the
officer for not having read the Riot Act to the natives. Commented John,
emotively, in his report on the debate:

> I should like to have seen Mr Buxton, surrounded by a mob of howling
> Matabeles, endeavouring to read the Riot Act while they were sharpening
> their spears to run through his well-to-do body.

There were, John added darkly, those in the House who would be
delighted if the Matabele defeated the British South Africa Company 'and its
brave men on the frontier'.

Mr Paul, the Liberal MP who had in John's view expressed 'irrelevant and
very unpatriotic' observations about the alleged brutality would, he said,
have been shot 'for want of patriotism' 300 years earlier. John added:

I do not think such a course would be desirable nowadays but it might prove very convenient at times and prevent a sentimental ignoramus talking rubbish.

A speech by 'Tommy' Maguire, the Irish Parnellite MP, was much more to Montagu's liking. Maguire spoke up for the Chartered Company and proved that he was 'a great friend of that pioneer of African civilization, Mr Cecil Rhodes'.

Three weeks later the Matabele War was in full spate, as the aggressive Matabeles under King Lobengula tried to conquer the more placid Mashonas. The British intervened and the Matabele were soon defeated near their capital, Bulawayo. Whilst the war was still being fought John wrote:

> What a curious way we have in England of doing these things. We give a charter to a company and allow them to have a little war of their own and take possession of enormous tracts of country, which we then claim as part of our Empire, the State itself having spent no money and having taken no trouble to acquire the territory. As soon as the Chartered Company is firmly established and has given Lobengula a thrashing, from which he will never recover, Mr Gladstone will, I suppose, make much of the fact that during his Government our Empire in South Africa has been increased by so many thousand square miles, where in reality the Colonial Office have performed their usual function of trying to delay the necessary action taken by the Chartered Company.

The Matabeles surrendered on 23 October 1893. Lobengula was driven into the bush, where he died the following year.

At this period of his life — he was now 27 — John was obviously viewing the problems of southern Africa strictly in black and white terms, in more senses than one. He tended to be unstinting in his praise of Cecil Rhodes and cruelly unsympathetic towards Lobengula, who despite his faults had in the past extended friendship towards white hunters and traders, and had granted the Chartered Company mineral rights worth millions of pounds. On the other hand, John was no more guilty of jingoism than most of his fellow Tory MPs. Reflecting their views, he made this comment in his column on 8 November 1893:

> The Chartered Company has scored another victory over the Matabele. Lobengula is not yet thoroughly suppressed but he has had a severe blow from which he will not easily recover. Mr Buxton made as good a defence of his policy as was expected of him. He is avowedly unpatriotic and it evidently was an unpalatable task to him to have to admit that the Chartered Company and our countrymen had gained a decisive victory. It does not much matter, however, as Mr Rhodes has the whole position in his hands and only lets the Colonial Office know as much as he thinks they

ought to know, by arranging convenient breakdowns in the wire to the frontier. I do not say that this is by any means a good precedent but it is inevitable under the present state of things and Mr Buxton has got himself and his sentimental colleagues to thank for it. Poor Lord Ripon. I am sure he is more grieved at the defeat than the Matabele themselves. A kind, good, old man is our Secretary of State for the Colonies and he does so hate a war, little or big, along with his fellow humanitarians. So much the better from his point of view that some of those Chartered libertines, the frontier colonists, should be killed; and let the savage still enjoy the faction fight, his doctored rum and his keen taste for white-murdering.

By now John's condemnation of those who did not look upon Rhodes as being a hero of our time, and on his cause as being comparable to that of the Crusades, was becoming irrational. Few politicians would use the description 'humanitarian' as an insult. Then, on 29 November 1893, the member for Northampton, Mr Labouchere, received a verbal lashing similar to that which John had handed out to Mr Paul some weeks earlier:

The member for Northampton endeavoured to make out that the wounded had been neglected by the Chartered Company after the battle. Mr Buxton's reply was better than most of his answers on this South African business. He said that he had received a telegram from the Board to say that there was not a shadow of evidence that other than humane treatment had been given to the wounded. Really, Mr Labouchere is degrading himself in the eyes of all respectable people by attributing brutal conduct to our countrymen who are fighting out in Matabeleland. I wonder who his informant is or whether he is a bear of the Chartered Company's shares ...
  Mr Buxton again stood up well to the unpatriotic member for Northampton and said that there was no evidence for the allegation.

At this point in the debate another member, Sir James Ferguson, said that Labouchere's allegations were 'scandalous'. Labouchere appealed to the Speaker, who assented to the use of the word, whereupon Labouchere commented: 'Then I beg to say that it is a scandalous action on the part of the honourable gentleman [Mr Buxton] to support such a wretched, rotten, bankrupt set of marauders and murderers as the Chartered Company.'
  John's pen must have flown across the page as he rounded off his commentary on that particular week at Westminster:

This childish outburst was received with good natured laughter all over the House. What Mr Labouchere really wants is the treatment that a pettish child gets, namely, a good smacking ... We all know that he is fond of self-advertisement but he is doing it now at the expense of his countrymen.

This, surely, was enough to show that John did not like Mr Labouchere, but two weeks later he again dipped his pen into his inkwell of vitriol:

Friday's sitting began with the usual questions from Mr Labouchere about his friend Lobengula. How fond some of these Ultra-Radicals are of this savage, in common with the other enemies of this country. One might almost be tempted to say 'Birds of a feather' but then of course no one could imagine Mr Labouchere with a row of beads on his head and a string of feathers round his waist.

By the spring of 1894, unrest among the immigrants and prospectors (known as *uitlanders* by the Dutch Boers) who had surged into the Transvaal after gold, was increasing, because they were still being denied the franchise and other political rights — even though, by developing the mines, they were helping the republic to become the richest state in Africa. But Stephanus Paulus Kruger had no intention of giving the vote to the *uitlanders* who outnumbered the Boers by three to one. 'There is sure to be trouble before long,' wrote John Montagu on 23 May, 'as the Boers have shown an utter want of consideration for the wishes of the English. If a disturbance arises, England must show a firm hand.'

In December 1894 a new agreement was signed by the British Government, giving Rhodes' Chartered Company additional rights south of the Zambesi. John told his *Western Gazette* readers that he wholeheartedly approved:

The bargain is certainly advantageous to the company and puts Mr Rhodes' administration on a much securer foundation. Gradually but surely the Transvaal and the Orange Free State are being surrounded by British territory and it is only a question of time as to their absorption into the Empire. It is to be hoped that the absorption will be of a peaceful kind but when, as at present, the English population of the Transvaal exceeds enormously that of the old Dutch settlers, it is improbable that the newcomers will much longer tolerate the harsh laws and unjust regulations imposed upon them by the present Transvaal Government. Some day the British public will wake up and find that by a 'coup de main' the Transvaal Government has been captured and although there will doubtless be some protestation on the Continent, and a good deal of rubbish talked by the 'Little England' party in this country, Mr Rhodes is not the sort of man to be influenced by either. As to the Chartered Company, it has undoubtedly a great future before it. With its present capitalization of a little over £2 per share the company's property works out at a value of 2d. an acre, which cannot be considered a high value; even granted that a good deal of it may be only agricultural or hunting ground. When it is known that a good many rich gold reefs exist and that population is flocking fast into the Chartered territory, he will be a wise man who buys a few Chartered shares and puts them away for future years.

These extracts from the thousands of words he wrote for the *Western Gazette* reveal a great deal about the young Montagu. They suggest that he was impressionable, immature politically and unskilled in the art of political invective. His 'sentimental ignoramus' taunt at Mr Paul and his 'birds of a feather' jibe at the expense of Mr Labouchere belong more to the under-graduate debating society than the political column of a sober provincial paper. But he was not without ability. He was learning to express himself on paper and had made his first — albeit stumbling — efforts to acquire journalis-tic skills which he would in time master and employ to better effect. He was also quick to size up situations and not without acumen, for Cecil Rhodes was indeed plotting a 'coup de main'.

Outside the Transvaal, at Fort Salsibury, Rhodes had an administrator called Leander Starr Jameson, or Dr Jim; together they secretly hatched a plan. Rhodes would instigate the armed supporters of a reform committee in Johannesburg to rise up and take over the city from the Boers. They would then hold it until Dr Jameson arrived with reinforcements. The British High Commissioner would intervene to restore order and the *uitlanders* would then set up a provisional government as a first step towards making the Transvaal a British colony. At the last minute, the entire plan went awry. Jameson was telegraphed not to come but he ignored the order. Bravely, foolishly and without Rhodes' permission, Jameson set off with his motley army, only to be intercepted and forced to surrender by Boer commandos. The entire operation was a shambles and Rhodes was forced to resign; Jameson and his troops were handed over to the British for trial; Kruger emerged a hero; the British government was implicated and relations between the Boers and the British deteriorated so rapidly that within three years they were at war.

Rhodes came to London in February 1896 and it is highly probable that John Montagu met him to discuss Rhodesia's political and commercial troubles. Despite the fiasco of the Jameson Raid, John still admired Rhodes and continued to support him and his Chartered Company. Indeed by now John had become a director of no less than six companies operating in Africa. Perhaps the most important of these was the Bulawayo Estate and Trust Company, a concern that had a capital of £250,000 and owned nearly a quarter of a million acres in Mashonaland, several properties in Bulawayo and shares in numerous other businesses. The other enterprises were the Africa Trust Consolidated Exploration and General Company; Matabeleland Cen-tral Estates; the Premier Tati Monarch Reef Company (which operated South Africa's first goldfield); the Rand Rhodesia Exploring Company and Salisbury Consolidated Estates (of which he was Chairman). Some of these ventures were closely connected with Rhodes' financial empire.

Worried by the situation in Africa, uncertain of his companies' future, John now decided to go out there to see for himself. On 10 February 1896 Rhodes set off on his return journey to Rhodesia, via Egypt, and on 29 February the weekly newspaper *South Africa* carried this announcement:

> The Hon. John Scott Montagu, MP, expects to leave England today to join Mr Rhodes at Bulawayo and will probably be absent for six months in South Africa.

By this time the Transvaal and the territories north of the Limpopo were in turmoil. A few days before John left England an explosion of 35 tons of dynamite wiped out Braamfontein, a suburb of Johannesburg, killing scores of people. Then, many refugees were killed or injured in a railway accident — one of the worst in history — on the line between Johannesburg and Natal. There was also unrest among the natives around Bulawayo, now under the shaky control of a scratch force of inexperienced Volunteers following the departure and subsequent capture of the regular police force during the Jameson Raid. In Pretoria Gaol the Johannesburg reform committee — whose members included Rhodes' brother Frank — were apprehensively awaiting trial for high treason.

John decided to go to South Africa mainly for business reasons but he was given one or two other assignments. His contributions to the *Western Gazette* over the past three years had earned him some recognition as a political writer and *The Times* asked him to keep them informed of any important developments. He also undertook to tell Lord Selborne, Under-Secretary for the Colonies, about any matters that would help the Government handle the delicate position from which it was trying to extricate itself.

Accompanied by his friend and neighbour Captain Maldwin Drummond, John sailed for Cape Town on the Royal Mail steamer *Athenian*, arriving in South Africa on 18 March.

Late the next evening, they boarded a train for Johannesburg. In those days the journey took about 60 hours and it was not until 22 March that they arrived, travel-worn, on the Rand, to hear bad news for anyone with investments in the region. Two days earlier 141 whites and many pro-white natives had been murdered in Matabeleland; the entire territory was ablaze with violence. The Volunteers and regular troops were being mobilized and the citizens of Bulawayo and other townships in the region had retreated into their fortified encampments, fearful of being besieged by the Matabele. Lord Grey, Jameson's successor as administrator of Rhodesia, was hurrying northwards from the Cape with his staff to take charge of the emergency. If John was seeking excitement and a personal insight into southern Africa's crisis, he had arrived in the right place at the right time.

John had several contacts in Johannesburg, including W.H. Somerset Bell and F.M. Woollan, fellow directors of Bulawayo Estate and Trust, and from them he learned that if he intended to continue his journey to Bulawayo, in spite of the Matabele uprising, he would have to travel via Mafeking since the direct mail, coach route to the north via Pietersburg and Tuli had been closed. John decided to try the alternative route and, whilst delayed in Johannesburg waiting for a coach to Mafeking and the necessary travel permit, he decided to go to Pretoria to meet President Kruger. An appointment was arranged for him by Sir Jacobus de Wet, Britain's Diplomatic Agent.

Afterwards, John told the Press about his meeting with Kruger:

Of course, much that passed is not for publication. His face is one of great strength and distinctly indicates a talent for — well, say, diplomacy. After shaking hands with him and exchanging compliments on both sides and after the same process had been gone through with Sir Jacobus, the President talked for a moment or two about the Transvaal. One incident occurred which, I think, I am justified in relating.

'The Transvaal', said the President, 'is like a pretty girl with many lovers, each one waiting to marry her or at least to get a kiss.'

I suggested that the damsel was not free but that she was engaged to England, and that England as the first and only legitimate lover was the only one who ought to be considered in her eyes.

The President shrugged his shoulders and made a reply to the effect that the lover had behaved very badly and had alienated her goodwill.

Whilst in Pretoria John was also able to interview the imprisoned members of Jameson's force and their *uitlander* collaborators.

By now the crisis in Rhodesia was deepening but John was still impatient to get to Bulawayo. On 30 March he was at last given permission by the Transvaal authorities to continue his journey. A few days later he arrived in Mafeking, only to be held up yet again by a breakdown in communications. During this time Grey and his aides arrived from the Cape and with John enjoyed the hospitality of the trading pioneer Julius Weil, who was later to become famous as the man who provisioned the town during its 280 day siege.

Later, news came through that a few travellers, including Dr Hans Sauer, who had been one of Rhodes' cabinet ministers, had managed to reach Bulawayo. Grey, John Montagu and their companions decided to follow suit.

Their three-day 450 mile coach ride was not without incident. They set off on 18 April and soon after crossing the Khami river they narrowly escaped being captured by a Matabele regiment. It was with some relief that they later met up with a military bodyguard that had been sent out from Bulawayo to escort them into the town, which was now 'in laager' and at the centre of an area in which both the rebels and the whites were trying to concentrate their forces. At the time of John's arrival, grim battles were taking place only a few miles from Bulawayo, where a large *impi* was holding its ground on the far bank of the Umgusa river. It was several days before the natives were finally forced to retreat, following repeated attacks by white patrols armed with machine guns.

After arriving at Bulawayo, John brought himself up to date with the affairs of his companies, and became involved in some of the military operations that took place during the siege of Bulawayo, despatching reports to *The Times* over the telegraph line to the south which, for some reason, the rebels failed to cut. However, he soon found that the role of part-time war correspondent conflicted with his position as a captain in the Volunteers and he therefore became a temporary member of the staff of Colonel Sir Richard Martin, who as Deputy Commissioner in Rhodesia was in charge of the Chartered Company's troops in Bulawayo. John was later awarded the Rhodesia 1896 campaign medal.

Whilst John Montagu was occupying himself with business meetings and military matters in Bulawayo, Cecil Rhodes was making his way to the beleagured city from Salisbury, on the last leg of the historic journey that was to take him, unarmed, into the Matabele stronghold in the Matopo hills for an *indaba* with the tribal chiefs: a mission that ended the rebellion. Rhodes arrived at Bulawayo on 30 May, just as John was due to leave. There Rhodes learned that the young MP had been speaking up in the interests of the Chartered Company and had been entrusted with a petition to the House of Commons in which the colonists and their officials called for the continuance of the company's rule.

John's own accounts of his visit to Bulawayo give a glimpse of the hardships endured there during the siege. 'Eggs were 40s. to 50s. a dozen', he wrote. 'Tins of condensed milk were sold for 7s. 6d. each; strong buyers, as the Stock Exchange would say. Enough bread for breakfast for one person cost a shilling.' He also noted that the Rinderpest cattle plague had killed most of the oxen in a country that was dependent on the ox wagon for transport. The plague had, in fact, been an immediate cause of the uprising; the Matabele tribesmen derived nearly all their wealth from their cattle herds, the finest in Africa, which had been slaughtered wholesale by the Chartered Company in an effort to eradicate the plague.

Before he left Bulawayo, John was a guest of honour at a banquet — modest, in view of the circumstances — at which he expressed his views about the Jameson Raid and gave his impressions of the Johannesburg reformers. Then, early in June, he departed for home. The regular coach service to Johannesburg was now operating normally again and when he arrived there he found that the political climate had been transformed. Those who had been sentenced to death in April had been reprieved and most of them were now free. Kruger had commuted the death sentences on the leaders to fines of

£25,000 and the two-year prison sentences on their followers had been remitted to fines of £2000.

Cape Town, though, where John arrived on 5 June, was in mourning for the many South African victims of the liner *Drummond Castle*, lost off the French coast with the loss of all but three of her passengers and crew.

John had booked his homeward passage on the *Tantallon Castle*, the pride of the Castle Company's fleet (the Union-Castle merger still being four years hence). More than 500 passengers — a record number — had booked for the voyage, among them many of the Johannesburg reformers, happy at the prospect of enjoying the sunshine and sensations of Piccadilly after their miserable sojourn in the gloomy gaols of Pretoria.

The *Tantallon Castle* sailed on 10 June and as the *Cape Times* reported, John Montagu was among the 'more or less distinguished' persons on board. His fellow passengers this time included the colourful Henri Bettelheim, who was the Turkish Consul in Johannesburg, Lord Borthwick and Baron Quarles de Quarles.

John arrived back in England in early July and was soon fulfilling his promise to the citizens of Bulawayo to oppose any alteration to the government of Rhodesia. To enlighten the British public, many of whose members must have wondered exactly what was going on out there, he undertook a series of lectures; the first, at Battersea Town Hall, was entitled 'British interests in South Africa'. His interest in Rhodesia remained strong for many years and he continued to be a director of various Rhodesian companies, even though, soon after he became immersed once more in parliamentary and constituency business, the advent of the motor car fired his imagination more strongly than Imperial affairs; and began to demand more and more of his time.

5

Revolution on the Roads

Arriving home from battle-scarred Matabeleland, John found that a rebellion of a more peaceful nature had been taking place during his absence. The motoring movement, which was already becoming well-established in France and Germany, was beginning to gather momentum in Britain. Westminster and Whitehall were at last waking up to the fact that the speed limit and other petty restrictions were hampering the emergence of a British motor car industry.

The Red Flag Act had been amended in 1878 leaving councils free to decide whether the attendance of the flag man was still necessary in their areas but the speed limits of 4 mph in open country and 2 mph in town were enforced everywhere.

Not unexpectedly the first British motorists took the law into their own hands, bending and frequently breaking the petty clauses of the Act in an attempt to speed up the rate of progress. Henry Hewetson, a London coffee trader, was the first to do so, in November 1894. Ten years later he described his experiences in a book entitled *Ten Years of Automobilism*, edited by John Montagu:

> I happened to be in Mannheim, where one of my friends owned a Benz car. He showed me the working of it and I then went to Messrs Benz and ordered a two-seater 3 hp car which cost me about £80. They explained to me that although motor cars were being used on the Continent I should not be allowed, on account of English law, to run it in England. This appeared to me so ridiculous that it made me all the more keen to buy the car.

For six weeks Hewetson drove happily and unhindered around London, until he was warned by the Police that he would be prosecuted unless he complied with the Act. Hewetson responded by employing a youth to reconnoitre his route on a bicycle and warn him if there was a policeman in sight. On such occasions Hewetson would slow down and his son would walk ahead of his car, bearing a piece of red linen two inches square attached to a pencil. That, explained Hewetson, was the obligatory red flag. And he

45

was correct, since the lawyers who drafted the Act had omitted to stipulate the size of the flag. Not for the first time, the law was an ass.

Red flags to those early motorists were as red rags to bulls, and whilst John was adventuring in southern Africa between February and July 1896 moves were being made to repeal the Act. The Conservative administration of 1895 had, in fact, inherited the draft of a Light Locomotives Bill that had been prepared by Mr Shaw Lefevre, a member of the outgoing Liberal Government. The Bill made provision for motor cars to use public roads and although the Tories were not especially keen to change the law, several events prompted them to blow the dust off the Liberal draft and introduce it, somewhat half-heartedly, in the spring of 1896, by which time about 180 self-propelled vehicles existed.

The first of these events had been Britain's first motor show, held on 15 October 1895 at Tunbridge Wells and organized by the Mayor of that borough, Sir David Salomons, a highly respected engineer. The show was held soon after M. Levassor had made motoring history by driving 732 miles in just over 48 hours in the Paris-Bordeaux motor race. This achievement excited the public's imagination because it was only the second motor race ever held and the first in which a petrol-engined car had achieved the fastest time. Inevitably the interest aroused by this early triumph of the 'internal combustion' engine helped attract attention to Salomons' show, especially as one of the exhibits was a mechanical duplicate of the 4hp Panhard which Levassor had driven in the race. This exhibit was demonstrated by another opponent of the red flag, the Hon. Evelyn Ellis.

Then, a few weeks after the show, Salomons formed Britain's first motoring organization, the Self Propelled Traffic Association. This soon became a powerful pressure group in the motorists' campaign for emancipation and when Henry Chaplin, President of the Local Government Board, at last decided to introduce the bill that was to give the motor car the freedom of the roads, Salomons was able to exercise considerable influence on the way in which the new law and its regulations were drafted.

The activities of another influential figure, a company promoter by the name of Harry J. Lawson, also helped persuade the Government to change the law. At about the time that Salomons formed the SPTA, Lawson founded the Motor Car Club, a more commercially-minded organization. Lawson's greatest coup was a reception held at the Imperial Institute in London in February 1896 to promote an exhibition of motor cars due to take place there the following May. The guest of honour at the reception was the Prince of Wales, the future King Edward VII, who arrived in an electrically-powered carriage and then enjoyed his first ride in a petrol-engined car — a German-built Daimler driven by Evelyn Ellis, whose cousin Sir Arthur Ellis was the Prince's equerry. His Royal Highness was highly impressed by this new form of transport and from then onwards was a keen supporter of 'automobilism'.

There can be no doubt that with the motor car now tried, tested and approved by the future King of England, the Government felt obliged to make the confounded contraption legal. By the end of June 1896 Chaplin's bill had had its second reading in the House of Commons and on 14 November it became law. The occasion was celebrated by the famous Emancipation Run from London to Brighton, an event commemorated today by the RAC's annual Veteran Car rally along the same route. The Emancipation Run was the first major show of private motor vehicles on public roads, with the exception of the strictly illegal dashes around town by Hewetson, Ellis and their contemporaries. Although they had sought unfettered freedom the new Act imposed a speed limit of 14 mph on open roads, subsequently reduced to 12 mph by a Local Government Board regulation. It was, though, a tentative step in the right direction and the events leading up to 14 November 1896 were to change the lives of every Englishman, not least that of John Montagu, who within a year joined the group of pioneers who were to make motoring part of everyday life. The Prince of Wales announced, soon after buying his first motor car in 1900: 'I shall make the motor car a necessity for every English gentleman'. John was one of those for whom that declaration very quickly came true; before long it was true for thousands more.

One day during the autumn of 1897 an open Panhard automobile rattled westwards along the Bath road from London at the frightening and illegal speed of 16 mph. Small children yelled rude remarks from the roadside; their parents took refuge indoors; terrified horses reared up on their hind legs and bolted. Driven by his friend Hugh Weguelin, John Montagu was enjoying his first ride in a motor car. Their destination: Windsor.

For several months John had been reading about the amazing new motor cars that the law had lately let loose on the roads of Britain, and had seen several of the few hundred 'self propelled' vehicles that made their appearance within twelve months of Emancipation Day. Because neither the cars nor their drivers were registered or licensed, no one knows exactly how many of them were out and about during this first year of 'proper' motoring, but some indication can be gained from the fact that when it was formed in August 1897 the Automobile Club of Great Britain (forerunner of today's RAC) had 163 members. John later estimated that there were 650 motor cars and motor cycles in use by the end of that year.

His noisy, uncomfortable ride to Windsor was enough to convince John that the motor car was the key to road transport's future. 'There was no screen to protect us', he said in a broadcast from Savoy Hill 30 years later, 'and as we had no goggles and wore ordinary overcoats we soon began to feel very cold. But the fascination of speed made one forget all other discomforts. I could hardly sleep that night. It was difficult to think of anything else for a few days afterwards and I at once determined to get a car for myself.'

Having been initiated on a Panhard, John was inclined to follow the example of other motoring pioneers and buy a similar model. However this proved to be far from easy. Balked by tiresome negotiations he decided, in the spring of 1898, to order a Daimler. It was a sensible choice. The Prince of Wales had given the marque a unique distinction by making it the first petrol car to convey English Royalty and although the one that had been demonstrated to him in 1896 had been built in Germany, Daimlers were also being assembled in Coventry by the time Montagu decided to take up motoring. The Prince was soon to establish the long association with the Royal Family that Daimler enjoyed for many years, and the Daimler habit was quickly adopted by the nobility. John Montagu was one of the Coventry factory's first aristocratic customers.

His car, a 6hp six-seater, was delivered during the summer of 1898 and his own account of its features and foibles gives a fascinating insight into the hazards and pleasures of driving what was, in its day, one of the most advanced automobiles money could buy. This is how John described his new toy to those who tuned in to Savoy Hill in 1928:

> The engine was two cylindered, with tube ignition. There were two platinum tubes heated by a forced draught petrol flame and by this means the mixture of air and petrol vapour was exploded. The body consisted of a yellow wooden wagonette, the hind seats being sideways as in a horse drawn vehicle. The car had tiller steering, was chain driven and the gear change was beside the front seat on a metal pillar, on which there were two levers on a dial. One of these moved the bevel wheel in or out of its connection with the drive, while the other lever operated four speeds in the gearbox. There was no radiator but a tank containing about 12 gallons of water was carried at the back, the water being pumped through the cylinder block by a semi-rotary pump. As soon as the water had boiled away the tank had to be refilled. One tankful generally lasted for about 20 or 30 miles. The brake consisted of a footbrake operating a wood lined metal band on the countershaft, while the handbrake was merely a metal shoe which could be applied to the tread on the hind wheels. One of the anxieties of those early cars was that if there was a strong wind the ignition lamps blew out. When they had to be relit it was a risky job, for the petrol which had not been consumed after the lamp had been blown out occasionally exploded. As to the steering, if one struck even a small obstacle on the road the tiller was nearly wrenched out of one's hand. The

John at the tiller of his first car, a 6 hp Daimler wagonette, pictured outside Palace House in 1898.

springing was primitive and the bumping severe on any except a really good road.

Difficult to start, steer and stop; these were John's impressions of the first Daimler to be delivered to him at Beaulieu. From then on, John became regarded by many of his friends and relations as 'a nasty vulgar person who has lost caste beyond all hope, because I went about in motor cars'. But he was proud as well as critical of his new steed:

> I cannot describe the joy this first car gave me. I began to realize at once that the mechanical vehicle was going in time to produce a wonderful revolution in our transport methods. Often I waxed eloquent before older men about its possibilities but was generally laughed at and severely snubbed. Later on, when some of my prophecies came true, I became much disliked, especially by my 'horsey' friends. Such is the fate of most prophets.

John experienced his full share of the suspicion, resentment and outright hostility directed at those who ventured out in horseless carriages into a world still traversed by horse-drawn transport. On two occasions hotel keepers refused to provide accommodation. At Aldershot the horses of a cavalry detachment fled into an orchard when he approached, entangling their riders in the contents of a washing line strung between the boughs. At the Wheatsheaf Inn on the Winchester road some mutes and professional mourners pelted the Daimler with flints when the noise of its engine frightened their horse. At Hounslow his car skidded into some railings and fractured its petrol pipe. Panic ensued when an onlooker threw a match into the fuel dribbling into the gutter and started a fire. A police sergeant and two constables arrived on the scene and threatened to prosecute John for arson.

At the time he was running-in his first car, the organization that was to become the motive force in the continuing fight for the rights of the motorist was celebrating its first anniversary. This was the Automobile Club of Great Britain and Ireland, formed in 1897 by two former officers of the Motor Car Club — Frederick Simms (of magneto fame) who had introduced the Daimler into England, and C. Harrington Moore. The nascent Automobile Club included among its earliest members such luminaries as Henry Hewetson, Evelyn Ellis, Hiram Maxim, Alfred Harmsworth (the future Lord Northcliffe), Paris Singer, the Hon. Charles Rolls (one of the founders of Rolls-Royce), Henry Edmunds (the man who was to introduce Rolls to Henry Royce) and many others. The club's Secretary was Claude Johnson, who had started his career as Chief Clerk at the Imperial Institute at the time of the 1896 motor show and was later to become Rolls-Royce's chief executive.

John Montagu, then as always a gregarious fellow and by now a committed motorist, was inevitably attracted to the Automobile Club, not only because he sympathized with its aims, but also because he saw that its premises in Whitehall Court could conveniently provide him with a base for the busy social life that he enjoyed during his frequent visits to London as a Member of Parliament. The somnolent atmosphere of some of the London clubs where politicians gathered would not have been to his liking, whereas one whose members were full of enthusiasm for the new cause of motoring was far more congenial.

John became a member of the Automobile Club in January 1899. A few weeks later he ordered his second car — another Daimler, but much more powerful than the 1898 model because it was one of the first to have a four cylinder 12 hp engine. The car embodied several other advanced features, as *The Autocar* soon reported:

> The gear case and all the underframe are of aluminium, as also are the lubricators, carburettors and float chambers. The car is fitted to be used with either gravity or pressure burners. The engines (sic) are also fed by gravity, the car being thus made much safer in case of accident or of the pipe breaking. The aluminium bronze used in the gearing is wearing remarkably well, more than fulfilling all that was hoped of it, being almost noiseless and transmitting to the wheels with as little loss as may be the power of the engine.

The car was not delivered until May so it was in his 6 hp Daimler that John, accompanied by his motoring mentor Hugh Weguelin, drove the seven miles from Beaulieu to Lyndhurst on 1 April 1899 to take part in his first major outing with the Automobile Club. The occasion was the club's Easter Tour, which took a leisurely three days to make its way from London to Bournemouth. Its members then spent part of Easter Monday as John's guests at Palace House — the beginning of Beaulieu's long association with the motor car that has culminated in the village becoming a motorists' mecca, due to the establishment there of the present Lord Montagu's National Motor Museum.

A week or two before the Easter Tour, John had made his first significant contribution to motoring history by being the first motorist to take a future British Prime Minister — in the person of Arthur Balfour, then Leader of the House of Commons — for a drive. The elder statesman and his young chauffeur lurched over the 'bumpy macadam' of the Thames Embankment during a short spin from the Palace of Westminster. Within a few months Balfour bought his first car, a 4½ hp De Dion. After Balfour became Premier in 1902, and started to drive up to London from his country home, John commented: 'In years to come other Prime Ministers and their motor cars will stand outside No. 10 Downing Street. Possibly even aerial machines may

At the wheel of his second car, an 1899 12 hp Daimler, with his chauffeur Jack Stephens.

arrive by way of the roof and hurriedly drop in on a National Defence Committee meeting.' A prophetic statement, as proved by the use of helicopters for such purposes more than 50 years later.

When Balfour resigned in November 1905 the press reported incredulously that he had used a car to remove his household goods from No. 10. Said John: 'This is one of the many uses to which a large car can be put. There is nothing remarkable to thus shift his official papers and personal treasures in this safe manner than to trust them to the danger of a four wheeler or hansom'. Today it is common practice, when the early results of an election suggest that a change of government is imminent, for a removal van to be parked discreetly round the corner from Downing Street, ready to facilitate a swift change of occupancy.

Back in 1899, though, soon after John's dedication to motoring had carried him into the Automobile Club and, six months later, on to its committee, he began to use his 12 hp Daimler to travel up to Westminster from Beaulieu and an unofficial speed contest seems to have developed among the small coterie of motoring MPs, since in July *The Autocar* carried this report:

> Mr Montagu came to town recently on a motor car. He left his father's place at Beaulieu on the outskirts of the New Forest at 5.40am and reached Clapham at 10.30, doing the distance of 105 miles in less than five hours. This, says the *Daily News*, beats the record so far as it has been set up in the House of Commons.

(It also beat the speed limit and later a similar exploit was to earn John a £5 fine at Basingstoke for careering through the countryside at 17mph, committing what the magistrate called 'a very serious breach of the law').

One Monday evening, just before he set the 105 mile 'record', John came up against the full force of the law when he attempted to drive his Daimler into Palace Yard, Westminster — the open space near the House of Commons. Horse-drawn carriages had been using the area for years and they had recently been joined by the electric autocars belonging to Sir Samuel Montague and Mr J.H. Dalziel. But when John first drew up at the entrance to Palace Yard in his petrol-powered car the policeman on duty refused to allow him to enter: 'Them things is excluded by the order of the Speaker', John was told, 'because we never know when it might set the building on fire'. The order emanated, in actual fact, from the Office of Works, which had banned all spirit-powered vehicles from the precincts of the House.

Reluctantly John parked his car outside the gates but immediately appealed to the Speaker, contending that the ban was contrary to the privilege members enjoyed for 'free ingress and egress' to the Commons. Mr Speaker accepted John's argument and ordered the Police to allow the Daimler to enter the Yard. Next evening, accompanied by Hercules Langrishe, John again drove up to the gates but this time he was waved through without any objection.

'The sergeant at the gate told me he had received no orders to prevent my entry, so I drove in', John told a *Daily Mail* reporter. 'After the occurrence of Monday I saw the Sergeant at Arms who told me that he had given no instructions with respect to petrol driven cars as distinguished from electrical vehicles. I naturally claim the privilege as a Member to go to the House exactly as I please but it was intimated to me that no further opposition would be offered, so I just ran in on Tuesday to prove this.'

By now John had placed himself in the vanguard of the motoring movement. During the same session of Parliament in which he established the right of MPs owning petrol cars to use Palace Yard he was made Chairman of the Parliamentary Automobile Committee, a position from which he was able to exert great influence. His five-hour drive up to London and his altercation with the policeman gained him useful press publicity — and in 1899, as

In the Borough of Basingstoke, in the County of Southampton.

To *The Honourable John Scott Montagu of Palace House, Beaulieu, in the said County of Southampton.*

Information on oath [or affirmation] has been laid [or **Complaint** has been made] this day by *Thomas Hale*

of the said Borough *Superintendent of Police*

for that you on the *twenty-eighth* day of *March* One thousand

nine hundred and *two* at and in the Borough of Basingstoke

aforesaid, did *then being the driver or person in charge of a certain Light Locomotive on a certain highway there situate called Winchester Road, unlawfully did drive the said Light Locomotive at a greater speed than twelve miles an hour on the said highway, contrary to the Regulations contained in "The Light Locomotives on Highways Order 1896" duly made and published by the Local Government Board in that behalf and which said Regulations were at the time of the commission of the said offence and still are in force, and*

contrary to the form of the Statute in such case made and provided.

You are therefore hereby summoned to appear before the COURT OF SUMMARY JURISDICTION, sitting at the Town Hall in the said Borough, on Tuesday, the *twenty-second* day of *April instant* at the hour of TEN in the FORENOON, to answer to the said information [or complaint].

Dated the *fifteenth* day of *April* One thousand nine hundred and

[signature]

A Justice of the Peace for the
Borough of Basingstoke aforesaid.

The summons that led to a £5 fine for speeding.

throughout his career, he seldom missed an opportunity to attract the attention of the media.

As the 19th century drew to a close more and more wealthy men — and a few women — took up motoring, encouraged by the example set by the leading trend-setter of the day, the Prince of Wales. His short excursion at the Imperial Institute was followed, in November 1897, by a demonstration at Buckingham Palace of two motor tricycles and a brace of Coventry-built Daimlers. Then, in June 1898, the Prince had his first, albeit brief, ride in a petrol-powered motor car on a public road, when J. S. Critchley drove him from Warwick Castle to Compton Verney in a 5½ hp Daimler. By this time the Prince was seriously considering buying a motor car, and his decision to do so seems to have been prompted by a long drive through the New Forest in Montagu's 12 hp Daimler.

In August 1899 John Montagu was invited to lunch at Highcliffe Castle, some 17 miles from Beaulieu, where the Prince was staying with his friends the Cavendish Bentincks. Sometime before, or during, the meal it was suggested that the Prince should go for a drive and as a result, early that afternoon, the portly heir eased himself into the front passenger seat of John's

John and Edward, Prince of Wales, at Highcliffe Castle after their drive in the 12 hp Daimler.

John's son Edward, 3rd Lord Montagu of Beaulieu, and Charles, Prince of Wales (a great-great-grandson of Prince Edward), on the 12 hp Daimler many generations later.

motor, which was parked at the main entrance to the castle. Two lady companions made themselves as comfortable as possible on the hard, narrow rear seats, which they reached by clambering over the back wheels, the entrance to the rear compartment being similar to that of the horse-drawn dogcarts of the Nineties.

After crossing the London & South Western Railway at Hinton Admiral, John turned right and headed east along the road to Southampton for eight miles, before turning back to Highcliffe. At this point he allowed the car to build up speed and the ladies in the back — whose attire was hardly suited to fast motoring — had to struggle to prevent their elaborate hats being carried away in the slipstream. John later wrote this account of the journey:

> The King, enjoying the unwonted speed, chaffed his fair companions in his cheery way and made the true remark that motoring would force ladies to adopt some special form of head dress. Remember, this was said in 1899, before hardly any ladies were motorists and before special costumes for

motoring were invented. I distinctly remember that His Majesty displayed immense interest in the details of the car, asking the most intelligent and penetrating questions as to the machinery, and with his wonderful alertness of mind he had evidently grasped what a remarkable effect upon the locomotion of the world the coming of the motor car would have. After some conversation as to the sort of car which might suit him, His Majesty bade me farewell.

A few weeks later there was a sequel. John was asked to take his Daimler to Marlborough House, where it was examined by several Royal officials. Shortly afterwards the Prince ordered his first car. This was a 6 hp Daimler Mail Phaeton, now owned by Her Majesty the Queen. At the present Lord Montagu's suggestion the car was restored by the National Motor Museum at Beaulieu as a gift to mark the Queen's Silver Jubilee in 1977. Evidently the Prince was not too pleased with the car, probably because it was underpowered and uncomfortable. In 1900 he ordered two 12 hp Daimlers, one of which — a 14-seater for his beaters — had a similar engine to the one that had so impressed him during his ride in John Montagu's car the previous summer.

In 1899 the Automobile Club decided that the time had come for Britain to be represented in the great long-distance road races that had been taking place in France since 1894. No one was more aware than John Montagu that if the British motor industry were to catch up with its Continental rivals, it would have to prove that its cars were capable of running reliably at high speeds over long distances. As John saw it, the motor car was not merely a mechanical substitute for the horse-drawn carriage but a means of accomplishing long journeys, for business or pleasure, in the quickest possible time.

The major motoring event of 1899 was the 201-mile Paris-Ostend race, in which Britain was represented by Charles Rolls and John Montagu. They were the first Englishmen to race motor cars on the Continent in an official competition and Montagu had the distinction of being the first Englishman to enter a British-built car in such an event. Rolls' career as a competitor in Rolls-Royce motor cars was still several years in the future and his steed in the Paris-Ostend event was an 8 hp Panhard, built in France.

Despite his lack of motor racing experience John must have felt fairly confident as he and Rolls set off for Paris towards the end of August 1899. By now he had covered more than 3000 miles in his 12 hp Daimler and realized that if he could maintain the speeds he had achieved on his runs up to London from Beaulieu, he would have an excellent chance of acquitting himself creditably. His friend Rolls had the advantage of a car with a lighter body but the Daimler's more powerful engine might just give it an advantage over the Panhard. True, he and Rolls were racing for Britain, not competing with each other, but a friendly rivalry nevertheless prevailed between them.

The men who accompanied Montagu and Rolls as their obligatory passengers during the race included Julian Orde (a future secretary of the Automobile Club) and mechanic Jack Stephens in John's party, and Claude Johnson, Robert Bird and Staplee Firth in Rolls'.

John's 1899 Daimler in France at the time of the Paris–Ostend Race.

Trouble occurred before the race even started. The Daimler and the Panhard had been put aboard a ship at Southampton and carried to Le Havre without incident but John's car was so clumsily unloaded that the metal tube between the cylinder head and the radiator fractured and had to be brazed. This done, John set off to join the 29 other competitors due to line up for the start of the race at St Germain on 31 August — seven cars, 11 motor cycles and 11 voiturettes. These comprised the event's Tourist Class, which was allowed two days to complete the course, whereas the larger and more powerful cars in the Speed Class were to drive non-stop to Ostend on 1 September.

The prospect of 30 assorted vehicles starting simultaneously and jostling for an early lead amidst the inevitable clouds of dust and exhaust smoke must have been a daunting one as John motored towards the starting line just before 9.30 am. But a moment or two later he had to cope with a more immediate hazard. The cooling tube had broken again and whilst the other contestants roared off in a 'hurricane of noise' John was left on the line, desperately trying to find a way of repairing the pipe. This he eventually did by inserting a rubber hose between the two broken ends: one of the first occasions, perhaps, when a flexible pipe was fitted in the cooling circuit of a motor car.

By now, though, the other entrants had gained a lead of 130 minutes; but not all of them were enjoying a trouble-free run. The motorcyclists, not unexpectedly, had taken the lead but already one of them had taken a tumble and was lying unconscious at Conflans. An electric car had been delayed in the Forest of St Germain by what a reporter called 'a slight derangement', whilst several more competitors met with an assortment of setbacks on a steep hill and sharp bend at Bois-de-Molle. Among the victims there was M. Marcin, whose electric car broke an axle.

Rolls, too, was in difficulties. At first his Panhard ran very roughly but after 40 miles it settled down and he was able to draw ahead of the other cars. Twenty miles from St Pol, however — the stopping point for the first day — Rolls had to drive off the road to avoid a horse and cart. A tyre was punctured and during the 45 minutes it took to repair it, M. Creux swept by in his 10 hp Peugeot to take the lead. John Montagu, battling bravely along in the wake of the race and enjoying the benefit of a clear road, reached St Pol in 4 hr 57 minutes, covering the 113 miles at an average speed of 21 mph, which was only slightly slower than Rolls. However the time he had lost at the start counted against him, leaving him with little real chance of making a serious challenge unless his rivals experienced problems during the final leg.

Soon after leaving St Pol he was boxed in by two other competitors, whilst Rolls and Creux cantered ahead; then he had a puncture, which lost him another 12 minutes. He arrived at the finishing line on Ostend race course in third place, the medal he received to mark his achievement being the first prize that had ever been awarded to a British driver racing a British car (albeit of German design) on the Continent. Creux won, Rolls came second. But John Montagu could claim a moral 'dead heat' with the winner, since his average speed of 23.9 mph was exactly the same as that of Creux. Justly, but unfortunately, the 130 minutes he had taken to mend his cooling pipe brought his average down to 18.7.

John ordered a new 22 hp Daimler from the Coventry factory's representatives, who were watching the finish of the race and then he stayed on in France for another two weeks with the intention of entering the Paris-Bordeaux Race. Engine trouble forced him to withdraw but the 12 hp Daimler's career was not quite over. Within little more than six months the car and its owner were to face the toughest test that the Automobile Club had yet been able to devise for those 'nasty vulgar persons who went about on motor cars'.

6

The Thousand Miles Trial

An hour after sunrise on Monday 23 April 1900 an unfamiliar cacophony drowned the creak and rumble of horse-drawn carts, the jingle of halter and harness and the clatter of iron-shod hoofs that normally aroused the residents of the West End of London from their slumbers.

For most of those who lived and worked in the mews, squares and thoroughfares within earshot of Hyde Park Corner the dull, cold dawn was the beginning of just another day; but for 65 'automobilists' and their passengers a great adventure was beginning. As contestants in the Automobile Club's great Thousand Miles Trial they were literally about to put motoring on the map of England and Scotland.

Through Knightsbridge, Pimlico, Piccadilly and Park Lane they revved and rattled their way to the starting point in Grosvenor Place, gazed at in open amazement from the kerb and peeped at in disbelief from lace-curtained bedrooms. But how many of the casual onlookers who happened upon that strange spectacle were aware that, from that day onwards, life in London and Britain's other big cities would never be quite the same again? Daily travel in and between towns was to change in a way that few could imagine, thanks to the curious contrivances that had been groomed, fuelled and watered whilst London was asleep and coaxed into raucous life soon after first light.

For an organization that was facing many vicissitudes, the trial was an ambitious undertaking. Lack of support among the rank and file members had dogged the Automobile Club during its first two years; then, in June 1899, it had held a motor show in Richmond Park that ran up a loss of £1600. The club seemed to be dying on its wheels and a major effort was needed to boost membership and further its founders' aims of 'protecting, encouraging and developing automobilism'. But what could be done? And how could enough money be raised to do it?

Two remarkable men, both of them close friends of John Montagu, dragged the club out of its difficulties; its Secretary, Claude Goodman Johnson, a brilliant organizer and publicist and Alfred Harmsworth, the wealthy newspaper tycoon. Few were more enthusiastic about the future of motoring than young Harmsworth. Driving a fast car, he would say, was 'like being massaged in a high wind'. Whilst the idea of publicizing the automobile and the Automobile Club by holding a nationwide rally may have been Johnson's, it became a reality only because Harmsworth agreed to sponsor the event by indemnifying the club against any further losses and by donating £452 to its prize fund.

John Montagu was an enthusiastic supporter of the thousand mile trial from the moment it was first discussed by the club committee and was one of the first to register as an entrant; as the only Member of Parliament to take part his presence gave the event added prestige. One of the purposes of the trial was to test the competing cars to the limits of their reliability and performance, short of pitting them against one another in an out-and-out road race, which in any case would have been illegal. There was also another, equally important, objective and this was to demonstrate the capabilities of the motor car to the general public and explain, to non-motorists, what motoring and motor cars were all about. With this in mind, hill climbs were held during several stages of the trial (thus launching motoring as a 'spectator sport') and there were exhibitions and concomitant civic receptions at all the major towns en route. As a committee member, motoring MP and, by now, a trustee of the newly-formed Motor Vehicle Users' Defence Association, which was pledged to fight legal oppression, John was already a formidable spokesman for the motoring cause and during the trial he concluded his long stints on his Daimler by sharing the speaking duties with Charles Rolls, Henry Sturmey (editor of *The Autocar*), Lord Kingsburgh and Claude Johnson.

The significance of the trial and the value of the public relations campaign conducted during it by John and his colleagues, can only be appreciated by taking into account the many unanswered questions about motoring that existed not only in the minds of the general public, but among automobile owners themselves.

In 1900 when there were about 1500 cars on the road in Britain, the motoring fraternity was still divided on such fundamental matters as to whether steam or petrol engines were the best form of motive power, belts or chains the best way of transmitting that power to the wheels, water or air the most suitable means of cooling the engine, and so forth. In Britain these arguments had scarcely been put to the test, since very few advocates of any of these technologies had driven their cars so much as a hundred miles at a stretch, let alone a hundred miles or more day after day, as the trial required. The reliability of the bewildering designs on offer to motoring enthusiasts was, naturally, one of the factors that the trial would resolve. To enable fair comparisons to be made the competition was divided into two sections — one for vehicles entered by motor manufacturers, the other for privately owned vehicles entered by club members or their friends. Clearly it was the cars, not their drivers, who were on trial (even though success depended largely on skilled driving) and the decision to judge manufacturers' and privately-owned vehicles separately enabled like to be compared fairly with like.

It was, therefore, as supporters of a common cause who had yet to agree exactly how the cars of the future should be built that the 65 starters trundled to Hyde Park Corner in the grey light of that April morning more than 80 years ago. John had stayed overnight with Cis at his parents' home in Tilney Street so it would have taken him only a few minutes to drive his high-built Daimler down Park Lane to Grosvenor Place, where the contestants were being marshalled opposite St George's Hospital, forming an orderly line alongside the spike-topped ten-foot wall that surrounds the gardens of Buckingham Palace. Among those present were many men and machines who were to become household names, including Herbert Austin at the wheel of a Wolseley, George Lanchester and Archie Millership in Lanchesters, S. F. Edge in an 8 hp Napier, Charles Rolls in a 12 hp Panhard and J. D. Siddeley in a Daimler. In fact the event was dominated by Daimlers: there being no less than 12 among the 30 vehicles competing in Section II, the private vehicle class. And although the trial is today remembered as the first event in which motor *cars* travelled the length and breadth of the country, what is sometimes forgotten is that other motor vehicles, in the shape of motor tricycles and quadricycles, also competed.

At 7 am the starter, Lyons Sampson, lowered his flag. Fitfully, the trial began. John, with Cis and two others as passengers, carefully steered his Daimler down St George's Terrace, regulating his speed by gently applying the woodblock brakes — taking care not to engage them too fiercely, since they were liable to smoulder and catch fire on lengthy descents. Despite the early start a large crowd had gathered and the convoy had an unofficial escort of cyclists all the way out into the western suburbs of London, where the water-bound macadam roads of the metropolis gave way to the gravel, sandstone and flints that were to puncture the Daimler's tyres many times during the miles ahead.

Apart from the cold weather, against which their overcoats, caps and gloves afforded reasonable protection, John and his party had to contend with the clouds of dust that inevitably plagued all but the leading car in a motor rally in those pre-tarmac days. Goggles and veils, though hardly becoming, were imperative.

Three miles beyond Maidenhead, on a long and wide stretch of the highway leading to Reading, John encountered the trial's first 'speed trap'. This comprised two plain clothes policemen standing by a milestone, checking and timing each car as it passed, whilst colleagues concealed in a knot of spectators outside an inn a mile and a half further on performed a similar task. The speed limit here, as everywhere else, was 12 mph. Not all the contestants exercised the required restraint once the law was safely out of sight; John, we can be sure, was among those who later made the most of the many opportunities that arose to prove that their cars were capable of faster speeds than the law allowed. On the Reading road, however, he avoided prosecution; it was to be another two years before he received his first summons for speeding.

The destination for the first stage of the trial was Bristol, 118½ miles from Hyde Park Corner. The journey exemplified one of the problems that the new long-distance road traveller would have to face for some years to come: a shortage of places where food and drink could be obtained. As for the car, its needs could be catered for by carrying spare cans of petrol, or planning journeys so that calls could be made at chemists, blacksmiths or drysalters known to stock the essential fluid. A decent meal for the driver and his passengers, in comfortable surroundings, was another matter. However, Claude Johnson had kept all this in mind when planning the trial and the contestants managed to find hostelries and hospitality all along the way. En route to Bristol they called by invitation at Harmsworth's country estate at Calcot Park, where a champagne breakfast was served in a large marquee and where, in view of Harmsworth's interest in motoring, there were facilities for refuelling the cars and attending to minor mechanical problems.

John Montagu and Rolls were among the first to arrive at Bristol that evening and on the next day they and the other contestants took part in the first of the public motor exhibitions that punctuated most stages of the trial. Then, early in the morning of 25 April, the contest resumed with a run to Birmingham where the meet-the-people routine was repeated. By now John and his friends had assumed the role of motoring missionaries, since for most of the spectators who lined the village streets in the more remote regions traversed by the trial, and indeed for many of those who gathered at the finishing points and flocked to the exhibitions, the event was their first opportunity to see a motor car at close range. Not everyone became a convert to this new form of locomotion. 'Mad in one thing, mad in all', said one old-timer who watched the proceedings. 'You're blind even if we're mad', retorted John, temporarily forgetting that he was supposed to be helping to generate goodwill towards motorists. 'Twelve miles an hour on the road. Most dangerous. Never ought to be allowed!' was the old man's reply.

Like most of the contestants, John completed the early stages of the trial without major incident, but greater demands were imposed on the cars and their drivers as they ventured northwards, where the scenery became more spectacular, the hills steeper and the bends sharper. More and more competitors began to drop out because of mechanical trouble, and between Birmingham and Manchester the survivors tackled the first of the four hill climbing trials they were obliged to enter. This took place on Taddington

Hill, a long but not especially steep ascent of two and three quarter miles near Buxton, the highest town in England. John Montagu's Daimler was placed fourth among the cars, completing the climb at just over 11 mph; his friend Charles Rolls swept to the summit at 17.7 mph.

John arrived early at the day's finishing point, the Botanic Gardens in Manchester, which were the humid setting for the trial's third and most successful exhibition to date. This was opened by the Lord Mayor of the city and, in seconding a vote of thanks to His Worship, John spoke of the goodwill that had been extended to the competitors in every town and village they had passed through. Manchester, he commented, had been the birthplace of the railways and he hoped the city would now take an equally progressive attitude towards the motor car.

When the trial resumed at 7 am on 30 April the going was decidedly slippery due to heavy rain the previous day. First the stone setts of central Manchester had to be negotiated; next, a succession of industrial towns and villages, most of them paved with cobblestones, stretched ahead for 30 miles. John's Daimler was made the pilot car for this part of the day's journey. Overtaking was forbidden and, as Henry Sturmey noted, the vehicles proceeded 'almost in procession at a steady and moderate pace'. The rules of the competition allowed the vehicles to be driven by their owners or 'their substitutes or servants' but if, as is likely, John was still at the wheel at this particular time he would have felt more like a conquering hero than a motoring missionary. Sturmey, a passenger in one of the leading cars, reported that they 'crawled through dense throngs of factory hands and children'.

Once past Preston, on the edge of industrial Lancashire, the vehicles headed for Kendal and on the way they had the option of competing in a hill climb up notorious Shap Fell, the summit of which is more than 1300 feet above sea level. John opted out; Rolls, needless to say, accepted the challenge and won, being not only the fastest car to climb the hill but the fastest vehicle of any kind, whereas at Taddington a motortricyclist had beaten him by 1 mph.

The following day, during the fifth stage of the trial, John experienced serious mechanical trouble for the first time in more than 400 miles of increasingly arduous motoring. The rally was now making for Carlisle; Dunmail Rise, between Kendal and Keswick, had been chosen for the first really stiff hill climb test. Even the optional struggle up Shap had been long rather than steep. The two miles to the top of Dunmail included gradients of 1 : 9 and 1 : 10, quite a challenge to vehicles of no more than 12 hp. Several cars came to grief and a slipping bevel — a common enough fault — slowed John's Daimler to less than 6 mph, placing him well down in the list of stragglers.

The stage from Carlisle northwards was a momentous one, since it took the trial over the border and on to Edinburgh. The route covered exactly 100 miles and John was able to compensate for his disappointing performance the previous day. Birkhill Summit, the hill chosen for this stage's test, was admittedly the least taxing of all; it was also the last hill climb contest and its attraction to those who had not fared too well earlier on was that it gave them an opportunity to regain lost prestige. The climb up from Moffat to the control point at the foot of the hill was in itself something of a test for the less powerful cars, and nearby Moffat Water provided a convenient source for drivers who needed to refill their boiled-out radiators before proceeding any further. Reported Mr Sturmey: 'Mr Montagu arrived with Lady Cecil Montagu and a friend on their car, her ladyship being a keen automobilist and anxious to make good time up the hill'. Her anxiety was rewarded; the Daimler averaged 10.4 mph and was the seventh fastest car among the 45 vehicles that conquered the hill.

John in the passenger seat of his Daimler (right) at Edinburgh, half way through the Thousand Miles Trial. The car following him belonged to J.S.Critchley.

Edinburgh, 556 miles from London by the route the trialists had taken, was both the halfway mark and the turning point for the 50-odd vehicles that were still roadworthy after such a long pilgrimage. The city was already well acquainted with the motor car, a fact that John stressed when thanking the Lord Provost for opening the club's exhibition in Waverley Market. Then, on 4 May, the great trek home began — a downhill run, in the sense that the final stages were free of hill climb tests. For unrecorded reasons John took advantage of the rule allowing substitutes or servants to share the driving and instead of following Rolls — by now the trial's acknowledged leader — out of Waverley Market he took an express train to Berwick, racing by with a wave from his carriage at a point where the railway ran alongside the road. He rejoined his car at Berwick for the remaining 60 miles to the next overnight staging post, Newcastle upon Tyne, where in the rather overcrowded confines of the Drill Hall the Mayor welcomed the travellers to 'the greatest engineering city in the world'. John, once more the club's official responder, said he was sure the contestants in the trial would find 'a more than usually intelligent audience' in George Stephenson's birthplace. The club's object, he added, was to demonstrate that the manufacture of cars had reached a point where they could be considered thoroughly safe, reliable and trustworthy in the varying conditions of road, wind and weather. And he was right, for by and large the cars and their drivers were proving that in May 1900 motoring had, quite definitely, arrived.

With overnight halts and one-day exhibitions at Leeds, Sheffield and Nottingham and briefer shows at smaller towns along the way, the trial carried motoring's message through Yorkshire and the North Midlands, an ignition fault being John's only real cause for concern on these largely

John drives his Daimler to the starting point for a speed trial during the Thousand Miles Trial.

John in 1910, during celebrations marking the tenth anniversary of the Thousand Miles Trial.

trouble-free final stages. Curiously, it was in Sheffield that the trial attracted least interest. The arrival of the vehicles early one evening was watched by only a few spectators and the next day's exhibition was poorly attended, although John tactfully refrained from commenting on the city's evident apathy when he thanked the Master Cutler for declaring the show open.

Before reaching Nottingham the drivers were given a rare opportunity to indulge in some official 'scorching' when a speed trial was held on the Duke of Portland's estate at Welbeck Park. Here a 14-mile privately-owned road had been prepared on which, free of the fetters of the speed limit on public highways, the drivers could take a flying start at a measured mile and accelerate without scanning the ditches and hedges for policemen with stopwatches. Fourteen drivers entered the contest, stripping their cars beforehand of extraneous weight in the shape of petrol cans, baggage, back seats and spare tyres. No one could match Rolls, who averaged 37 mph, but John was satisfied with fifth place at just over 26 mph.

Nottingham was the trial's last night away from home and here, as before, the competitors and their companions were able to obtain bed-and-breakfast in comfortable hotels for about 3s.6d. (17½p) and a splendid dinner for another 5s. John and his friends indulged in the time-honoured practical joke of swapping around the newly-cleaned shoes left outside the guests' bedroom doors — an escapade rendered all the more hilarious because clergymen as well as motorists were staying at the hotel that night.

The run to London began at 7 am on Saturday 12 May — the 20th day of the trial, although there had been no activities on any of the Sundays because driving cars on the Sabbath was frowned upon. This final stage of just over 122 miles was the trial's longest, and before many miles had been covered the drivers met an unadvertised challenge. Ahead, near Rempstone, loomed Bunny Hill, which rises 110 feet in 1490 yards and finishes with a flourish on a gradient of 1:7. This was steeper than any of the test hills that had been encountered and John's car was one of many that had to be pushed to the top by its passengers. Nevertheless the Daimler was among the first cars to check

Members of the RAC at Queen Eleanor's Cross, Northampton, during the Thousand Miles Trial anniversary rally.
Left: John at the wheel of his first Rolls-Royce Silver Ghost, which he called 'Dragonfly'. His passengers were Charles Freeston in the front passenger seat and Charles Sykes (left) and G. Foster Pedley in the rear. Basil Joy and F.B. Browne are in the Vertex car behind the Rolls. Henry Edmunds ('the godfather of Rolls-Royce') and Mrs Edmunds are aboard the next car in the line, A12 (Edmunds' rally number in 1900).

in at the Automobile Club in Whitehall that evening. Of the 65 vehicles that had set off from Hyde Park Corner on 23 April, 35 completed the course under their own power.

Rolls, as everyone had forecast long ago, took the gold medal, this being awarded to the most meritorious vehicle to be accompanied throughout by its owner and driven or steered by him or her for at least half the distance of the trial. Silver medals went to vehicles which successfully accomplished the trial with their owners on board all the time and at the wheel at least half the time. Finally there were bronze medals for vehicles — of which John Montagu's Daimler was one — which successfully completed the trial without qualifying for a 'gold' or for a 'silver'.

As a test of technical merit and as an exercise in public relations the Thousand Miles Trial was a triumph. For John Montagu it was a turning point in his career. Soon after the event he began making plans for a venture that would enable him to devote nearly all his time to furthering the cause of motoring. As a Member of Parliament and committee member of the Automobile Club he was in a position of some influence; he had much to say on the subject of 'automobilism' and all he needed now was a means of putting his message across in his own way. The Press was the obvious medium, but its attention could not always be guaranteed: it had other topics of general interest to report, apart from the advent of the motor car. Montagu therefore decided to launch his own weekly motoring magazine.

7

John Montagu, Publisher

In 1900 Lord Salisbury called for a general election so, instead of going ahead with his plans for a new car magazine, John Montagu plunged enthusiastically into helping his party obtain votes. Lack of an opponent in his own constituency provided him with the safest of seats but his campaign became memorable because it was one of the first in which an MP used a motor car whilst electioneering. This enabled him to address up to five meetings an evening at places several miles apart, an unprecedented schedule for those days. Later he described his experiences for the *Daily Mail*:

> The greatest difficulty a candidate for a country division has to face is the necessity for his attendance at every village and hamlet in the constituency within the shortest possible time before the poll. During the last few days before the election every effort is made by both sides to have the last word with their candidate in attendance at every important place in the constituency. This means that at least four or five meetings must be held every night of which hitherto the candidate has only been able, by means of horse vehicles, to be present at two.

To make the best use of his motor car, John explained, the candidate had to keep to a timetable. This, he went on, is how it should be organized, presuming five meetings were to be covered:

> The meeting at village A must begin not later than 7.30. The candidate would then, after delivering a speech of 12 to 15 minutes, depart three miles — nine minutes at twenty miles an hour — to village B. Here two and a half minutes must be allowed for his entrance, taking off his coat and handshaking, and 15 minutes again allowed for a speech. Two and a half minutes more will be consumed in departing, in acknowledging cheers or escaping from eggs and another three or four miles have to be covered to the next village, C. Here, two and a half minutes must again be allowed for entrance, 15 for speech and two and a half for exit. It is absolutely necessary, moreover, that at this and subsequent meetings the speaker who is orating when the candidate arrives should sit down immediately or valuable time will be lost. Thus on again to villages D and E. Thus the candidate will have held five meetings. He will have spoken for 75

71

minutes, travelled anything from 20 to 50 miles and be home for supper in three to four hours.

Dashing about like this was typical of John, propelled as always by a restless spirit and boundless nervous energy and turning the journeys between his engagements into events that became almost as important as the appointments themselves. Almost, but not quite. Mindful, as always, of the importance of the media, without whose attention his efforts would largely have been wasted, he warned would-be motoring politicians not to leave the Press behind:

> The reporters of the two chief local organs must also be conveyed or no reports can be expected to appear and the rest of the constituency will not realize how energetically the work is being done. Therefore the car should convey the candidate, his agent, the two reporters and the motorman who, during this flitting by night (if the candidate drives himself) will probably have to sit upon the step.

John's words convey a comical picture of his open tourer roaring through the darkened New Forest, whilst his agent and reporters clutch their bowler hats and his whey-faced motorman clings to the bodywork inches from the churning gravel. Today's high-powered and highly mobile vote-catching itineraries have stemmed from John's 1900 campaign. He concluded his advice with a prophecy and a warning:

> The motor car is a great force at elections and will become a greater one year by year. Therefore I advise candidates not to express anti-motorist opinions or indulge in diatribes against motorists, thinking to curry favour with a misguided magistrate here or an out-of-date farmer there. Be tolerant and keep your opinion to yourself, and if you are a motorist already don't be ashamed of being one, for you are on the winning side in the near future and when polling day comes you will find local automobilists keen and ready to help you.

John remained an enthusiastic campaigner at general elections for the rest of his life, attending meetings night after night. Because eating a heavy meal before making a speech was liable to bring on an attack of asthma, he was sustained at these times by cold chicken sandwiches before each meeting and a bowl of soup afterwards.

Once the election was over, John was able to concentrate all his energies on planning his motoring magazine. For advice he turned to Alfred Harmsworth, owner of the *Daily Mail*, to which Montagu was a regular contributor.

There had never been a publisher like Harmsworth before, and there were those who hoped there would never be one like him again. Eleven months older than John, he had been a brilliant freelance journalist in his youth and in the 1890s he was quick to realize that thanks to compulsory education, founded on the Elementary Education Act of 1870, the literate population of the country was increasing, creating a new and ever-expanding market for popular newspapers. The age of mass communication can be said to have started with Harmsworth's *Evening News* and *Daily Mail*, in which he pioneered the familiar elements of modern journalism, human interest stories, campaigns, competitions and a pithy reporting style based on concise sentences and paragraphs in which facts, ideas and arguments were set out one at a time, clearly and simply.

Their backgrounds could not have been more different: Harmsworth, self-made, power-hungry, eccentric; Montagu, the wealthy aristocrat, anxious to make his own way in the world, yet at the age of 34 still looking for a way of channelling his energy and enthusiasm into a sound business venture. But Montagu and Harmsworth had much in common (though Cis did not like him), for both had been quick to appreciate the importance of new methods of communication, first bicycles, then motor cars, later aeroplanes and radio. It was the second of these that drew them together at the turn of the century; and when, a year or two later, John decided he wanted to launch his own motoring periodical it was to Harmsworth that he turned for practical advice on journalism and publishing. John was by no means a novice with words, but his political contributions to the *Western Gazette* and his despatches to *The Times* from South Africa in 1896 were the kind of commissions any MP would expect to be asked to undertake. They were a far cry from the kind of writing and editing that would earn anyone a living, and there can be no doubt that John wanted his magazine to be a commercial success, not merely a rich motorist's mouthpiece.

Harmsworth invited John to work at the *Daily Mail* for a while to learn how the various departments were run. Little is known about his time as a temporary staffman on Britain's million-copies-a-day paper, but one of his first assignments was recalled many years later by the obituary writer there who reported his death. John, it seems, was sent down to the Thames Embankment one night to report on the plight of London's homeless, who slept rough along the waterfront. His article touched the heart or conscience of one reader, who sent £20-worth of half crowns to the *Mail* office. John was then sent back to the Embankment to distribute the money among the down-and-outs and write a follow-up on their reaction to their unexpected largesse.

Once equipped with professional insight into the publishing world, John set about finding premises and recruiting staff for his new weekly magazine which he had decided to call *The Car Illustrated*. Initially he rented offices at Piccadilly Mansions, on the corner of Shaftesbury Avenue and Sherwood Street, overlooking Piccadilly Circus — 'the hub of automobilism', as he hopefully called it. John and his staff would rush to the windows whenever they heard a motor car, so novel were they. Four years later traffic was still sparse by modern standards: a photograph of Piccadilly Mansions published in *The Car Illustrated* showed only a dozen or so vehicles circulating around Eros in the foreground, and most of them were horse-drawn.

The first and second floors of Piccadilly Mansions were the home of the Montagu publishing empire until 1906, when it moved half a mile westwards to 168 Piccadilly. These premises, facing Bond Street, provided the benefit of a suite of offices on the first floor and a shop at street level from which the magazine and its associated books, maps and other publications could be purchased. Six years later *The Car Illustrated* and its offshoots moved to their final home, 62 Pall Mall, a town house opposite Marlborough Gate, where John worked in a fifth floor office behind a large semi-circular window — still a feature of the Pall Mall skyline — which gave him a commanding view across St James's Palace to the Surrey hills.

Although, as its title implies, *The Car Illustrated* gave priority to motoring news, it was launched as (and remained) *A Journal of Travel by Land, Sea and Air*. This all-embracing sub-title made it necessary for John to recruit, as employees or as freelance contributors, a versatile team of experts and commentators on all aspects of transport. He also needed experienced personnel to concentrate on the business affairs of the journal. Whilst John was personally involved in both the creative and the management aspects of his venture, he delegated some of his commercial responsibilities to G. Butler Morris, who was his publisher for five years, when they parted company after a disagreement. A young man by the name of Claude Wallis, who later became Chairman of the Iliffe publishing group, sold advertising space for Montagu and would boast proudly to his clients that *The Car Illustrated* was read in all the best houses.

Reports and comments on travel on land were contributed by such luminaries as Charles Freeston, who became a famous pioneer of Continental — and especially Alpine — touring; G. Foster Pedley, formerly manager of the Daimler works at Coventry; Lawrence Cade, the motorcycling expert; and John's cousin George Montagu MP (the future Earl of Sandwich), who was a great railway enthusiast.* 'Travel by air' in the magazine's first year was restricted to balloons and the early airships, since the Wright brothers' first aeroplane flight would not take place for another 18 months, but Charles Rolls, who was as keen on ballooning as he was on motoring, could always be relied on to keep John up-to-date with news of lighter-than-air aeronautics

---

* Interviewed in 1980, George Montagu's son, Victor (the former Viscount Hinchinbrooke), recalled how, some 60 years earlier, as a 15-year-old boy, he had been allowed to drive John Montagu's open Rolls-Royce along private roads at Beaulieu. Victor Montagu recalled that John Montagu (his godfather) was 'a sweet-tempered man with a kind face'.

and the journal soon signed up an ideal aviation correspondent in the person of J. T. C. Moore-Brabazon (later Lord Brabazon of Tara), who in 1909 became the first British pilot to fly an all-British aeroplane around a closed circuit of one mile. The feat won him a prize of £10,000 offered by Lord Northcliffe, who by this time was sponsoring aviation with the same enthusiasm he had applied to motoring ten years earlier.

Two other people who became closely associated with the early days of *The Car Illustrated*, were Charles Sykes and Eleanor Velasco Thornton. Sykes, who was 27, had won a scholarship to the Royal College of Art and had then decided to settle in Chelsea instead of returning home to Newcastle upon Tyne. A mutual friend introduced him to Claude Johnson and through him he met John Montagu. For many years Sykes contributed highly individual illustrations and superb artwork to *The Car Illustrated* including some of the most beautiful pictures of early Rolls-Royces ever to grace the pages of the Edwardian press.

Despite the grand names by which she insisted on being called, Miss Thornton was registered as plain Nelly when she was born in South London in 1880. She and her younger sister Rose (who married Gordon Hayter, a member of Montagu's staff) were pupils at the Grey Coat Hospital, the well-known school for girls near Westminster Abbey. Nelly became Claude Johnson's secretary at the Automobile Club and Rose went to work for Lord Northcliffe. Nelly, or Eleanor as she now called herself, was at the age of 22 a vivacious and attractive young woman; talented, intelligent, ambitious and free living, she was a true 'New Woman' of the Edwardian era. Montagu was impressed by the way in which she ran Claude Johnson's office and captivated by her good looks. In 1902 — just before Johnson left the Automobile Club to become Charles Rolls' partner at C. S. Rolls & Co., motor dealers — she joined John Montagu's staff at *The Car Illustrated*. Eleanor Velasco Thornton, more than any other individual, helped John tackle the multitude of problems he had to face whilst planning and launching his journal.

Although motoring was still in its infancy when *The Car Illustrated* was started, motor makers (a description first used officially in the 1901 census) and motorists already had their own trade press; there was the Automobile Club's own members' *Journal, The Autocar* (price 3d.), *The Motor Car Journal* (1d.) and *The Automotor Journal*. But John Montagu's new weekly was destined to be quite different from any of these because it would cover all forms of transport, would be printed on glossy paper to ensure good quality reproductions of the monochrome photographs with which it would be liberally sprinkled, and would eventually contain colour pictures. It was moreover to be an 'up market' venture with a cover price of 6d., reflecting the owner's aim of reaching a wealthy readership at the top end of

Eleanor Velasco Thornton, businesswoman. Photographed at the offices of The Car Illustrated.

the social scale, to whom coverage of the social life of the motoring aristocracy was as important as articles on the latest trends in motoring. Technically and visually *The Car Illustrated* was to be superior to its contemporaries.

The first issue of *The Car Illustrated* appeared on Tuesday, 28 May 1902 and its style and content established a pattern that was maintained, week after week, for the next 14 years. The journal could hardly have made a more auspicious debut for there, on the frontispiece, was a photograph of Britain's most eminent motorist, the still uncrowned King Edward, seated behind the wheel of the editor's latest car, a massive (for those days) open 24 hp Daimler, the third of the six Daimlers of ever-increasing power that John had bought in the years before he became a Rolls-Royce convert.

A few weeks before *The Car Illustrated* went to press, the King had visited Beaulieu whilst convalescing aboard the Royal Yacht in the Solent. The occasion had provided John with an 'exclusive' for his first edition, as well as great personal prestige, and it is possible that publication had been held so that page one treatment could be given to the Royal visit. When the King had landed at Bucklers Hard, the tiny harbour three miles downstream from Palace House on the Beaulieu River, John and his Daimler had taken him on a drive through the New Forest. Followed by his staff, who travelled in a 12 hp Panhard lent to John by Lord Wimborne, the King had been shown around Palace House and the nearby ivy-clad ruins of Beaulieu Abbey and then driven to Lyndhurst, Wilverley Post, Brockenhurst and Lymington. The route back to Beaulieu involved crossing the Toll Bridge at Lymington, where an altercation with the toll keeper briefly delayed the Royal progress.

Earlier in the day a motorist had sped across the bridge without paying his toll, and when John and his distinguished passenger arrived they found the gate across the bridge shut. The keeper was unmoved by John's insistence that they should be let through. 'King or no king, who was it who rushed my gate?' he asked. Placated by a payment of the statutory toll and, no doubt, a tip, the keeper eventually allowed the Daimler to pass.

The tour ended at the Bungalow, a curious corrugated iron building that John had purchased for £100 at the Royal Show at Southampton and re-erected on his estate by the Solent shore for use as a weekend retreat and guest-house for his London friends. They were, in the eyes of Beaulieu residents, an odd bunch. At the Bungalow that afternoon in 1902, King Edward enjoyed — or attempted to enjoy — an impromptu meal of plovers' eggs with John and Cis. John had gathered the eggs earlier that day but most of them had been spoiled by a late frost, with the result that a jet of foul-smelling liquid spurted on to the King's waistcoat when he started cracking his eggs. Cis took over the task, remarking: 'This is very hard on me, Sir', to which the King replied: 'On the contrary, it is very hard on *me*'. Eventually a dozen sound eggs were found and later the Royal guest posed for the photograph that was to become

*Royal visit to the Bungalow, 1902. This is the photograph that John signed for Eleanor
Thornton.*

famous as the first to show Edward as King aboard a motor car. Another
photograph taken on the same occasion shows John at the wheel and Edward
at his side. The original print still survives in the Montagu family archives
and is signed 'Miss Thornton, from John Montagu, April 1902', signifying
the close relationship that was developing between them even before *The Car
Illustrated* first appeared. Inside that first issue, in an article entitled 'The King
as a Motorist', John told his readers all about the Royal excursion:

> I was very much struck by His Majesty's extremely intelligent interest in
> every part of the car. His Majesty, like the good Englishman that he is, has
> always given his support to English-made motor cars. In 50 years a picture
> of the first King of England and Emperor of India who adopted the motor
> car as a means of locomotion will be historical. Her late Majesty, Queen
> Victoria, when she first travelled in a railway train, was thought by many
> to be running a great risk. There are those who take the same view of the
> motor car today, although happily they are decreasing in number.

The King's health was at this time concerning his admirers, all of whom

King Edward VII takes a back seat in John's 22 hp Light Daimler in July 1904, en route from Hinton Admiral railway station to Highcliffe Castle where he was the guest of Mr and Mrs George Cavendish Bentinck. Lady Savile is on the King's right. His equerry, the Hon. H. Legge, is the front seat passenger.

knew the kind of life he was leading and marvelled at his ability, in his 60th year, to lead it. Concluding his article, John confided:

> Let me record for the benefit of those alarmists who are always assuring us that great personages are either very ill or likely to become so shortly, that in His Majesty's case such rumours are absolutely false. Not only this, but as every motorist knows, good nerves are a sign of good health and in this respect I can honestly put His Majesty in the very front rank.

Ironically, three weeks after these words were published it was announced that King Edward had perityphlitis. Surgery was necessary and his coronation had to be postponed for six weeks.

John certainly made the most of his social connections in that first issue of *The Car Illustrated*. A.J. Balfour, then Leader of the House of Commons and soon to become Prime Minister, contributed a message of support. 'The problems of locomotion are of the greatest social significance', he wrote. 'The

most effectual means for dealing with congested populations and traffic will
be found in the cheapening and improvement of methods of locomotion. Any
enterprise which, like your own, is likely to promote the invention of new
methods and spread knowledge of those already discovered ought to meet
with healthy support.'

Alfred Harmsworth was more forthright. As to be expected of the man
who likened motoring to being massaged in a high wind, he contributed an
article on the more sensual aspects of driving, saying:

> I believe that the brain, nerves and blood are stimulated by rapid transit
> through the air. I know of no better means for quick recuperation after
> illness or great mental effort than a day in a rapid motor car. Working all
> day at some pressure in London, taking a considerable railway journey
> followed by half an hour in a horse-drawn carriage, I formerly arrived
> home too tired to enjoy exercise. Now I drive the whole distance by road
> in such time as I will not mention for the benefit of the Police, and am able
> to walk or play tennis, anxious afterwards, rather than the reverse, to dine.
> We do not sufficiently realize that much time is taken in getting our tickets,
> finding our platform and reaching our train — the process being reversed
> at the other end of the journey, with perhaps a change of railway carriage
> in between. The motor has changed all that. Anything that takes one away
> from the railway is not time wasted. Almost any other form of travel is
> leisure by comparison.

Not every contributor was as enamoured with motoring as Balfour and
Harmsworth. Gilbert Parker, one of John's MP friends, grumbled: 'Though
it produces an exhilarating effect by reason of the swift passage through the
air, it leaves an unpleasant irritation of the nerves behind'. Harmsworth's
nerves, obviously, were of stronger fibre than those of Mr Parker.

By launching *The Car Illustrated* at the end of May 1902, John was able to
publish a topical account of an historic motor contest which had been staged
by Lord De la Warr that Whit Monday at Bexhill-on-Sea, Sussex. Dis-
counting a three-car event held in 1901 on the Crystal Palace cycle track, this
was Britain's first official motor car race. It had long been John's ambition to
introduce motor racing into Britain and he first suggested the idea to Lord De
la Warr when he met him at Monte Carlo in February 1902. The idea was
soon followed up, for by Easter preparation of the track on the De la Warr
estate was under way. Even though the course proved to be too short for the
most powerful entrants to make a proper flying start, some high speeds were
reached by, among others, M. Serpollet's steam powered 'Easter Egg', thus
described because of its streamlined body. John rode with Serpollet during
one of the races and enthused:

> Never, except on the footplate of a locomotive, have I felt the sensation of

speed so intensely. Before the finish was reached I felt certain that well over a mile a minute was being accomplished.

John donated a challenge cup for the main event of the day, which was won by Charles Jarrott in a 40 hp Panhard, with Charles Rolls in second place in his 40 hp Mors. Just as the Thousand Miles Trial of 1900 was the beginning of motor sport in Britain, so was the Bexhill meeting the start of motor racing in this country. 'Where Bexhill has led, others may follow', wrote John. He went on to urge other seaside towns to hold similar events. 'This would be a source of great benefit and bring much local prosperity, besides being a new attraction to people who visit seaside resorts, the life at which is sometimes the very essence of boredom.'

Serious thoughts like these were the pith of John's journal, but there was a generous leavening of lighter material. 'Cecilia' (Cis) contributed a motoring diary of her adventures on the road with 'Jack' in the 1890s in their first motor car. 'Jack' himself, none other than John Montagu of course, offered advice in his weekly Editorial Jottings on anything and everything directly or indirectly connected with motoring, including this coy gem entitled 'Cars and Courtship':

> However fond you may be of the lady, disaster will result if you endeavour to steer with one hand and entrance your lady with the other. The motor car is a jealous animal and wants your whole attention.

Cis also contributed a weekly feature called Costumes and Chatter, signing herself 'the Goddess in the Car'. The emphasis was on motoring apparel and the aim was to advise lady motorists and passengers how to dress fashionably, whilst keeping as warm and dry as possible. No easy task in 1902. Muriel Beaumont, the future Lady Du Maurier, posed prettily in her 16 hp Napier for the first issue to illustrate 'a new motor hat with removable hood'. A few weeks later, Lillie Langtry was photographed snuggling into her new coltskin motor coat and an expensive sable. In due course George Montagu's sister, Lady Olga Montagu, and Laura, Lady Troubridge, took over the authorship of the fashion page.

The Car Illustrated provided motorists with many benefits other than hours of interesting and amusing reading. Annual subscribers were given free life insurance (£1000) and free disability insurance (£6 a week) to cover them against death or injury in motoring accidents; other classes of insurance of almost every description were also offered, since John's business interests included directorships of insurance companies. A Touring and Information Bureau was set up along lines similar to those later followed by the motoring organizations; here, motorists could obtain help on all kinds of matters, ranging from advice on road conditions throughout the country to technical reports on second-hand cars. A thriving sideline was the publication of motoring guides and books, written or edited by John. One of his most ambitious ventures was a set of five guide books entitled *Roads Made Easy*, written by Claude Johnson, who toured the countryside with Brownie box cameras mounted on his car so that he could take photographs of major crossroads and junctions. These were published alongside the text and showed readers whether to turn left, right or drive straight ahead. 'Follow the telegraph wires' was another way of telling drivers which road to take. *Roads Made Easy* established a format rather like that adopted later by the Michelin Guides. John was fascinated by maps, signs and guides and he formed a company at Beaulieu called the Terraforma Syndicate which made maps that had the attributes of contour models, even though they were flat.

John's weekly magazine was, perhaps, the most important legacy he left to those who today study the early development of the motor car and its social

Earliest known photograph of employees of The Car Illustrated, *seen during an outing somewhere in Surrey in June 1914.*
Daniel Hill of Wisconsin (seen seated second from right, front row, as a boy of 14) supplied the picture and is probably the only surviving member of the staff. Among those who can be positively identified are the manager, Mr Gillingham (standing second from left), Wherry Andersen, acting editor (wearing a bowler hat and framed by the archway) and Mr Baily (immediately to Mr Andersen's left).

ramifications. Launched before King Edward was crowned, it survived the entire Edwardian era. It was, though, a financial liability and a sister monthly publication, *The Car Magazine*, had to be abandoned when its losses became too high to bear. Although one of the first magazines to have coloured pictures *The Car Illustrated* made a profit in only five of its 14 years in John's ownership, so commercial success as an editor and publisher eluded him even though his brainchild helped motoring to become accepted and respectable. In 1911 his journalistic responsibilities were increased when he took over the Royal Automobile Club's struggling *Journal*; Harold Lafone, one of his employees, became its editor.

The Car Illustrated, like John Montagu himself, was born in an age of optimism and progress, when major advances were being made in transport and communications. In 1902 the world was only just becoming accustomed to such innovations as pneumatic tyres, municipal buses, electric 'tube' railways, wireless telegraphy, Zeppelins, and monarchs and Prime Ministers who rode around in motor cars. That same year also saw the publication of H. G. Wells' cumbersomely-titled *Anticipations of the Reaction of Mechanical and Scientific Progress upon Human Life and Thought*, a book which quickly ran to eight editions and established Wells as a political prophet. The author forecast the development of privately-owned motor carriages 'capable of a day's journey of 300 miles or more', travelling 'at a reasonably controlled pace' on ordinary streets and at high speeds 'on specialized ways restricted to

'A car of the future', as depicted in The Car Illustrated.

swift traffic'. John met Wells several times and today the two men can be seen as fellow visionaries, making predictions that were often greeted with sheer disbelief. Soon after *Anticipations* was published John commented: 'Mr Wells deprecates the folly of spending public money on tramways. As I have often pointed out, tramways are four times as expensive as a single line of railway and should the population shift to a new locality the rails cannot be shifted with it, whereas the motor omnibus can follow the line of population. The motor car may be the rich man's vehicle today but it will be the poor man's friend tomorrow.'

John's prophecies adorned nearly every issue of *The Car Illustrated* and as 1902 was the year in which he began to establish his reputation as a motor transport seer, the course his career took in the latter half of his life will be easier to appreciate if some of the ideas he floated during his first years as a professional writer are touched on now.

As even the very first issues of his magazine reveal, John regarded the motor vehicle as the transport of the future because it would enable people and their goods to be carried from door to door. Despite his boyhood enthusiasm for railway locomotives and his later prowess as an engine driver, John came to the conclusion — probably long before the Thousand Miles Trial — that vehicles running on rails had only a limited usefulness. Trams, he told the House of Commons in June 1902, would soon be replaced by cars in many parts of London. A month later he questioned the advisability of building railways for the Army on Salisbury Plain. Good roads for motor cars would be more use, he said, as this would enable the Royal Engineers to gain much-needed experience in operating motor vehicles — it being 'most probable' that the troops would have to manage large numbers of them in the future. Considering that the British Army was then still dependent on horse-drawn transport, and steeped in the traditions of the cavalry, John's proposal that soldiers should learn how to get about in cars was a bold one. He had already told the Government in 1901 that Britain should follow the example of Germany and France and re-equip its cyclists corps with motorcycles. Newly promoted to the rank of major in the Hampshire Volunteers, he knew a thing or two about motorizing the military. His brigade had used four cars whilst in camp and found them invaluable for scouting and staff duties. He reported:

> Staff supplied with vehicles could perform longer distances than horses in a shorter time. In war a thousand men on motor bicycles or tricycles could easily ride a hundred miles in one night, appear behind the enemy's lines, cut off all means of communication and take possession of the whole district before their presence was known. A corps of motorcycle scouts might be of immense use in the defence of the south coast against any sudden invasion.

Some of his friends held similar views, having formed themselves into a body known as the Army Motor Volunteers, which provided transport for senior officers during manoeuvres on Salisbury Plain in August 1901. In July 1903 the War Office, perhaps with some reluctance, formally approved the creation of a Motor Volunteer Corps. Twelve years later John was able to put into practice some rather more ambitious ideas for equipping soldiers with motor transport.

Fuel for motor cars, and the roads the cars travelled on, preoccupied Montagu as much as the cars themselves. In 1907 he regaled his readers with an article on the 'sea of petrol' that existed in Britain in the form of the ever-increasing quantity of motor spirit used by the nation's expanding fleet of motor vehicles. Even though at that time petrol was extremely cheap by today's standards, John thought the time had come to discover an alternative fuel. He devoted several editorials to his proposals to encourage the use of alcohol instead of petrol, since the former could be produced more cheaply from almost any substance, including sawdust, leaves and fruit. He even regarded the production of alcohol motor spirit as the answer to the economic problems of Ireland, whose derelict distilleries could, he said, make alcohol from the country's abundant crops of potatoes. His scheme for running cars on alcohol developed into a full-scale campaign, in which he urged the Government to exempt non-potable alcohol from tax and thus encourage its use by motorists. The supposition that the Government would agree not to tax a commodity that was likely to become in greater demand was, perhaps, naive but today the need for a liquid motor fuel that can be made from renewable resources is more evident than ever.

John also saw a future for electric cars — although unhappily they, too, later reached a technological dead end. Noticing that the new steam-powered central corn mills were putting windmills out of business, he suggested:

> If these were to be fitted-up with small electric dynamos and a few accumulators, they would form very valuable charging stations for electric cars. In the near future, by the help of such stations, electric vehicles will be used for cross-country travelling.

This charming idea of electric cars silently drawing up beside windmills to recharge their batteries was one of John's less realistic proposals.

Whatever their source of energy, motor cars are at their most efficient on straight, uncongested, well-metalled roads and it was the lack of these that exercised John's mind throughout his motoring career. He published a regular feature in *The Car Illustrated* entitled 'The Best Ways out of London', to help drivers avoid traffic jams, and he devoted page after page to the need for brand new highways for motor traffic — for which the term 'motorways' had already been coined. In 1902 he advocated a new road to the west from

London, avoiding 'the narrow gut of Brentford', and in 1923 — 36 years before the M1 was opened — he campaigned for the construction of a motorway from London to the North.

But although constantly thwarted in his campaign for new roads he had some success in improving the surfaces of old ones. Built from dirt and stones, these quickly disintegrated under the onslaught of more and more rubber-tyred motor vehicles. The dust they raised was even more of a nuisance than their noise and smell. In King Edward's day, living beside a road frequented by motor traffic was, in its way, as unpleasant as living alongside a motorway today. All types of devices were fitted to cars in an attempt to stop them raising clouds of dust as they passed by but, as John commented, little could be done 'until the day dawns when science discovers a process by which dust can be effectively and cheaply laid on the high roads'.

To bring that day nearer John set up a Dust Fund (Balfour was an early contributor) to sponsor dust-laying experiments. It was a modest start to what turned out to be a gradual, if in John's view inadequate, improvement in Britain's road system. From these experiments stemmed the wider application of tarred and asphalted surfaces. The road to John's seaside bungalow at Beaulieu was one of the first to receive a treatment of 'tarmac' when the fund was established, and a full report on the experiment was given by John to the Royal Commission on Motor Cars in 1905.

However it was as a platform for his campaign against the 12 mph speed limit and the severe fines imposed on those caught exceeding it, that *The Car Illustrated* initially became popular. 'You can beat your wife, steal, get drunk, assault the police and indulge in many other crimes and felonies', he said, 'and you will find it cheaper than to go at $12\frac{1}{2}$ miles an hour.' A regular cartoon showed the scales of justice weighted heavily against motorists compared with other minor offenders. Not all his readers agreed with him. One, a JP, responded to an especially fierce editorial by writing to John in this vein:

> I shall be happy to meet you with a view to our better acquaintance in the Court of Petty Sessions at Ashby-de-la-Zouch, over which I have the honour to preside, when I trust to make it clear to you how much you are indebted to the legislature of this country.

John, who had been a magistrate for ten years and would soon become the Chairman of his local bench, wryly replied that the letter exemplified the impartial spirit of the judiciary. In 1902 and 1903 he started to rally support for what was to be the greatest parliamentary battle of his career. He was to emerge, bloodied but triumphant, with a new deal for motorists. Curiously, it was a victory that did not win him their universal acclaim.

8

Coup d'état at the Automobile Club

The notion that it was dangerous to travel at more than 12 mph on the roads of Britain was, in the early years of this century, so deeply entrenched that in some places express trains were expected to slow down to this pace whilst traversing level crossings. At such times, it was argued, locomotives on railways became locomotives on highways and must observe the speed limit that had been imposed when Henry Chaplin's Bill became law in November 1896.

John Montagu appreciated that repealing the 'Emancipation Act' would be no easy task, and that despite sympathetic noises emanating from Whitehall, a strong tide of public opinion was still running against any proposal to give motorists the greater freedom they so earnestly sought. Whilst there were those, such as Walter Long, President of the Local Government Board, who favoured new legislation to encourage motoring, reactionaries such as Cathcart Wason, MP for the Orkneys, had to be contended with. 'A few people claim the right to drive the public off the roads', he would thunder. 'Harmless men, women and children, dogs and cattle, have to fly for their lives at the bidding of these slaughtering, stinking, engines of iniquity.'

In June 1902 John secured the first reading in the House of Commons for his Motor Vehicles Registration Bill, drawn up in consultation with some fellow members of the Automobile Club, which now had about 2500 members. Supported by such well-known pro-motoring MPs as T. P. O'Connor and Leicester Harmsworth (brother of Alfred) the Bill was the next item on the House's agenda after a statement by its Leader, Arthur Balfour, on King Edward's emergency operation and the postponement of his coronation. The Bill proposed to abolish the speed limit and discipline erring motorists under an Act of 1835 prohibiting 'furious' driving. The Act, still in force, was intended for horsemen but Montagu thought it could equally be applied to motorists. In return for being allowed to travel safely at any speed, car owners would be obliged to register their vehicles and carry number plates so that they could be identified readily if they broke the law or were involved in accidents. The Bill was to receive many set-backs before, more than a year later and much amended, it became law as the Motor Car Act.

A month after the Registration Bill received its first reading a dashing Australian by the name of Selwyn Francis Edge, driving an unproven 30 hp car designed by Montague Napier, gave Britain her first victory in international motor racing. As Edge was the first to acknowledge, he had luck on his side. His rivals in the 350-mile race from Paris to Innsbruck dropped out because of mechanical trouble and accidents and Edge only had to complete the course in order to win the race.

The trophy that Edge won for Britain's Automobile Club was donated by James Gordon Bennett, a flamboyant American publisher and playboy, for annual competition between national motor clubs. Thus distinguished from other motoring honours, which went to individual drivers or car manufacturers, the Gordon Bennett Cup was in its day motor sport's most prized piece of silverware.

Motor racing was eight years old by the time Britain at last found an international champion, and the speed restrictions of the Red Flag Act and its successor were obviously the main reasons why success was so long coming. The Automobile Club was unable to hold national road races in Britain, nor were its budding racing drivers able to practise on anything but private tracks. No wonder France and Germany gained an almost invincible lead both in motor racing and in the design of fast touring cars. In achieving belated prestige for Britain in 1902, Edge and Napier thoroughly deserved the hospitality and congratulations bestowed on them when they were guests of honour at an Automobile Club banquet on 24 July. But, as everyone present was aware, the rules of the competition required that the race should be held in the country that held the cup. And Britain, with its 12 mph speed limit, was in no position to stage such an event. Another of the rules stated that the race should cover a distance of 550 to 650 kilometres, making the use of public roads essential since an event of this length held on a private closed circuit would be monotonous to competitors and spectators alike. At the banquet the club's Chairman, Roger Wallace, said he hoped that the Government would help the 1903 Gordon Bennett Race to be held in England and thus give a new stimulus to the motor industry. Proposing a toast to the French Automobile Club, winners of the cup in 1900 and 1901, John Montagu touched on the impending problem by remarking that luckily there was no legal limit to the rapidity of human progress.

Later, he was one of the supporters of a resolution expressing the club's determination to hold the race in Britain. Its Secretary, Claude Johnson, started to gather suggestions as to where the race could take place — Lincolnshire, with its flat, deserted roads being one of the venues proposed.

At this stage in the club's plans there was at least a possibility that, by 1903, the Motor Vehicles Registration Bill would have led to the abolition of the speed limit, paving the way for the race to be held somewhere in Britain. But as 1902 drew to an end it became increasingly evident that the Bill was not going to have an easy passage. John therefore started agitating for action and on 31 December, when it seemed that Britain would shamefacedly have to ask if the race could be held elsewhere, he devoted an editorial in *The Car Illustrated* to the problem:

> It is impossible to exaggerate the good that would accrue to the automobile industry if the race takes place in this country ... really the difficulties are not very great ... and the race would bring thousands of pounds into the racing districts. The popularly supposed accidents arising from mere speed on the road are remote and the effect on the attitude of bucolic bodies towards motor traction would be most valuable.

By now the question of a venue had to be resolved quickly. The rules decreed that the race should take place between 15 May and 15 August and although it had been decided that the first two places in the British team would be taken by Napier cars, an eliminating trial was being organized to fill the third place. The closing date for entries for the trial had passed whilst the argument about where and when the cup would be defended was still in progress.

Knowing that a furore would be created if, regardless of whether or not the 1896 Act was repealed in time, the Government allowed the race to be held in England or Scotland, John swiftly supported a suggestion that it should be staged in Ireland, which had a network of passable roads running through sparsely populated countryside. The suggestion came from a group of influential Irishmen, tempted by the estimated £20,000-worth of benefits that would be spent in the region where the race was held.

In January 1903 the club started collecting signatures for a petition calling on the Government to allow the event to take place in Ireland. This paved the way for the introduction, by John Montagu, of The Light Locomotives (Ireland) Bill, which was of great historical significance because it was the first attempt to legalize motor racing on public roads in the British Isles. It set a valuable precedent and even though, for various reasons, road racing never became established in Britain, John's efforts ensured that the Gordon Bennett Race was held on home territory in 1903, giving British motor sport a boost at a crucial period in its history. Had the Automobile Club been denied the opportunity to host the event, Britain's tentative progress towards becoming a fully fledged motoring nation would have experienced a serious setback.

John's failure to obtain a second reading for his Registration Bill had left him only too aware of the difficulties in changing the legal status quo. His

Gordon Bennett Bill sought to close certain roads in Ireland so that they could be used solely for the race, and to suspend the speed limit on those roads during the event. It ran into trouble soon after it was presented. Mr Galloway, the Member for South-West Manchester, blocked its second reading on the grounds that the Bill had not been circulated properly to Members beforehand. What had happened was that John had distributed all the copies in his possession to interested MPs and lobby correspondents the previous evening and had none left for the rest of the House. Nevertheless, the rules of Parliament had to be obeyed, and there was a delay until John obtained the required extra copies. From then onwards the Bill had a surprisingly smooth passage through both the Commons and the Lords.

King Edward had mixed feelings when he gave the Bill the Royal Assent at noon on 27 March. By now he was a confirmed motoring enthusiast and had not been easily dissuaded from using a motor carriage instead of the traditional horse-drawn coach during his coronation procession through London. But motor racing was a different matter. 'None of your record driving, Mr Montagu,' he had warned before being taken on his excursion from Beaulieu in 1902. In February 1903 he again expressed his dislike of competitive driving by trying to prevent the Gordon Bennett Race from being held in Britain. He instructed his Private Secretary, Lord Knollys, to write to the Home Secretary:

> The King thinks it would be very dangerous for the occupants of the motors, and still more so for the public, and he is strongly opposed to any such proposals, which might be made, being favourably entertained.

The King later withdrew his opposition on learning that arrangements for the race were being made following the introduction of John Montagu's Bill but he renewed his objections in May after several competitors and spectators were killed in the Paris-Madrid Race. This 'race to death', as it became known, created widespread opposition to point-to-point motor races between cities, and from then on circuit races of the kind that had already been agreed for the 1903 Gordon Bennett were adopted, these being easier to control. King Edward told Balfour, now Prime Minister, that he was afraid that serious accidents would occur in Ireland, but his fears were not realized. Whatever he may have thought of John Montagu for his initiative in making the race possible, it did not spoil their friendship and in the summer of 1904 John once more took the King for a drive in his 22 hp Daimler.

In his last important act as Secretary of the Automobile Club, Claude Johnson had selected a course near Dublin for the Gordon Bennett Race. It consisted of a number of stretches of road which, taken as a whole, formed a figure-of-eight 90 miles long, around which the cars would lap until they had covered 550 kilometres. The club had to pay for improvements needed to bring the circuit up to racing standard and this was done by launching a Road Fund through *The Car Illustrated*, which very soon passed the £850 mark.

Because Britain was defending the trophy for the first time, in a country where motor racing had never been seen before, the Gordon Bennett attracted greater interest in 1903 than in previous years. For the first time since the first race in 1900 four teams entered, Britain's challengers being France, Germany and the USA. The British cars were painted green — a tribute, it has been said, to the shamrock. This is believed to have been the origin of British Racing Green as the national colour of British motor racing. On 25 March, John announced that the time had come for the race to have a second prize and he offered to donate a £200 trophy, which the Automobile Club decided to award to the team achieving the best aggregate performance. The Montagu Trophy was motor racing's first international team prize. Designed by Charles Sykes, it depicted a nude female figure, cast in silver, standing on a bronze pedestal and holding aloft a silver-winged motor car. Eleanor Thornton is said to have been Sykes' model for this creation, which is today on show in the National Motor Museum at Beaulieu.

Held on 2 July, the 1903 Gordon Bennett Race was won by Germany for the first time. The French drivers took the next three places, thus winning the Montagu Trophy. The British team put up a disappointing performance; two of its cars crashed and though S.F.Edge finished the course he was disqualified because someone gave his car a push to help it move off from one of the control points. Britain ensured that the competition was memorable for spectators and drivers alike by making it the main event in an Irish Fortnight, which included motor tours and trials and a motor boat race at Queenstown for the Alfred Harmsworth International Cup. This undoubtedly kindled John's interest in speed boat racing, which he was to take up seriously two years later; meanwhile he spent most of his time in Ireland enjoying his first long motor tour since the Thousand Miles Trial. He took his 24 hp and 22 hp Daimlers to Ireland, and in the latter managed to beat Charles Rolls by four yards in one of a series of contests organized to give visitors another taste of racing after the Bennett and Montagu trophies had been claimed.

John returned to London after Irish Fortnight to resume his campaign to abolish the speed limit and bring the laws of motoring into the 20th century. By now his Parliamentary Automobile Committee was supported by 86 Tories and Liberals, among them a bright young politician by the name of Winston Churchill.

The Registration Bill had failed to receive a second reading in 1902 because, as Balfour explained, there was no time for it to be dealt with during that session of Parliament. John reintroduced the Bill in the autumn, with similar results. Determined to persevere, he was dismayed by the stubborn resistance among some members of the Automobile Club, who opined that

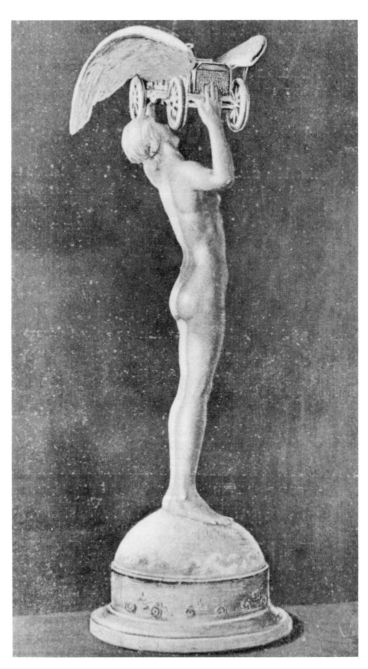

The Montagu Trophy, team prize in the 1903 Gordon Bennett Race.

Montagu and the club's legislative committee had no mandate to agree to the registration and numbering of motor vehicles in return for the abolition of the speed limit. Their views were reflected in a leading article in *The Autocar*:

> The registration of cars will no doubt ... prove very distasteful. The experiment is a risky one and we are inclined to believe that it would be safer to leave things alone, speed limit and all, than to tamper with the numbering clause. We are opposed to the numbering compromise on account of the fact that it will put a very dangerous weapon in the hands of the Police and other persecutors. The ideal is the removal of the speed limit and it would be better to ask for what we really want.

Motorists were divided on this question throughout the winter of 1902-3 and in some quarters John was accused of being solely responsible for the proposal to number vehicles. In December 1902 the Automobile Club rallied to his defence by explaining that registration had been agreed unanimously by the entire legislative committee composed of members regarded as being best able to judge what the law should be, taking into account, first, the automobilist's point of view and, second, what would be acceptable to the House of Commons. John Montagu, it was explained, had put before Parliament a Bill that conformed to the committee's recommendations. 'If Mr Montagu has sinned he has sinned in very good company, and it is not fair that those who do not agree with the policy should place the responsibility entirely on his shoulders.'

Throughout the controversy, John patiently explained to his more reactionary fellow members that they could not expect to win the right to drive at any speed without accepting some form of restriction and identification.

By the spring of 1903 three factions in the campaign for new motoring legislation could be identified. At one extreme were those who were so opposed to the motor car that they wanted stricter speed limits and compulsory registration. Diametrically opposite them were the motoring diehards, who favoured neither speed limits nor registration. Between these two sides stood Montagu and the moderates, willing to register and number their cars in return for the right to drive at whatever speed they considered safe, taking prevailing road conditions into account. In a referendum conducted by the Automobile Club there was a two-thirds majority for John's policy and this encouraged him to introduce the Bill yet again. He did so on the advice of Walter Long, who in February 1903 advised him to have the Bill ready as there were no proposals for motor car legislation in the King's Speech. But in July there was a change of heart in the Cabinet and the Government introduced its own Motor Car Bill. Since this offered the moderates what they wanted, John abandoned his Bill and without much difficulty persuaded his parliamentary colleagues to muster behind the Government's line.

The Bill was introduced in the House of Lords, emerging unscathed even though, behind the scenes, Cathcart Wason and a group of like-minded MPs and peers were urging the imposition of a 20 mph speed limit. Lord Camperdown put this forward as a formal amendment to the Bill but was defeated. John scornfully commented that there was not one practical motorist among Wason's committee, nor anyone remotely aware of what constituted a dangerous speed. 'From the point of view of public safety', he said, 'twenty miles an hour is as dangerous as thirty if the speed is in an unsuitable place. Upon the driver should fall the responsibility of using his vehicle wisely.'

Thanks to the House of Lords there was now, for the first time, a real prospect that speed limits would be swept aside, just as the red flag had been seven years earlier; but when the Bill reached the Commons, Walter Long was faced with such an overwhelming demand to retain speed restrictions that he found that it would be blocked unless a compromise could be reached. John and his supporters were isolated and among the more hysterical proposals they had to stomach was one that suggested, in all seriousness, that motorists caught speeding should be flogged. Long had little choice but to promise to consider introducing a 25 mph speed limit at committee stage. Thus appeased, the Commons gave the Bill a second reading without a division.

As expected the Motor Car Bill caused as deep a rift in the Automobile Club as its predecessor, the Registration Bill. Some members — probably the majority — were happy to let the legislative committee and its friends in Parliament take whatever action they thought would be in the best interests of motoring and the community at large. Others, more vociferous, continued to argue that the committee had no mandate to propose or support new legislation, and when the Bill was being discussed in the Lords they became highly agitated about the powers that the Local Government Board, the Police and the courts were likely to be granted if and when the Bill became law. The club committee (as distinct from the legislative committee) tried without success to force John Montagu's group to consult the club before deciding on its tactics. When the imposition of a speed limit became a virtual *fait accompli* after the second reading in the Commons, the club asked Montagu to block the Bill, so that one more favourable to motorists could be introduced later. John refused, accepting Long's proposed 25 mph as being reasonable in the circumstances, and seeing no advantage in killing the Bill and forcing motorists to resume their fight another day.

On Thursday 6 August, Montagu wrote to Long, detailing the concessions the parliamentary motorists would seek with regard to the penalties for motoring offences proposed in the Bill. With some hope that these would be granted, in return for their acquiescence over the 25 mph limit, John and his friends assembled in the Commons at noon next day for the start of a debate that was to change the course of motoring.

Before the session started rumours were circulating in the lobbies that the Government would be unable to win a majority for the 25 mph restriction and would have to settle for 20 mph. John resolved to resist this and was dismayed when the opening speaker, Mr Broadhurst, proposed an amendment seeking a limit, not of 20 mph, but of 15. Amidst cries of 'No' from the motorists, Sir Frederick Banbury then suggested that 20 mph ought to be an acceptable compromise. The House divided, and the 25 mph limit proposal was defeated by 183 votes to 42. The 15 mph proposal was also lost. With the temperature of the House thus gauged there was no need for a vote on the 20 mph proposal, which was accepted without a division. John had lost a battle, but not the war.

The hopes and fears of motorists and anti-motorists alike hinged on the debate; it was a pity that such a highly controversial and complex piece of legislation had to be thrashed out at an increasingly hectic pace. The parliamentary recess was imminent and some members of both Houses were becoming distracted by thoughts of the pleasures that awaited them on the grouse moors on the Glorious Twelfth. Anxious to have the Bill passed before the recess, the Government had to push many clauses through quickly, without proper consideration, but even so the debate did not end until 3 am on Saturday, 8 August. Later that day, embellished with the 20 mph limit and other amendments, the Bill went back to the Lords for their final approval. Government and Opposition spokesmen alike reasserted their aversion to speed limits, but nevertheless the upper House bowed to the commoners' wishes and passed the Bill without more ado.

Thus, what had started life as Montagu's Motor Vehicles Registration Bill, and had been translated almost measure for measure into the Government's own Motor Car Bill, became, on 1 January 1904, the Motor Car Act. Bitterly criticized by motoring's backwoodsmen as being too restrictive, and by the enemies of motoring as being too lenient, the Act was — despite its admitted imperfections — instrumental in making motorists accept that, like all other sections of the community, they had certain social responsibilities. The Act was Britain's first charter for the motorist; in return for fairer treatment under the law, he was now obliged to register his vehicle (on payment of £1), display number plates, and obtain a driving licence (renewable annually). What is surprising, in view of all the brouhaha in the Commons about the dangers of motoring, is that the new law did not require a motorist to prove that he was a competent driver before he could obtain a licence. John Montagu had proposed that drivers should have to pass a test before being licensed but this idea was defeated. Driving licences became as easy to obtain as dog licences. For better or for worse, the Motor Car Act influenced the development of motoring for much longer than had been intended, for there was no further radical reform of road traffic legislation until the 1930s, when the general speed limit was abolished, the 30 mph limit in built-up areas imposed, and driving tests introduced.

AA 19, an early 'cherished' registration number, seen on John's 1903 24 hp Daimler.

Applauded as a hero by some, and despised as a traitor by others, John wearily left the House of Commons in the early hours of 8 August and that weekend started to write the first of many long articles on the Bill, a subject that filled page after page of *The Car Illustrated* in the weeks that followed. After 16 hours of talking and listening, drafting and bargaining, relieved by only two half-hour breaks for meals, he was exhausted. 'Never in 11 years of parliamentary life have I felt so done up', he confessed. A letter from Alfred Harmsworth revived his spirits:

You have made a splendid fight against prejudice and have made possible an Act that, compared with the legislation that is coming into being in the United States and Germany, is not unfavourable. We have to recognize that thanks to the road hog on the one hand and prejudice on the other, the whole world is closing its ranks against the motor car. We in England have to recognize that our sport is infinitely more dangerous in this country than in most others by reason of the narrow, winding, hedge-lined and populous roads. My impressions were that there would be *no* extension of the speed limit. The considerable number of road hogs who are timed at 20 and 30 miles an hour through populous villages have rendered the task of those of us who set out to convert public opinion very difficult.

Not all John's friends were as understanding. Even Claude Johnson was reported as saying that instead of accepting the 25 mph proposal, John should have flung Walter Long's previous arguments against fixed limits back in his face. The Automobile Club's main and legislative committees held an emergency meeting and unanimously agreed that motorists would be better off under the 1896 Act, 12 mph limit and all, than the new one. The Chairman, Roger Wallace, and his Administrative Secretary, Rees Jeffreys, reported that they had tried to have the Bill withdrawn but had failed because John and his colleagues had accepted it and had agreed to help it become law. In their collective wrath the committees passed two resolutions. The first of these called on John to tell the House of Commons that he had accepted the 25 mph speed limit without the club's sanction, and that the club disassociated itself from the views that had been expressed during the debate by those regarded as being its representatives. It was a clear vote of No Confidence in John Montagu. The second resolution, preceded by a declaration that the Bill was 'fatal to motoring', stated that the speed limit would be vexatious and inefficient. Wallace and Jeffreys then led a deputation to the Commons to try to muster opposition to the Bill at its report stage but, as they said afterwards, they received 'little encouragement in the attitude of the recognized representatives of automobilism'. That week the club's *Journal* published an article headed 'Killing an Industry', in which an extraordinarily pessimistic view was taken:

> The outlook of the British automobile industry is black and depressing due to the efforts of parliamentarians who have seemingly forgotten that one of their first duties is to foster and assist British traders and manu- facturers and have given the industry a set-back from which it will never be able to recover.

The club had not merely reacted to the Bill, it had over-reacted. The idea that automobilism had been dealt a fatal blow was, in John's opinion, just plain silly. After itemizing the major concessions that his parliamentary group had won for motorists, ranging from rights of appeal against convictions to the abolition of a clause that would have sent infringers of the speed limit to prison, John proceeded to demolish the charges that had been levelled at him by Wallace and Jeffreys, under the auspices of the *Journal*. If motoring really was doomed, said John, the club might as well go into voluntary liquidation. How could the 'set-back' be one from which the industry would *never* recover when motorists in other countries with similar restrictions were combating anti-motorist opinion instead of wallowing in 'foolish pessimism'? To the accusation that Wallace and Jeffreys had received 'little encouragement' when their deputation went to the House of Commons, John retorted: 'I am sorry I was not there but I was working with my lawyer at amendments. I only wish I had been there, as I might have explained how impracticable were the views of the Automobile Club committee.'

The tenor of John's response was that the Bill was nowhere near as bad as some of its opponents made out, and that the club should stop bellyaching and concentrate on creating a climate of public opinion that would enable more liberal legislation to be enacted in the years ahead. Walter Long hurried to John's defence. Angered by the Automobile Club's attacks he wrote:

> The attack made upon you is most unjust. You fought your case with rare courage and skill. If you had taken any other line I am sure the great majority of the House would have insisted upon passing a more drastic measure. The King's highway belongs to the public at large and not to one section of it alone. If this campaign of calumny and abuse is continued it will intensify feeling against motors ... and do more to retard the development of this very valuable means of locomotion. Many sensible and moderate men who dislike the Bill are grateful to you for the hard work and courageous attitude by which you did so much to weaken the force of public opinion which was so strong and united against you.

Sensible and moderate men gradually won recognition. One by one the committee members who had supported Wallace's condemnations wrote to John expressing their regret at what had been said, adding that, had they realized the position he was in, they would never have supported the resolution. By 2 September most committee members had written to John along these lines and although he had not received an apology from the club or the *Journal*, he decided to refrain from publicly commenting further on accusations which, he said tartly, had been made by those 'whose sense of the fitness of things and of what is due seems so wanting'. On 12 October, at the club's first meeting after the passing of the Bill, John received his apology, framed in the form of a resolution expressing appreciation for his parliamentary efforts.

The Automobile Club *Journal*'s campaign against John's methods and policies, and his counter-attacks in *The Car Illustrated*, were patently journalistic ploys for expressing, at an impersonal level, bitter disagreements between individuals. There is no evidence of a direct and outright conflict of personalities between Montagu and Wallace but there was certainly an unbridgeable gulf between the moderates and the club's hierarchy. In the six months that followed the great debate on the Motor Car Bill, Wallace and Jeffreys became involved in some amazing misunderstandings and one cannot help wondering whether the muddle in which the club found itself at the end of 1903 would ever have occurred if Claude Johnson, its first full-time (and arguably most efficient) Secretary, had remained in the post for another year, instead of branching out into a business career as a partner of Charles Rolls.

The 'old guard' of the club, dominated by Wallace, had appointed a three-man secretariat after Johnson resigned in December 1902. His post was filled by Julian Orde, who was later joined by Basil Joy as Technical Secretary and Jeffreys as Administrative Secretary. This arrangement did not work at all well but it was still in operation when, in October 1903, Jeffreys and Wallace clashed once again with Montagu over the way in which the club was being run. After a series of rows, John was to lead a successful *coup d'état* at the club's annual meeting in March 1904 and his private diaries for the years 1903 to 1906, hitherto unavailable to motoring historians, throw new light on a fascinating and long-forgotten struggle for power among pioneer motorists in the years in which, thanks to the Motor Car Bill, they became socially responsible.

Incensed by the public attacks on him in the Automobile Club *Journal*, John began in the autumn of 1903 to deal with what he called 'the ACJ question'. At his insistence a sub-committee was appointed to consider the *Journal*'s future and he had long discussions on the subject with Julian Orde. They also talked about Wallace's attitude to the battle of words that the *Journal* had initiated. John took the view that the publication had failed to give the club's rank and file members an unbiased account of his actions in Parliament. Before much longer, he was in trouble with the club committee for publishing what it regarded as confidential information about the *Journal*'s financial position. The *Journal*, wrote John in *The Car Illustrated*, had made a loss of £257 in six months. The committee's denial, which stated that the actual loss was £292 over nine months, was hardly reassuring. On the question of confidentiality, John told the committee that club members had a right to know how their subscriptions were being spent and to know that what they had been led to believe was a paying concern was, in reality, the reverse. As to the actual figures, he said he would be pleased to publish what the club considered to be the true state of the *Journal*'s finances. There the argument petered out. John recorded in his diary that he had been outnumbered at the committee meeting, where Worby Beaumont, Colonel Crompton and J.D. Siddeley had spoken against him and only S.F. Edge had backed him up. An expected ally, Arthur Pearson, proprietor of the *Daily Express*, had failed to attend.

By now John was openly intent on reforming the Automobile Club by overthrowing its officers and committee at the annual meeting and in the last months of 1903 the club's membership was closing ranks around two factions — the 'Wallace clique', as John called it, and what emerged as the Reform Party. John lost no opportunity to try and win round Wallace's supporters. On 4 November a fellow member, Roger Fuller, called at John's office to show him samples of the number plates that motorists would soon have to display. John noted Fuller's visit in his diary that evening:

> Saw that he was 'on the other side', therefore had a straight talk to him, impressing upon him had no desire to split up club but wanted reformation and meant to have it. He leaves far more convinced and reasonable, probably realizing that J.M. is a stronger man than most take him for. He may be regarded by the old 'uns and cranks as a 'young enthusiast' but his ideas are sounder than one would think.

John also recorded a discussion with Eddy Stanley (Lord Stanley's son) over lunch at the Carlton Club. Stanley told him he should start a rival motoring organization because the Automobile Club was 'appallingly weak and rotten' but John disagreed, commenting: 'I do not wish to break, only to mend'. Next day he lunched with Wallace and had what he described as 'a straight talk to a young man' (a curious expression, Wallace being the older of the two):

> I told Wallace, though it was not a nice thing to tell anyone, that he was most unpopular and must resign. I put forward scheme for running the *Journal* as monthly technical or scientific paper, dispensing with R.J. and devoting his salary to Wallace who would act as legal adviser to the Automobile Club. After a very long talk he seemed to see my point and has gone away considering deeply.

John obviously wanted 'R.J.' (Rees Jeffreys) to be sacked and the *Journal*'s editorial policy to be changed drastically. Whilst his motives for making this suggestion were probably inspired by a wish for the *Journal* to become impartial in matters on which members were at loggerheads, he may have seen the *Journal* as an unwelcome rival to *The Car Illustrated* — not, perhaps, in terms of circulation but of influence. Be that as it may, the future of the *Journal* was hardly an issue on which John could reform the entire

Automobile Club. He certainly had other ideas up his sleeve, but fortuitously matters were rapidly brought to a head when the much-disliked Jeffreys played straight into his hands by sullying the club's reputation in the shires.

On Thursday 3 December readers of *The Times* were astounded by the publication of a letter that Jeffreys had circulated a few days earlier to all the county councils in Britain. He kicked off with an astonishing introductory paragraph:

> A considerable number of enquiries has been addressed to the Automobile Club by members asking the advice of the club as to the counties in which they shall register their cars. Under the provisions of the Motor Car Act, automobilists are at liberty to register their car in any county they please and it appears to be the desire of these enquirers that their fees of 20 shillings per car shall be paid to those counties which are most anxious to adapt their roads and their administration to modern requirements.

Continuing in this vein, Jeffreys said that the club committee was considering drawing up a list, for the guidance of motorists, naming the councils that had shown a desire to encourage the development of motoring. The list, he went on, would 'secure to those counties a considerable proportion of the revenue to be derived from registration fees'. There then followed a list of questions asking each council how much it spent on road improvements, whether it authorized 'Police traps' and so forth. The anonymous council officer who passed the letter to *The Times* commented: 'The communication is an offer to authorities, in their public capacity, of a pecuniary inducement to exercise duties that are a public trust in a manner to promote the wishes of those on whose behalf the bribe is offered'.

John Montagu was more scathing, remarking that the circular might have been written by the Tsar of all the Russias, attempting to dictate to the county authorities. He refuted Jeffreys' claim that the matter had been considered by the Automobile Club committee, saying that he could find no proof of this. As a Vice-Chairman of the club John was well placed to find proof, had it existed. The letter was 'an extraordinary piece of folly'. Jeffreys was forced to issue a rather clumsy explanation of his actions and he apologized, somewhat ungraciously, for wording the letter in such a way 'as to be open to misconstruction'. But he maintained that the club committee was still considering advising members where to register their cars. John's suspicions were not allayed and he would return to the matter later.

By now it must have been obvious to all motorists that the committee and the club's members were seriously out of step. First the committee had, through its *Journal*, criticized John over the Motor Car Bill, only to be forced to climb down once he had had the chance to explain what had actually gone on in Parliament. Next, members had learned that their *Journal* was not as sound, financially, as they had been told. To cap it all, Jeffreys was writing unauthorized letters to county councils, suggesting that they would lose valuable revenue unless they came up with satisfactory answers to some very loaded questions. But this was not all; the row over Jeffreys' circular was still simmering when, in January 1904, the club committee suddenly decided to contribute £500 to a motor show which Charles Cordingley (proprietor of *The Motor Journal*) was to hold at the Agricultural Show, in competition with the 'Crystal Palace Show' organized by the Society of Motor Manufacturers and Traders. Earlier the club had decided to remain neutral until the sponsors of the two rival shows had settled their differences. Montagu doubted the probity of the *volte-face*, especially as the club's President, Lord Shrewsbury, was Chairman of the Automobile Mutual Protection Association which was backing Cordingley's show.

At about this time Roger Wallace announced that he intended to resign as Chairman of the club at the annual meeting. Despite having personally advised him to resign during his 'straight talk to a young man', John publicly thanked Wallace for having fought hard for the club 'at the expense of his private convenience and his pocket'. Wallace's announcement left the future control of the club wide open and in the few weeks remaining before the annual meeting on 10 March, Montagu and Claude Johnson hatched a plot to topple the committee and replace it with Reform Party nominees.

On 17 February, in a long letter headed 'How to save the Automobile Club', a correspondent who signed himself An Old Member told the readers of *The Car Illustrated* that the club had lost its prestige, especially by taking sides in the squabble between the SMMT and Cordingley. He went on to recommend 50 members for positions on the club's committees. John Montagu was on the list, as was Claude Johnson, who, said the writer, would be a most valuable addition, even though he had recently declined to be nominated for the Chairmanship.

Old Member was, essentially, Johnson himself, who had shown John a draft of the letter on 9 February. This became the basis for Montagu's reform scheme. 'Greatly taken with the idea, though it requires many alterations', were his first impressions of Johnson's draft. 'Shall publish it.' He revised the letter next day, probably inserting the suggestion that Johnson should serve on the committee, and on Saturday 13 February he called on the man he wanted to be the club's next President, the Duke of Sutherland. The duke provisionally agreed to be nominated. John then collected Lord Stanley, Postmaster-General in Balfour's Cabinet and drove him to Crystal Palace for the SMMT Motor Show's inaugural luncheon. Stanley, who figured in John's scheme as a future Vice-President of the club, made a speech in which he congratulated John on his parliamentary performance in the Motor Car Bill debate. In his diary John gleefully wrote: 'Quite a study to watch the expressions on the faces of the old club hands. When a Minister of the Crown speaks publicly of the want for reform, things are coming to a pretty pass.'

The letter from Old Member was followed up by the distribution by John of the Reform Party's manifesto. This called for the formation of a supreme council to run the club, a dignified settlement of the row over the motor shows, better relations with Parliament and local authorities, the suppression of 'reckless and objectionable' driving by club members, and the relaunching of the *Journal* as a private, non-controversial communication between members. The manifesto also sought to prevent the club from being run to suit the interests of any particular section of the motor trade or 'the fads of amateurs'.

As 10 March approached, John became busier and busier. 'Claude Johnson is constantly in the office', he noted. 'Many are the letters to be written, plans to organize, Press men to be seen and meetings arranged.' As had happened when John launched his parliamentary campaign the previous summer, *The Car Illustrated* became the mouthpiece for reform, this time speaking for those who wanted to reorganize the Automobile Club. The club's *Journal* sided with the Establishment and was involved in yet another argument with John because it printed letters from Lord Shrewsbury and Wallace, and their list of committee candidates, in bolder type than the Reform Party's list. The club also refused to give John the addresses of its members, which he needed so that he could invite them to vote for his nominees by proxy. Since Shrewsbury and Wallace were able to use the address list in order to distribute their proxy papers, the reformers were stymied. The argument seemed to have been settled amicably when the club agreed to mail the Reform Party's papers at the same time as those published by Shrewsbury and Wallace, but later John discovered more skulduggery. The reformers' proxies, he said, had been posted separately, in Fleet Street and had been delivered to their addressees up to a day later than the other proxies, which had been posted in the West End. Nevertheless, John managed to gather in his proxies well in time for the meeting.

The future of the Automobile Club was decided between 5 pm and 9 pm on 10 March at the Institution of Mechanical Engineers near St James's Park in London. It would be seven years before the club moved to its world-famous palatial premises in Pall Mall, and the co-operation of the 'mechanicals' had to be sought so that a sufficiently large meeting room for the automobilists could be obtained. Even so, John found the room 'packed to the doors' when, after calling briefly at the House of Commons to collect some mail, he arrived at the meeting and took his place on the platform beside Wallace and the other vice-chairmen, Colonel Crompton and Mark Mayhew.

Throughout the evening Wallace and his colleagues had to answer a barrage of questions over the bumbling way they had handled the club's affairs during the previous seven months. The Motor Car Bill was not debated but the notorious Jeffreys' Letter was, and its author had to admit that he had not shown it to the committee but only to three of its members — Wallace, Crompton and Beaumont. Wallace said he did not remember seeing it. Crompton and Beaumont claimed that they had seen a draft, and had altered it, but that it was very different from the letter as circulated. It was all most embarrassing and the matter was left rather in the air. After the meeting John wrote:

> It is now clear beyond all doubt that Mr Wallace, Colonel Crompton and Mr Beaumont received the draft letter from Mr Jeffreys and that all were responsible, especially Mr Jeffreys, for the form in which it went out and probably, if the truth is known, for the foolish criticism of the parliamentary party in August.

John and the reformers carried the meeting on every item in their manifesto and 49 of their 50 candidates were elected onto the committees. The 'old guard' had had its day. What emerged was effectively a New Automobile Club, with the Duke of Sutherland as President, Lord Stanley, Lord Dudley and Earl Onslow as Vice-Presidents and Colonel H.C.L.Holden as Chairman. Jeffreys and Basil Joy lost their secretarial positions and became heads of the club's legal and technical departments.

On 1 January John had written in his diary:

> 1904. A new year. Full of hope, full of the promise of work and of footholds to be carved on the great rock of ambition. The past year has been one full of work and much worry. It has its bright side, though, for *The Car Illustrated*, which has now become a thing of daily thought to me, has built itself up into a recognized power and property.

Nine weeks after writing this he already had cause to believe that his hopes and promises were being fulfilled. In 1903, on his initiative, international motor racing had been introduced into Britain and the antiquated laws of motoring had been repealed. By March 1904 he had reformed the motorists' citadel, the Automobile Club. Ahead lay other absorbing projects; and in only 20 months he would inherit even greater responsibilities.

9

Battle for the Standard

Whilst attempting to scale 'the great rock of ambition' that confronted him in 1904, John Montagu tried to take over one of Britain's principal newspapers. Had he succeeded, the name Montagu would have been added to the roll of now-legendary Press barons — Beaverbrook, Camrose, Kemsley, Northcliffe, Rothermere — who were the founders of modern Fleet Street. John's bid failed, but whilst he was making it his friendship with Alfred Harmsworth developed into a close business relationship, thus ensuring his future success as a freelance journalist.

Harmsworth had revolutionized Fleet Street with the attention-grabbing style of journalism he pioneered in his *Evening News* and *Daily Mail* and in the spring of 1904 his latest innovation, the generously illustrated *Daily Mirror*, was beginning to become profitable after a disastrous debut as 'a newspaper for gentlewomen'. By now Harmsworth's achievements had encouraged imitators and rivals to emerge, notably the *Daily Express*, whose proprietor, Arthur Pearson, was on friendly terms with John Montagu. At an early stage in John's campaign to overthrow the 'old guard' at the Automobile Club, Pearson was one of the comparatively few members of the original committee to be nominated by the reformers for a seat on the new one, although his name did not appear on the final list of candidates published just before the stormy annual meeting of 10 March.

During the weeks immediately after the Automobile Club coup John met Pearson and Harmsworth, separately, on several occasions. On 12 April, acting as an emissary for the Conservative Party, he had lunch with Harmsworth at the Savoy, to invite him to stand as Tory candidate for Weybridge at the next election. Predictably, Harmsworth declined, having received a severe drubbing nine years earlier at Portsmouth, where in his first (and only) attempt to become a Member of Parliament he was defeated by the Liberals in a campaign he afterwards likened to 'wading through a sea of filth'. On 19 April Pearson was John's lunchtime companion; their conversation soon turned to the tribulations of publishing newspapers and periodicals and Pearson told John that he would like to buy *The Car Illustrated*, should John ever decide to sell it. His publishing business was at this period experiencing financial difficulties that were becoming more serious week by week, which makes it all the more surprising that only four days after his talk with Pearson, John became embroiled in a scheme to purchase a newspaper that was later to become part of Pearson's Press empire.

That newspaper was the *Standard*, which had been founded in 1821 as a London evening journal (the forerunner of today's *Standard*) and had launched a morning edition in 1857. At one time the *Standard*, always staunchly Conservative in policy and outlook, was a serious competitor to *The Times* and although by 1904 it was ailing financially it still, to quote Pearson, had a great hold on the 'sober thinking classes' and was valued by businessmen for its coverage of commerce and industry.

All the leading serious and popular newspapers were involved in an intense battle for circulation in 1904 and this was one reason why the vulnerable but influential *Standard* was regarded as a desirable object by Pearson and Harmsworth. What has been overlooked in the annals of the formative years of the British national Press is the fact that an outsider, John Montagu, at one time saw the *Standard* as his opportunity to join journalism's first division.

John's diary is the only record that has survived the 80-odd years that have elapsed since he fought and lost the one major takeover battle of his career. His cryptic entries, usually made within a few hours of each stage of the negotiations, tell the story of eight months of frustration and eventual disappointment. The first hint of what lay ahead is contained in an entry dated Saturday 23 April which reads:

Proposal re 'S' taking root.

Two days later John dined with Artie Johnstone, a member of the family that owned the *Standard*. Afterwards he noted: 'Nothing definite arranged. Figures not discussed but evidence given that they are not averse to JM's proposal to take it over'.

By 4 May something more definite was in the air and the arrival of a note that afternoon from Johnstone, asking John to meet his solicitor, caused him to have self-doubts or second thoughts about what he might be taking on. At this stage he had probably not yet worked out exactly how he proposed to run the *Standard* or raise capital for what was bound to be a risky and expensive venture. 'The 'S' scheme has flown along so quickly; almost leaves J. Mont. unprepared for it', he wrote. 'Do not want the business rushed. Wants a lot of careful consideration. Afraid almost too big a thing.'

Alfred Harmsworth invited John to dine with him that evening at his London home in Berkeley Square. Not for the first time Montagu sought his friend's advice, telling him about his interest in the *Standard* and admitting that he was not sure how to handle the discussions he was due to have with Johnstone and his solicitor. To John's astonishment, Harmsworth told him that he knew all about his scheme. A mutual friend, referred to in the diary as 'old A.E.T.W.', in whom John had confided, had revealed all when he met Harmsworth the previous evening at the opera. 'Old A.E.T.W.' was Alfred Watson, editor of the *Badminton Library*, a series of books on sports and pastimes. John was at first alarmed by his friend's lack of discretion but that was not the only surprise in store for him that evening, for Harmsworth next disclosed that he had been trying to buy the *Standard* for the past two years.

Suddenly, what had started as an attempt to do a deal with the Johnstone family had become an attempt to acquire a newspaper that the most powerful man in Fleet Street had been, and evidently was still, hoping to purchase. What, John wondered, should he do now?

Harmsworth quickly suggested a way in which they could work together on what became known as their S Project. He suggested that, as he had always hoped to own the *Standard*, he should buy it through John, who would become Editor-in-Chief. John would have full editorial powers but Harmsworth would reserve the right to exercise a veto on the paper's policy in the event of a Government crisis. John saw this as an ideal partnership, which suggests that it was the editorship of an influential newspaper, not necessarily the ownership of one, that he was really after. The loose tongue of 'old A.E.T.W.' had, John noted, proved to be 'the means to an end — an end which at present J.M. is rather afraid of; not actually afraid of the scheme itself, as that has long been an ambition, but of being rushed into it before ready'. Harmsworth had been 'very nice indeed' about the project and whilst working out their plan to run the *Standard* as a joint venture he had told John 'many interesting and confidential things about his vast business and its working'.

Before leaving Berkeley Square, John suggested to Harmsworth that a mutual acquaintance, a businessman named Claude Watney (founder of the London Motor Garage Company) should look after the day-to-day details that would arise during their take-over bid and liaise between Montagu's and Harmsworth's offices. It was an arrangement that was not to work smoothly; Harmsworth regarded Watney as 'a difficult man', even though John had confidence in him.

Next day John met Watney and told him about his discussions with Harmsworth. Although 'much excited' by the project Watney said he was unwilling to become involved if Harmsworth was going to run the show, but he changed his mind when it was explained to him that no one was to know that Harmsworth was involved and that John was to have absolute editorial control. A few hours later Harmsworth called at John's office and it was agreed that John would conduct all the negotiations with the Johnstone family's representatives, and that if John could not find enough financial backers, Harmsworth would 'see to it' — that is to say, raise the balance of the finance himself. Harmsworth's involvement, it was again emphasized, was to be kept 'absolutely dark'. The reasons for this must have been the likelihood that the Johnstones would raise their price if they knew that wealthy Alfred Harmsworth was after their paper and that other publishers would join the bidding if they knew that their rival Harmsworth was trying to gain control.

At 3.45 pm on Friday 6 May John met Harmsworth in a lawyer's office in Ely Place, Holborn, to draft and sign a formal agreement setting out the powers and responsibilities they would enjoy if and when they acquired the *Standard*. At 4.50 John caught a train from Waterloo Station, homeward bound for a weekend at Beaulieu. As his train left the suburbs of London and headed into Hampshire he reflected that the S Project had 'simply romped along' in the 48 hours that had passed since he and Harmsworth had first discussed it. He would, he again told himself, have liked more time to think about the project but, as he wrote in his diary, Harmsworth had put his name to a 'very generous' agreement. Against this entry John noted, in shorthand, '£5000 a year settled'. This was to be his salary as Editor-in-Chief: a generous sum in 1904.

After a Saturday of political speech-making in the New Forest and an idle Sunday at Beaulieu, John returned to London 'feeling seedy' as he put it — the effect of one of the recurring asthmatic attacks he suffered that year, especially when his business affairs were causing concern. During the following two weeks he had further discussions with Harmsworth and approached several people who, he hoped, would back his S Project financially, including Lord Londonderry (who promised to help and to seek the support of Lord Derby) and Sir Francis Burdett. Then, newly appointed to the rank of colonel in the Hampshire Volunteers, John spent the last week of May in camp with his battalion near Winchester. This must have been a frustrating chore, keen as he was on part-time soldiering, because it left his S Project in abeyance. Nevertheless a week in the fresh air — albeit wet fresh air, because of incessant rain — cleared up his asthma, at least for the time being. He returned to London in a much healthier state, ready to deal with the next stage of the project, which was marked by ever-increasing insistence from the Johnstones' solicitors, Castle & Co., that John should name his backers and make a firm offer for the *Standard*.

John's problem now was that he did not yet have binding commitments from those whose support he had been canvassing, even though he was fairly sure that, given time, he could raise enough money for an acceptable bid. There was, of course, always Harmsworth's promise to 'see to it' to fall back on. John certainly had little or no money of his own to spare for the venture. On Thursday 16 June, when Castle & Co. again requested the names of his backers, John wrote despairingly in his diary that he needed to find a thousand pounds for *The Car Illustrated* from somewhere. During the day he tried to arrange an urgent meeting with Harmsworth, so that they could decide how to handle Castle & Co., but the summer social season was under way and Harmsworth was spending the day at Ascot. They eventually met, briefly, next day at the Automobile Club and Harmsworth invited John to spend the weekend at Sutton Place, his country mansion in Surrey, where they had several long discussions. John was disconcerted by some of his host's remarks about Claude Watney and on returning to London was obliged to give Watney what he called a 'friendly hint' not to quarrel with Harmsworth's staff. Whatever decisions Montagu and Harmsworth reached at Sutton Place, they managed to keep Castle & Co. happy for the moment and by the end of the month John was more optimistic that his project would succeed — even though he was still doubting his ability to run the paper. On 30 June he wrote:

> Scheme now takes a big leap forward. Am beginning, now that the thing is so near and probable, to doubt JM's capacity to do the job. It's a very big thing to undertake.

How right he was. Running a weekly motoring magazine, with the help of fellow enthusiasts, was hardly likely to provide a man with sufficient experience to edit a daily newspaper.

Whatever shape the 'big leap forward' of 30 June may have taken, the *Standard* affair dragged on for many more months. Throughout June and into July the main impediment was John's inability or reluctance to state the price that he and his backers (if by now they had committed themselves) were prepared to pay. Every time he was pressed to do so by Castle & Co. he was obliged, naturally, to consult Harmsworth before answering. Harmsworth, for his part, professed to be as keen as ever secretly to acquire control of the *Standard* via Montagu but when the question of putting in a firm bid arose, Harmsworth held fire. He did so despite the advice of his brother, Harold, the future Lord Rothermere. After a detailed discussion on 6 July with Castle & Co. about the financial aspects of the proposed sale of the *Standard*, John went to see Alfred Harmsworth, who for the first time told Harold what they were up to. Alfred said he was in favour of waiting a few months before stating a figure, since he thought that newspapers were about to experience a drop in advertising revenue: a factor that would reduce their profitability and weaken the negotiating position of any proprietors wishing to sell their newspapers. Harold, though, argued that they should strike a bargain with the Johnstones immediately. But Alfred won the argument.

Matters threatened to come to a head on 13 July when Castle & Co. wrote to John and asked him to make a definite offer by the 19th. Again he had to stall, saying he would reply by the 21st. Again he tried, unsuccessfully, to contact Harmsworth but this time John was unable to make use of an intervening weekend to talk things over because he had a long-standing, and unbreakable, engagement to meet King Edward at Hinton Admiral Station on Saturday 16 July, drive him to the Cavendish Bentincks' place at Highcliffe and spend the weekend and Monday morning chauffering the monarch and his party around the purlieus of the New Forest. It was not until the Monday afternoon that John arrived back in London, as a passenger on the Royal train. Office work and parliamentary debates then prevented him from seeing Harmsworth until the morning of the 21st, by when Castle & Co. were expecting a reply to their letter of the 13th.

John had drafted a reply but Harmsworth picked this to pieces and dictated one of his own, which John signed and posted. A figure of some kind was mentioned but Castle & Co. responded by saying that it was totally inadequate. Yet another deadline for a firm and final offer was imposed: 2 August. And once again Harmsworth was away from his office at the crucial time. John acted alone on this occasion, replying that the price that was being asked for the *Standard* was much too high.

For the next three months the S Project went into low gear. John kept in touch with Castle & Co. Harmsworth — now Sir Alfred Harmsworth — kept in touch with John. No one, though, made any significant moves and it appears that whilst John's backers and Harmsworth had no intention of increasing their 'totally inadequate' bid, no one else was bidding for the *Standard* at that time — even though Castle & Co., by their repeated requests for firm offers, may have been trying to give the impression that the *Standard* was a hot property.

In October Harmsworth invited John down to Sutton Place for another long chat about their mutual interests. Doubtless, the dormant S Project was mentioned but John was in no fit state to revive the project for several days. He had felt 'seedy and feverish' whilst travelling to Sutton Place and had to spend the next two days there, lying in bed or in front of the hall fire, fussed over by Lady Mary Harmsworth, whose doctor had diagnosed influenza. 'Weak and dicky and still feeling very shattered', John returned to his office to deal with outstanding correspondence. He recovered slightly whilst spending the weekend at Beaulieu, only to have a relapse when he returned to London on the Monday. On the orders of his doctor he spent the next three days resting in his London flat. During his absence Castle & Co. telephoned his office but by the time he heard about this he was due to catch a train back to Beaulieu where the Prime Minister, Arthur Balfour, was to be his guest for the weekend after speaking at a big Tory rally in Southampton on Friday 28 October. John had no time to return Castle & Co's call. Had he done so, he might have found a way of regaining the initiative in the *Standard* affair. Instead he participated in what, in view of his poor health, was the 'ordeal' of the Tory rally, at which he had to make a speech which left him feeling 'done for'. He then drove Balfour to Beaulieu, where he found an opportunity to brief him on the S Project. Afterwards John noted:

> Premier was kindness itself to J. Mont. He was greatly interested and promised his support if we were successful in obtaining the *Standard*. Very pleased to get this from him.

But as the telephone call from Castle & Co. was probably intended to reveal, the *Standard* now had another prospective buyer, Arthur Pearson, whose offer of £300,000 certainly exceeded anything that John had hoped to raise. Unaware of Pearson's offer, John kept to his pre-arranged schedule during the days that followed Balfour's visit. Instead of returning to London on the Monday morning, his usual habit, he remained at Beaulieu because he was due to attend a County Council meeting at Winchester on the Tuesday. He was then looking forward to a day's shooting on the Wednesday — a rare mid-week break — before returning to London on the Thursday.

When he returned home from shooting late on Wednesday afternoon he was handed a telegram from Eleanor Thornton, asking him to return to London immediately. He caught the 7.40 train, arriving at his office at 10.20 to find, not surprisingly, that the place was deserted. Puzzled as to what all the fuss might be about but unable to discover Eleanor Thornton's where-abouts, he went to the Beafsteak Club, one of his favourite haunts, for a late supper, where Eleanor eventually found him. She explained that Harmsworth had wanted to see him because another party, rumoured (correctly) to be Pearson, had made a bid for the *Standard*. Harmsworth had wanted to counter this but could not do so without Montagu's help. By the time John heard the story from Eleanor Thornton, it was too late to make a move until the next day.

In the morning John found that Harmsworth was out of town again. They met, at last, on Friday 4 November and John then hurried to Castle & Co. to hear that Pearson had paid the Johnstones' asking price without a murmur.

John could hardly believe this, since the price greatly exceeded the *Standard*'s market value. Although he nursed a faint hope that, as Pearson had not yet actually signed a contract, the sale was not yet final, he nevertheless called at No. 10 Downing Street to give Balfour the news and warn him that the *Standard*, under Pearson, could not be relied upon to support Government policy as it had in the past.

After calling at Downing Street, John dejectedly caught the 4.50 from Waterloo and spent a miserable weekend at Beaulieu ruminating on his misfortunes. 'Coming so suddenly, this is more of a blow than it would have been if worked up to', he wrote. 'I find, now that the thing slips, how hopes and ambitions were built upon it. Seem to have missed the chance of a lifetime.' He brooded for a week and his depression was not relieved when some business friends, who had no inkling of what had been going on, told him they would have liked him, rather than Pearson, to have secured the *Standard*. Their comments provoked another comment on the affair in his diary:

> Little do they know how he had striven for it and what hopes he had built upon it, not for himself but for the party. If only the capital were at once available, it seems now is the time to start a staunch old Conservative paper. The Government no longer have one to support them. Such an organ would rally the party and save it.

He discussed the idea of launching such a newspaper with some of Balfour's aides but soon became engrossed in other projects, and the idea gradually died. But why, backed by a heavyweight like Harmsworth, did John fail to acquire the *Standard*? Although he lacked Harmsworth's expertise in buying and running publishing businesses, and although he was clearly unable to raise sufficient capital from his own resources and by his own efforts, he had, after all, been given an assurance that Harmsworth would buy the *Standard* through John and 'see to it' if financing the venture became a problem. The initiative, it seems, was lost on 6 July when Alfred Harmsworth told John that he favoured waiting a few months before making a bid, even though brother Harold was all for striking a bargain immediately. At that stage there were probably no other serious bidders and had John been able to make an offer then, he might well have succeeded. Later that month, under further pressure from Castle & Co., he was able to make some kind of offer, but this fell short of being a firm and final bid and was, in any case, regarded as being inadequate. Harmsworth continued to play a waiting game and by doing so it would appear that he and John then started to lose control of the situation. At what stage Harmsworth's rival, Arthur Pearson, started seriously to consider buying the *Standard* is not known, but it was not until 2 November that Harmsworth heard about Pearson's move. From then onwards, events moved too quickly for Montagu and Harmsworth. Whether, had they been able to meet before 4 November, they would have attempted to put in a higher bid will never be known but it is unlikely. John, and doubtless Harmsworth too, were obviously surprised that Pearson had agreed to pay a price way above the *Standard*'s market value. Harmsworth, on whom the responsibility for finding the extra capital would have fallen, was surely too experienced to pay over the odds for a newspaper which, although it would have been a useful addition to his empire, was not essential to his future plans. He certainly wanted to own a 'serious' daily newspaper and within a few years of the failure of the S Project he realized his ambition by taking over *The Times*.

One of the commitments that took John Montagu's mind off the dis-appointments of the *Standard* affair was his nightly stint at the *Daily Mail*, as the newspaper's special parliamentary correspondent. He started hankering for this job long before the S Project began to occupy so much of his time and mental energy, and here too his reasons for wanting to branch out into other fields of journalism may have been that *The Car Illustrated*'s prospects were far from rosy. The magazine had made a small profit in its first year, during which sales reached a higher level that they would ever maintain again but in 1904, despite a slight increase in advertising revenue, it made a substantial loss. The main financial burdens in 1903 and 1904 were the continuing losses sustained by its sister publication, the monthly *Car Magazine*, which John insisted on subsidizing—unwisely, one feels—until as late as February 1906, when even a reduction in its cover price from 1/- to 6d. had failed to revive it. His diary is full of references to his discussions with his staff on the desperate need to cut costs. Talk of redundancy was in the air and even Charles Sykes was regarded as a possible victim. Fortunately he was reprieved, for as we know today—and as John must have realized then—*The Car Illustrated* without Sykes' illustrations would have been like *Vanity Fair* without Spy. Nevertheless, the fact that John was contemplating drastic economies suggests that, in 1904, he thought he had little prospect of earning a living as a publisher of motoring periodicals for much longer and was looking for more secure employment—or at least hoping to add a few more strings to his bow.

He had cut his journalistic teeth as a temporary reporter on the *Daily Mail* and since then he had given Harmsworth's staff numerous tip-offs about political developments at Westminster. Towards the end of 1903, through his associate Claude Watney, he had tried, unsuccessfully, to persuade Harmsworth to make him an official correspondent; he tried again on 6 January 1904, when he kept a lunch appointment with Harmsworth at the Savoy. He hoped that the occasion would give him a chance to put a firm proposal to Harmsworth—and provoke a definite answer, one way or the other. Unfortunately Harmsworth brought one of his editors along, the chain-smoking foul-mouthed Kennedy Jones, the epitome of the hard-bitten journalist and one of the most hated men in Fleet Street. He and Harmsworth were too engrossed in discussing the imminent war between Russia and Japan to pay much attention to John's proposal and John later noted: 'I am inclined to think K. Jones does not approve of it, he apparently being one of the many who designate me as a rich man working for a fad'.

All Harmsworth would agree to do was to pay John for his tip-offs, but this was not what he wanted at all. Two months went by and John tried again, attempting to sweeten Harmsworth by passing on, via Watney, some news he had just gleaned at the War Office. 'AH does not know all the chances of tit bits he missed when our *Daily Mail* scheme was rejected', he complained. 'Nor does he know the extent to which JM helps the DM.'

Watney, though, was no more successful as John's leg man in this project than he would be in the *Standard* business. On more than one occasion John had to have a quiet word with him about his 'attitude to the DM folk', asking him to 'work amicably with all of them and not quarrel'. In time, after the excitement and failure of the S Project, John had his way. He had another chat with Harmsworth and it was agreed that, as from February 1905, Montagu would contribute a political article every night whilst Parliament was in session. For this he received an annual retainer of £500. It was the beginning of a successful but arduous new phase in the story of John Montagu, journalist, for in addition to coping with his duties as an MP, editor and publisher, his other business interests (which included directorships of insurance companies) and his activities as a county councillor and part-time Army officer, he now had to dash along the Thames Embankment to the *Daily Mail* every night after Parliament adjourned and finish writing his contribution to the next day's paper. On the many nights on which Parliament sat late, he often had only 15 minutes to complete his piece.

John contributed to the *Daily Mail* and other national newspapers for the rest of his life, eventually earning £1500 a year — not bad for those days — from his freelance writing activities. He was able to prove to Kennedy Jones, who was in day-to-day charge of the *Daily Mail*, that he was not merely 'a rich man working for a fad' but had the talent to survive in Fleet Street's rat race.

John Montagu was not totally preoccupied with ambition and survival in the jungle of journalism in 1904. One of his strongest characteristics was that whenever he was dogged by business or personal difficulties or laid low by bouts of asthma, his enthusiasm for some new challenge or project would revive his spirits and help him put his problems, or the past, behind him very quickly. This characteristic came to his rescue during the turbulent months of the S Project and the financial crisis at *The Car Illustrated*.

In 1904 many of John's fellow motoring pioneers were becoming as accomplished at piloting boats or air balloons as they were at driving cars. Although, despite being a lifelong advocate of aviation, he derived little personal enjoyment from flying, John did for a while become one of Britain's speed boat aces.

Motor boats share their pedigree with motor cars and whilst J.J. Etienne Lenoir was the true father of both, it was Gottlieb Daimler who made petrol-engined motor boats a commercial success, overcoming suspicions about their safety by festooning his boats with cables and porcelain insulators to fool his passengers into thinking they were driven by harmless electricity, not flammable gasoline. By the turn of the century motor launches were 'catching on' in England and 100 ton motor yachts were becoming popular, an innovation that prompted John to be one of the first people to prophesy that oil would one day replace coal as a fuel for seagoing vessels.

'Oil could so easily be carried in the bunkers of a ship instead of coal', he wrote, 'and could be replaced with water when the oil was exhausted. The water line of the ship would therefore remain the same. There would also be the additional advantage of the use of oil in storms as the most powerful agent for preventing dangerous waves. Petroleum could also be pumped in from reserve tank ships at sea by means of a long flexible hose. Coaling at sea, one of the most delicate and dangerous operations in His Majesty's Navy, could be avoided. Huge oil tanks instead of coal stores would then be necessary at all our foreign coaling stations and oil would not deteriorate, as does coal.'

In November 1902 John proposed a 'sea racer', 60 foot long and powered by two 25 hp petrol engines, which could be used by the Navy for reconnaissance. Ordinary torpedo boats were too long and drew too much water for scouting in-shore and in shallow waters, he said, but a 'sea racer' would need a draught of less than three feet, even though it would be capable of 30 knots. 'There would be no funnels or smoke to attract the enemy and with an underwater exhaust the boat might be almost silent. If built low in the water it would be difficult for the enemy to observe and still more difficult to hit. I am thinking of having one built for myself, with power sufficient for 35 knots.'

John steering Napier ' *in which he and Lionel de Rothschild won Alfred Harmsworth's British International Trophy in 1905.*

Some of the readers of *The Car Illustrated*, for whom these comments were written, may have had a mental picture of John skulking in the shallows, the exhaust of his petrol engines bubbling quietly beneath the surface, whilst he spied on enemy battleships. That, of course, was not what he had in mind. John intended to use his 'sea racer' for the purpose that its name implied but it was not until the summer of 1904 that he acquired his boat. This turned out to be not as large as the one he had in mind but almost as powerful.

As already mentioned, John's interest in fast motor boats had been boosted by one of the sideshows at the Irish fortnight held during the previous summer. This, the first-ever major race for motor boats, had been held in Queenstown Harbour. There, three contestants competed for the International Challenge Cup, donated by Alfred Harmsworth, applying his flair for sponsorship and publicity to motor boat racing, having successfully helped motoring on its way by supporting the Thousand Miles Trial. The term 'international' belied the true nature of the first contest for his cup since Germany's entry, *Mercedes*, holder of a water speed record of 22.36 mph, was destroyed in a fire shortly before it was due to be taken to Queenstown. This left the field open to the other three entrants, all from Britain — *Scolopendra*, *Durandel* and *Napier*. This last, powered by a four cylinder 80hp Napier engine, was built by Montague Napier of motor car fame for racing driver S.F. Edge. With another pioneer motorist, Campbell Muir, at the helm it won the cup and set up a new speed record for petrol launches of 24.9 mph. A month later John Montagu borrowed *Napier* and tested her on Southampton Water, reporting afterwards:

> Give me the sea for speed! Speed through water at 25 mph in a boat 40 ft long has charms that those who have not tried it cannot appreciate. I am sure that motor boat racing will find as many votaries as motor car racing and if this little Napier, the first speed craft of her kind, can do 21.4 knots an hour (sic) what speeds will similar boats do in the future? To those who love speed on land I say, Try speed at sea. You will find it well worth while.

These were just the kind of comments that Harmsworth wanted his sponsorship of motor boat racing to generate, and through *The Car Illustrated* John Montagu did much to establish the new sport. Edge sold *Napier* at the end of the 1903 season and bought two Napier-engined successors to defend the Harmsworth cup in 1904. These were *Napier Minor*, a 35 foot timber-hulled launch built for cruising as well as racing and *Napier II*, a purpose-built 40 foot racer, designed and built in steel by Alfred Yarrow. This was a highly advanced craft for its day and its builders, famous for torpedo boats, constructed several scale models and towed them on the Thames at speeds of up to 25 knots in order to evolve the sleekest and most seaworthy hull shape for the vessel's twin 45 hp engines.

The 1904 race itself was a shambles and must have left Edge wondering if his efforts had been justified. Competitors failed to arrive or withdrew because of accidents and breakdowns. In the end the race became a contest between the two Napiers and *Trèfle-à-Quatre-Feuilles* from France. Since only one of the Napiers could represent Britain in the final heat they had to race each other to qualify. *Napier II* won but had to withdraw from the final when her hull, which had hit floating debris in an earlier heat, began to leak. *Napier Minor* took her place, beating *Trèfle-à-Quatre-Feuilles*, only to be disqualified on the grounds that, not having won the qualifier, it was ineligible for the final. So the trophy went to France on a technicality.

Instead of repairing *Napier II* Edge had her rebuilt to improve her performance. What emerged from Yarrow's yard in March 1905 was a precursor of today's power boats, with a 'planing' hull that skimmed over the waves, driven by pepped-up Napier engines developing an extra 30 hp. During her first trials *Napier II* fractionally beat the existing water speed record. By now John's enthusiasm for motor boats had reached the point where he was determined to buy one at last — a venture in which he was encouraged by his friend Lionel de Rothschild, a rich young scion of the banking family who later moved to Exbury, an estate on the east bank of the Beaulieu River. John had stated his intention of buying a motor boat more than two years previously, but had no doubt postponed doing so because he had been so busy reforming the motoring laws and the Automobile Club's constitution, keeping *The Car Illustrated* solvent and plotting with Alfred Harmsworth to take over the *Standard*. In August 1905 John and Rothschild decided to compete in the forthcoming third contest for the Harmsworth cup, now renamed the British International Trophy. With an eye to future contests they had ordered a revolutionary new boat but as this could not be built in time they looked around for a suitable secondhand craft. They found it, in the shape of Edge's new *Napier II*. From his own observations, John knew that this was just about the fastest thing afloat, having beaten all 19 starters in a race across the English Channel on 15 July.

The British International Cup Race was held in the oyster-rich Bay of Arcachon, near Bordeaux. Eliminating trials to decide who would represent Britain were held in Southampton Water and in their first attempt at motor boat racing Montagu and Rothschild were left behind at the starting line. A cylinder head gasket in one of *Napier II*'s engines blew out, but even though it took them nearly two hours to fit a temporary joint Montagu and Rothschild eventually caught up with the other three competitors. Apart from *Brooke I* (a single-screw craft with a 300 hp engine) *Napier II*'s opposition consisted of familiar competitors from previous races — *Napier*, now owned by Lord Howard de Walden and *Competitor*, which was in fact *Napier Minor* with a new name, new 100 hp Siddeley engine and a new owner — Lt Mansfield

Cumming. Despite having to stop for several minutes whilst an ignition wire was repaired, *Napier II* put up the best performance in the trials and Montagu and Rothschild chugged home across the Solent that evening confident that they would be among Britain's representatives at Arcachon.

In rough seas and a gusting wind, four launches roared over the line when the starting gun on Arcachon Pier was fired at 2.30 pm on 11 September. *Napier* and *Brooke I* had been selected as Britain's other representatives but there was only one other competitor — M. Thurbon's *Mab*. So the event only just had an international flavour. *Napier II*, steered by John, soon took the lead and when *Brooke I*'s carburettor packed up and *Mab* became partially flooded, the race became a duel between *Napier* and *Napier II*. John had to stop twice to fix ignition faults and although beaten in two of the four heats, *Napier II*'s overall time was more than a minute faster than that of *Napier*. Thus, Montagu and Rothschild became the third holders of Harmsworth's cup. John also won the Deutsch Trophy in *Napier II* during Arcachon's six weeks of sailing and motor boat races. Nor was that the end of his seafaring successes in 1905, for two weeks after returning from France he and Rothschild won the British Motorboat Club's Flying Mile Championship at Burnham on Crouch at a speed of 30.74 mph: *Napier II*'s best-ever performance.

Whilst Montagu and Rothschild were careering around in *Napier II* in 1905, the boat in which they were to defend the British International Trophy in 1906 was taking shape in Sam Saunders' yard at East Cowes. Ordered from S.F. Edge in December 1904, this was quite unlike any previous racing launch because although it was in some ways similar to *Napier II*, it had a hull made of cedar and mahogany skins which were literally sewn together with phosphor bronze wire. This method of construction produced a light, strong hull capable of withstanding the severe stresses and strains imposed upon it by the new type of six cylinder Napier engine that Montagu and Rothschild had chosen. This drove a shaft and propeller made by Yarrow & Co., hence the boat's name — *Yarrow Napier*. Because she had twin vertical funnels in front of her cockpit to carry away the engine's exhaust fumes, *Yarrow Napier* was sometimes mistaken for a steam launch but her speed far exceeded that of steam boats, as was proved during the 1906 'BIT'. Her closest rival was the steam powered *Rose-en-Soleil*, owned by Lord Howard de Walden, which finished more than 30 minutes behind *Yarrow Napier*. A week later Montagu and Rothschild — world motor boat champions for the second year running — took their boat to Stokes Bay, on the Solent, to compete in the Motor Yacht Club's annual regatta. They won a cup donated by *Motor Boat* magazine for the fastest sea mile and also walked off with the Enchantress Challenge Cup. In September, at the British Motorboat Club's races at Burnham, they had a crack at the world water speed record of 33.8 mph, set up a year earlier by Emile Dubonnet's 50 foot launch, *Dubonnet*. *Yarrow Napier* was unquestionably the fastest boat in the flying mile contest but, restrained by a powerful ebb tide, Montagu and Rothschild could manage only 29.38 mph, although they did win the 100 Guineas Challenge Trophy.

John (standing) and mechanic Teddy Stephens on Yarrow Napier.

That, more or less, was John's swansong as a speed boat racer. In 1907 *Yarrow Napier* was renamed *Flying Fish* and raced with less success by Rothschild. America won the British International Trophy and soon started dominating motor boat racing, much to John's annoyance. He vowed to return to the sport and win the cup back for Britain but by now, as John Montagu, 2nd Baron Montagu of Beaulieu, he had claimed his inheritance and had sole responsibility for running the Beaulieu Manor Estate. Motoring, writing and publishing continued to occupy most of his time but motor boat racing was one of the activities he was forced to abandon.

10

A Little Kingdom
in the Forest

On the death of his father on 4 November 1905, John became Lord Montagu of Beaulieu, moved into Palace House and succeeded to a ten thousand acre estate containing one of the most lovely rivers in the country; he also inherited Ditton Park and the Honor of Clitheroe in Lancashire, from which he derived mining royalties.

Although he could no longer represent the New Forest in the House of Commons, he was proud of being what he called 'one of the forty working peers' and regularly caught the 11.41 am train from Beaulieu Road Station to Waterloo on Tuesday mornings to start his weekly stint as publisher, editor and freelance writer in London. During the early days of his peerage, he used his influence as a member of the House of Lords and his friendship with the railwaymen of the LSWR to have the Friday evening Bournemouth express stopped at Beaulieu Road. Travelling by train gave him time to dream-up new ideas and plan for the future.

One proposal was that fruit and vegetables should be grown on southward facing railway cuttings and embankments; another was that a motor road should be built beside the railway line, thus putting thousands of acres of unused land to better purpose. Although nothing came of these ideas, the 'roads beside railways' proposal was the precursor of a later plan to convert railways into trunk roads.

In the last year of his father's life, John had persuaded him to have a telephone installed, much against his will. The old man's reluctance probably stemmed from the reliability of the mail in those days, for letters posted in Beaulieu at 11 am were delivered in London by 9.30 that same evening, and a similar speedy service operated in the opposite direction. What, then, was the point of trying to speak to someone ninety miles away, using one of those new-fangled instruments, when a letter would say all that was necessary before the day was out? Nevertheless, John wanted to talk to his household from London and ring his friends in town from Beaulieu. After a prolonged argument, which both he and his father later regretted, a telephone was installed in Palace House with the number Beaulieu 06.

However, when he moved into Palace House, John realized that the telephone could be a nuisance as well as a convenience; it was all very well being able to call business colleagues at any hour of the day or night but they in turn were liable to reciprocate, intruding into John's well-ordered weekends, during which he wanted to devote all his time to sport, parties, the well-being of his tenants and the management of his estate. So Beaulieu 06 was disconnected and any calls John wanted to make or receive at weekends were made from Beaulieu 29, the telephone in the Manor Office. He did, though, have a private telephone system installed so that he could call his head gardener and senior staff from Palace House. It was not until towards the end of his life that he had his home reconnected to the public service and even then he would use the telephone only when it was absolutely necessary. To the constant puzzlement of his family and servants he would never telephone them from his London office; he relied entirely on telegrams, even when asking them to send a car to meet the train on which he intended to travel home to Beaulieu.

(above and right) *Beaulieu village, as John Montagu knew it.*

Except for this idiosyncrasy John made full use of the latest technology whilst gradually modernizing and improving his estate. At the time of his succession a tiny gas works on the outskirts of the village served Palace House, the parish hall (in the Domus, once the lay brothers' dormitory in the Abbey) and the lamps in the village street. The foundations of the retort are

to this day marked by a circle of bricks behind the cottage that was once the studio where John's Terraform maps were designed. John no doubt regarded gas lighting as smelly, primitive and dangerous and under his supervision Beaulieu became one of the first villages in Hampshire to enjoy electric lighting. A generating station was built behind the village inn, the Montagu Arms and soon barges carrying anthracite for the gas engines that powered the electricity generator were to be seen on the Beaulieu River, in company with those taking coal to the gas works on the opposite bank. Older tenants imagine that on still nights they can hear the 'chug chug' of the gas engines, and the station's surviving workers recall John's regular visits, when he would inspect the ashes that had been raked out of the stoves and ensure that no unburnt anthracite was being thrown away. Beaulieu retained its private electricity supply for many years and the estate's electricians travelled around the manor in one of John's old cars, a 1903 De Dion-Bouton, now a familiar sight on the London to Brighton Run. Beaulieu was not connected to the national grid until 1954. The present Lord Montagu recalls his relief when he no longer had to rely on converters which were necessary to enable modern appliances, like refrigerators and radiograms, to accept the Beaulieu generator's old-fashioned supply.

Improving the water supply was another of John Montagu's enterprises, at a time when many houses in the village still relied on wells and hand pumps. John was aided by the fact that, centuries earlier, the monks of Beaulieu had laid on a supply of water to the Abbey from a well in the woods to the north.

This fascinating photograph of Beaulieu Fire Brigade shows John and Cis and their daughter
Helen (right) with several tenants and employees of their estate.
Back row, left to right: Bill Holman, Joe Tupper, H. Wells, Bill Long. Driver: Tom Jones.
Middle row: H. Pattillo, Chapman (Christian name unknown), Tom Hindey, Chapman (Christian name
unknown). Messenger boys: Harold Buckland, Eddie Long. Officer on extreme right: Mr Jones.
Standing, left to right: J. W. Nash-Brown (estate clerk), Frank W. Wadley (the brigade's captain and
founder and engineer-in-charge of the electricity generating station, 1906-43). Standing centre:
Rev. R. F. Powles, Vicar of Beaulieu.
The fire engine was donated to Hull Transport Museum in about 1931.

Lord Henry had a new cast iron main installed from Monks' Well to the
village in 1889 and John tapped this when extending the supply. Tenants
were charged 6d. for a tap but there were those who thought this was far too
much, and for the rest of their lives they carried buckets of water home from
the nearest well. Houses outside the village were beyond the range of the pipe
from Monks' Well; the Master Builders House at Buckler's Hard, where
ships were built for Nelson's Navy, for example. When the house was
converted into an hotel for his old friend and colleague, George Foster
Pedley, John devised an ingenious system whereby water was fed by gravity
from a remote spring to tanks in the hotel's loft.

The villagers of Buckler's Hard were offered running water but petitioned
against it, because their children would no longer have been able to earn
pocket money by carrying pails of water to the homes of tenants unwilling or
unable to fetch their own water. It was not until after the Second World War

that mains water reached Buckler's Hard. John had an almost uncanny gift for discovering sources of fresh water at Beaulieu; this proved invaluable when, in later life, he decided to develop residential areas around the manor.

John devoted much thought to water, though it was draining it away, rather than supplying it to his tenants, that caused him most of his worries. The Beaulieu estate is difficult to farm because much of it is low lying, wet, heavy clay. John and his zealous agent, Captain Henry Widnell, were forever inspecting the land drains, outfalls and culverts on the manor and the subject held a fascination for John. One of his favourite ways of occupying idle minutes was to liberate tiny streams from puddles in the road, with the aid of his long hazel walking stick. Field gates became another of his obsessions. There were 1700 on the estate; Montagu and Widnell knew them all because of problems they had in keeping them in good repair.

Palace House, the Abbey, the village and Buckler's Hard are the places in and around Beaulieu that every visitor knows, but it is away from the beaten tracks that the places that give an extra insight into John Montagu's life and character can be found. North of the Abbey, where the river has yet to become the familiar broad, navigable waterway thronged with yachtsmen and anglers, there is what was one of John's favourite retreats, Hartford Hole, where he would cast from a sunny bank into a shaded stretch of water where the sea trout lurked. Just beyond the pool is Hartford Wood, where in 1910 he built The House in the Wood.

From time to time he would let Palace House in the summer and he, Cis and their younger daughter Elizabeth, born 19 years after Helen in 1909, would live in this secluded woodland. The rhododendrons that John planted around the house have now matured, forming a fragrant frame around the extensive views of the forest that can be admired from its lawns.

Two and a half miles downstream from Hartford Hole, Buckler's Hard commands a sweeping bend in the river and is today almost as popular as Beaulieu village itself. It was John, Duke of Montagu, who tried to develop the tiny 'hard' into an important port in the 18th century, largely to serve the ships he hoped would bring sugar to England from St Vincent, his island in the West Indies. The project was a failure but he had more success with his efforts to establish a shipyard at Buckler's Hard.

It was John, the 2nd Baron Montagu of Beaulieu, who gave the place a new life by publicising its history and inevitably attracting heritage-hungry sightseers. The hard is more or less on the southern edge of the area of the estate which the public is able to explore, but there is much private territory further to the south and west. Here are the woods where oaks were felled to build some of the ships that fought at Trafalgar and where, more than 100 years later, John Montagu went shooting, sometimes with one or two friends, at other times with large parties of sportsmen. He would plan his shoots

The House in the Wood. In the group are, left to right, John Montagu, Sir Thomas Troubridge, Count Terry and Lord Headford.

like a military campaign, rushing guns and guests, loaders and beaters, from one end of the estate to another in a fleet of motor cars. There is little doubt that he was one of the first to use cars to carry shooting parties and the first journalist to write on the subject, 'cars as an aid to shooting'.

One of John's shooting parties, as depicted by Charles Sykes.

Himself an expert shot, John had no patience for careless marksmen. Those who injured their prey instead of killing it cleanly seldom received another invitation to shoot at Beaulieu. The men of the manor loaded the guns, for which they were paid half-a-crown for their day's work, and their sons were paid 1s.6d. to act as beaters. As a bonus there was a bottle of ale or ginger beer, and at the end of the day guests and servants would gather for supper in the estate plumber's cottage.

Fishing and shooting were John's favourite sports but he disapproved of fox and stag hunting and would not allow the local hunt onto his land. Otters could be hunted, though, because they ate his fish, both in the river and in Sowley Pond — said to be the largest lake in Hampshire — which was one of the prides of his estate. Sowley Pond was created by the friars of Beaulieu and was an abundant source of coarse fish. Local legend maintains that the monks threw their Golden Madonna into the pond to prevent it being stolen by Henry VIII's men, and there was much speculation that this would be found when, in 1907, John drained the pond. His motive, much to everyone's disappointment, was not to search for treasure but to capture the lake's pike and restock it with trout. His efforts were in vain; pike spawn, conceived in neighbouring lakes, was carried to Sowley Pond on the legs of itinerant herons and the trout soon became the prey of predatory fish.

Ancient and Modern at Beaulieu. A Sykes cartoon for an RAC menu card.

Between Sowley Pond and the mouth of Beaulieu River there is a three-mile stretch of Solent shore where John spent many leisure hours, accumulating much of his almost encyclopaedic knowledge of natural history that so impressed his friends and family. The coastguard cottages at the most easterly point, Needs Ore, were converted into seaside homes by John Montagu and among their tenants was Col. Charles Hodgkinson, one of the remarkable Hodgkinson twins of Indian Cavalry fame.

West of Needs Ore there is a wilderness of undulating shingle where John created a bird sanctuary, the precursor of the 1300 acre National Nature Reserve that is today the home of several uncommon species, including a colony of little terns. John also constructed a golf links here; its greens, fairways and bunkers, now overgrown, provide a safe and secluded habitat for a host of wild creatures.

West of the golf course is Tin Town, a collection of corrugated iron buildings which included the Bungalow where he had brought King Edward to lunch in 1902. Rusting lamposts still mark the course of a gravelled track which is all that remains of the experimental tarmac road he had had built here. For this was where John and his friends would spend many hilarious hours, amusing themselves with such activities as fixing lighted candles to the backs of crabs and sending them scuttling down rabbit burrows. Among John's weekend guests were the Troubridges, Sir Thomas and Laura. Lady Troubridge, writer of Elinor Glyn-type romances, wrote thus of their visits to 'the Bung', as Montagu called it, in those Edwardian summers:

> Life at The Bungalow was a kind of glorified picnic. The food, though plain, was always excellent. Beaulieu oysters from the beds opposite Buckler's Hard, prawns, plovers' eggs and, in their season, pheasants, partridges, wild duck and teal. Those, with mushrooms, would compose a meal entirely produced by the estate. The social life of The Bungalow was passed on the broad verandah and that and one living room was all the accommodation, apart from half a dozen small bedrooms and two larger ones for the hosts. Privacy was certainly lacking and the visitors if they wanted it had to do a great deal of blind pulling.
> Of entertaining in the ordinary sense there was none, yet the tiny rooms were always full of friends, both old and new, who came again and again and were made to feel completely at home. Those summer days had a savour all their own, with the sea almost at the verandah steps and the lonely silence of the shore broken only by the strange, harsh cry of the gulls, contrasting with the stir and movement of life within the house.

In 1909 John sold a 99-year lease on 'The Bung', retaining the right to hold motor car trials on the lane leading to it. During the next few years he built a new seaside retreat, half a mile along the coast. Called The House on the Shore, this was as imposing as The House in the Wood on the northern edge of the manor and it was where John spent the last summers of his life. The house, like many hereabouts, is at the end of a long drive that winds through pine trees, rhododendrons and azaleas and whilst supervising its design and construction John used local craftsmen and, wherever possible, local materials.

Beaulieu was, in those days, self-sufficient in almost everything, especially building materials. The bricks for The House on the Shore came from Beaulieu brickworks, the site of which is now marked by a tall chimney and a jumble of rusting machinery beside a footpath that runs through the woods between Beaulieu and Buckler's Hard. The roof tiles came from a barn at Thorns Farm but there is little reason to doubt that they were made on the estate, perhaps hundreds of years before John found a new use for them. Oak for the floorboards, doors, rafters and exposed beams came from the manor woodlands, as did elm for the weatherboarding on the upper storey. Attached to the house there was what was still a novelty before the First World War: a garage. At that time the very word was new, for originally the place where a motor car was kept was called a 'motor house'. John's garage was doubly uncommon because it had a personal door leading directly into the house; an ordinary enough facility today, in the most modest 'semi', but *avant-garde* when The House on the Shore was built. The house was of such advanced design that its plans were exhibited at The Royal Academy.

John Montagu loved modernizing and improving his estates at Beaulieu and took an enormous interest in the detailed day to day running of affairs. His ability to absorb information on anything and everything under the sun was one of his best-remembered characteristics. Sir James Kingston Fowler, the eminent surgeon who became the first honorary Warden of Beaulieu Abbey and the author of a definitive history of the building, once said of John: 'He was an extraordinary man. There was only one table at the Beafsteak Club; John would come in when everyone was talking and within two minutes he would be leading the conversation. He could speak on any subject at any moment.'

Another of John's attributes, his paternalistic concern for his tenants, was recalled by Gilbert Malcom and his sisters Katie and Bessie, whose father was the first of five farmers who came to Beaulieu from Scotland during the agricultural depression in the 1890s. Whilst John did not call on his tenant farmers as regularly as his father had done, he took the same close interest in their welfare and the difficulties they faced in wresting a living from land that was of below-average quality. After one especially poor harvest he had no hesitation in reducing the farm rents. Every Christmas John held a party in the Domus for his tenants' children. The tenants and their children knew their place, of course; Katie Malcom remembers that whenever she heard Lord and Lady Montagu's brougham coming along the lane, she would hide behind a hedge in order to avoid having to give the obligatory curtsey.

Another, more significant, incident is still spoken of in Beaulieu by the Kitcher, Norris and Wadley families. One bitterly cold March morning John, who had just returned from his annual winter holiday at Valescure, in the south of France, heard three of his tenants coughing and sneezing outside the Manor Office. They were David Kitcher, clerk of works, Fred Norris, miller and saddler, and Frank Wadley, electrician. Remarking upon their evident ill-health John told the men that they ought to take a holiday in the sunny climes from which he had just returned. 'Not much chance of that, m'Lord', answered Norris, who had never had a holiday in his life. Impulsive as always, John turned to Harry Widnell, and said: 'Take them to France for a fortnight at my expense'.

More than 60 years after he was made responsible for the day-to-day running of Beaulieu, Widnell was able to recall in great detail the manners, mannerisms and lifestyle of the man known to everyone on the estate as 'Lord John'. Widnell had been immediately impressed by John's kindly attitude and smart appearance at his initial interview. He was wearing his brigadier's uniform and in Widnell's eyes bore a striking resemblance to Field Marshal Haig. Widnell was also struck by John's blue eyes, reddish hair, healthy complexion, rugged build — and by his elastic step, which gave him 'the ability to be in two places at once'. When discussing anything of urgency or importance he would grasp his companion by the arm and walk to and fro whilst holding forth with tremendous enthusiasm on whatever subject was on his mind.

Montagu in mufti cut a very different figure to the imposing brigadier who had first interviewed Widnell. When setting off from Beaulieu at the beginning of the week, to lead his 'London life', John invariably wore a business suit of blue serge but on Fridays he changed into an amply-cut lovat green tweed suit, complete with full — but not too long — plus fours. 'Lord John always looked exactly what in his innermost heart he knew himself to be: a typical country gentleman of his day', said Widnell.

In the summer John would discard the plus fours for grey flannel trousers, with which he wore a light flannel shirt and a tie that he passed through a gold ring, a Victorian fashion that Montagu perpetrated long after that era had ended. Another minor idiosyncrasy was his habit of looping his watch chain between the two top pockets of his waistcoat, instead of the lower pockets. In these and other little ways John was unconventional but never eccentric. Widnell recalled that John's clothes often displayed signs of hard wear and were discarded only when 'necessity demanded their retirement'. His soft grey and brown felt hats received similar treatment and for years he always carried but seldom wore a plaid motoring hat; this reposed in one of the cavernous pockets of his overcoat.

Outwardly at least — in the way he dressed, occupied his weekends and cared for his tenants — John exemplified the Lord of the Manor. But there were really two John Montagus — the one who went shooting and fishing and inspecting the drains at Beaulieu, whilst devoting two or three days a week to ruling his 'little kingdom', and the one who caught the train to London to spend the business part of the week embroiled in publishing, politics and writing.

11

Rolls-Royce and Brooklands

Life for a motoring lord was never dull midway through Edward VII's reign, which had become a true Golden Age for those who could afford to indulge in the new form of personal transport that — thanks to John Montagu's efforts in 1903 — now had the freedom of the roads of Britain; a freedom restrained only by the new speed limit and the simple, if contentious, formalities involved in obtaining the necessary tax and registration documents. Even though the statistics showing the number of private motor cars on the road in Britain in the years immediately following the introduction of the Motor Car Act are not totally reliable, there is little doubt that there were between 16,000 and 30,000 in use by the time the Act was 18 months old, compared with less than 9000 in March 1904. Unquestionably, private cars outnumbered all other kinds of motor vehicles and in a book he edited and published in 1906 to mark the tenth anniversary of the abolition of the Red Flag Act, John wrote prophetically about the future of what he and his contemporaries still insisted on calling 'automobilism':

> It will to a great extent replace nearly every other kind of traction upon the surface of the earth. It will help solve political and social problems but at the same time create others. It will affect values of land, towns and houses. Land in the country, on the outskirts of towns and in villages remote from railways will become more valuable because of the greater ease of access. On the whole, railways will lose because mechanical road transport is a new rival which will compel improvements in passenger and goods services. In most places motor carriages conveying the public will kill the trams. Populations will gradually tend to become less concentrated and be diffused over wider areas. Travelling will increase enormously and dustless motorways will be constructed between principal towns to carry the ceaseless traffic which will use them by night and day. Large towns will have special arterial roads to connect their centres with main roads outside.
>
> Europe in a few years time will become for the motorist one vast holiday area. Hotels will find the motorist the most profitable source of revenue. The country which has the best roads will in future become more and

more prosperous. Enormous sums will be invested in road making and
new vehicles all over the world.

These were brave words in 1906; John's ideas were derided in many
quarters but all around there were signs of things to come. Two Royal
Commissions were at work, examining the very developments that John was
forecasting. One of the Commissions, on London traffic, published a series
of 'Blue Books' with fulsome reports, plans and diagrams illustrating the
capital's present transport problems and those it was likely to face in the
future. The other Commission, which pondered over the very future of the
motor car itself — the dangers it created, the laws that controlled it and the
cost of building and repairing the roads on which it ran — collected evidence
throughout the autumn and winter of 1905 and 1906. Within days of
inheriting the Barony of Beaulieu, John told the Commission about one
aspect of automobilism that particularly interested him — the need for
dustless roads — and he was able to report on the latest activities of *The Car
Illustrated*'s Dust Fund, to which such eminent motorists as Arthur Balfour
and Alfred Harmsworth had donated £100 apiece to pay for tests to be
carried out with various chemicals which, in the opinion of their manufacturers if nobody else, could successfully seal and bind the surfaces of dusty
roads. The Commission proposed higher motor taxes and the creation of a
central Road Fund; from this stemmed the establishment of the Road Board,
which was responsible for improving existing roads and building new ones.
John was a member of the board from the time it was formed until it was
absorbed into the new Ministry of Transport.

The Royal Commissions were the precursors of the bureaucracy that
would soon be set up to cope with the changes in travelling habits that were
being brought about by the growing popularity of the motor car. What was
of equal, if not greater, interest to John was the new motoring hardware that
rapidly took shape during the years in which he became accustomed to the
powers and privileges of his peerage. The Rolls-Royce motor car and the
Brooklands motor racing circuit are two manifestations of the spirit of
progress that inspired the British motor industry in Edwardian times and
enabled it to take its place, somewhat belatedly, among the world's leaders in
automobile design and motor sport. John was closely associated with both
developments, which began to flourish in the summer of 1907 when the
soon-to-be legendary Rolls-Royce Silver Ghost completed its first endurance
trials and the first race meeting — at which one of the principal prizes was the
Montagu Cup — was held at Brooklands.

Rolls-Royce blossomed first and because two members of the triumvirate
responsible for the success of the enterprise were close friends of John, he was
better placed than most journalists to hear, at first hand, what was going on.

Later, when the founders of the company sought to topple the Daimler from its pre-eminent position in the market for luxury cars, it was the likes of John Montagu who first had to be convinced of the merits of the new breed.

The Rolls-Royce story began in November 1903 when Claude Johnson became Charles Rolls' partner at C.S.Rolls & Co., motor dealers and importers. Johnson's resignation from the Automobile Club had been one of the major topics of conversation in the motoring world in December 1902 and it was John Montagu who, in the Christmas edition of *The Car Illustrated*, first made the news public. Johnson stayed on at the Automobile Club for six months after handing in his resignation, joined Paris Singer in a new venture called the City and Suburban Electric Carriage Company and then went into partnership with Rolls, who was about to open his first motor showroom in the West End.

Soon after Johnson became his partner, Rolls began to wish that he could sell English cars, instead of imports, but because of what he called the 'sheer pigheadedness' of most British manufacturers, who were failing to match the technical excellence of their Continental rivals, he was unable to do so. He was unwilling to set up his own car factory, firstly because of his own lack of experience in building cars and secondly because of the financial risks involved. By coincidence a 40-year-old electrical engineer named Frederick Henry Royce was busy at work in Manchester building a 10 hp car which he was determined would be an improvement on the foreign motor, a Decauville, he had bought a year or two earlier. Rolls and Royce were complete strangers but they had a mutual friend, an electrical engineer and entrepreneur by the name of Henry Edmunds.

Thirty years earlier, Edmunds had been present when Thomas Edison first recorded sound. Subsequently, Edmunds introduced sound recording into England and pioneered electric lighting. Now, in May 1904, he once again helped make history by persuading Charles Rolls, his fellow automobilist in London, to go to Manchester to meet Royce, his fellow electrical engineer. Rolls was immediately impressed by the meticulous workmanship embodied in Royce's 10 hp car and realized that he had at last met someone who was capable of building British vehicles that could compete with the best that France and Germany could offer. At the end of 1904 C.S.Rolls & Co. became sole dealers for all Henry Royce's cars, which from the outset were named 'Rolls-Royce'. Later the enterprise became Rolls-Royce Limited, with Rolls as Technical Managing Director, Royce as Chief Engineer and Claude Johnson as Commercial Managing Director.

John Montagu took a keen interest in Rolls' and Johnson's new venture and although he was unable to visit the Paris Salon in December 1904, where Rolls-Royce cars, chassis and engines were exhibited for the first time, he was at the London motor show two months later when the most successful of

Royce's early designs, the four cylinder Rolls-Royce Twenty, was unveiled. Two lightweight versions competed in the first Tourist Trophy race on the Isle of Man in September 1905 and although one of them, driven by Rolls, broke down after performing promisingly in the practice laps, the other car, with Percy Northey at the wheel, came second and was only fractionally slower than the winner, John Napier's Arrol-Johnston.

Typically, Claude Johnson extracted every ounce of publicity for the new car from Northey's achievement and John Montagu was among those who, in the months immediately following the racing debut that set Rolls-Royce on the path to fame and fortune, ordered production versions of the 'Light' Twenty.

Johnson's role in promoting Rolls-Royce motor cars cannot be exaggerated. Rolls was a public hero by 1905 and no mean mechanic either; so his contribution was crucial. Royce was a brilliant engineer but a somewhat retiring figure and not one to thrust himself, or his work, into public attention. Johnson was certainly Rolls' equal as a salesman and publicist and he made strenuous and amply rewarded efforts to establish Rolls-Royce cars among the upper classes. John Montagu was one of his first conquests; he had been buying Daimlers more or less annually since 1898, so his decision to become the owner of a marque that was only just becoming familiar was a bold one, and a major coup for Johnson. Chassis number 40526 for John's Twenty left Royce's tiny factory in Manchester on 11 April 1906 to be fitted with its *Roi des Belges* open tourer coachwork — a style favoured by the King of the Belgians and named accordingly. In the early summer of 1906 John

John's Rolls-Royce Twenty during a hill climbing trial at Beaulieu in May 1907.

performed what was to be his last important service for Rolls-Royce's rival by taking his almost brand new 45 hp Daimler to Bavaria and Austria for the Herkomer touring car trials. Thirteen drivers from England took part; three of them, including John, won gold medals.

Family legend maintains that John's Twenty fell short of Rolls-Royce's impeccable standards but the company's records do not support this view. The car was still going strong in 1916, having required only the usual number of spare parts over the years. John's reputation *vis-à-vis* the formative years of Rolls-Royce has likewise suffered what may be an injustice. Soon after the 1905 TT, Claude Johnson and Henry Royce announced that the next Rolls would be a luxury town car, powered by a V8 petrol engine capable of running from 3 mph to 20 mph in top gear; driving around all the time in top gear, even up steep hills, was something of a fetish among Edwardian motorists. Because of its bonnetless body, achieved by hiding the engine under the driving seat, the V8 looked like an electric brougham. There was also a version of conventional appearance, geared so as to be incapable of exceeding 20 mph and called, excruciatingly, the Legalimit. Neither type proved to be anywhere near as popular as Johnson hoped; John Montagu is said to have been the instigator of the whole idea but this may be unfair. Lord Northcliffe was the only person to buy a Legalimit, so perhaps he was the culprit. This early and rare error of judgement by Rolls, Royce and Johnson was quickly forgotten and the company soon surged ahead, at a pace unprecedented even by its own standards, by developing the car that was to make the name 'Rolls-Royce' synonymous with excellence.

Between 1904 and 1906 Henry Royce methodically developed two cylinder 10 hp, three cylinder 15 hp, four cylinder 20 hp and six cylinder 30 hp motor cars; the six cylinder 40/50 hp Rolls-Royce of 1907 was his final and decisive contribution to the so-called 'battle of the cylinders' that was being waged by rival engineers, notably S.F.Edge, who believed that six cylinders rather than four would provide the smooth and comfortable ride, reliability, high performance and other attributes demanded by the carriage trade. Royce did not find it easy to produce a superior six cylinder car but when he succeeded it won universal acclaim. The Rolls-Royce 40/50, unofficially known as the Silver Ghost — after the thirteenth, and most distinguished model to come off the production line — quickly won John Montagu's approval and the coverage it received in *The Car Illustrated* helped it become famous and respected in, it now seems, less than no time.

Never one to do things by halves, Claude Johnson took the thirteenth 40/50, gave its bodywork a dazzling aluminium paint finish, attached various silver-plated lamps and other embellishments, and after a preliminary 2000 mile workout in May 1907 set the Silver Ghost off on a 15,000 mile journey during which it won a gold medal in the 629-mile Scottish Reliability

Trial and was then driven from Glasgow to London and back, over and over again, until it had covered a record 14,371 miles, stopping only for petrol, tyre checks and the obligatory Sunday rest days. A writer from *The Car Illustrated*, probably John himself, was a passenger during one night run from Manchester to London, reporting afterwards:

> The journey through the night hours had been perfectly delightful, owing to the almost eerie silence of the car, combined with a degree of restful comfort such as we had never previously experienced on a motor driven vehicle. The charm of these Rolls-Royce cars is derived from the fact that one scarcely realizes they are travelling at all. Never once through the journey, thanks to the splendid driving of Mr Johnson, was there the slightest contretemps on the road.

Contretemps on the road were common in those days. Motor cars were regarded with suspicion and even hatred by the horse-owning gentry and the dust they stirred up angered farmer and squire alike. Passing cars were often pelted with stones and clods of earth and on one occasion Lady Cecil Montagu narrowly escaped injury when a porcelain telegraph insulator was thrown at a car in which she was travelling.

Whilst the Silver Ghost was flitting in eerie silence between Glasgow and London, Rolls-Royce's plans to move from Henry Royce's original works in Manchester to a brand new factory in Nightingale Road, Derby, were well advanced. By March 1908 the company had decided to drop all other models from its range in order to concentrate on building Silver Ghosts.

Having proved its point in the 15,000 mile trial, Rolls-Royce had also decided to withdraw from competitive motoring and devote all its energies and hard-pressed finances to the business of making and selling cars. However the 1908 International Touring Car Trials proved too strong a challenge for Claude Johnson and two non-standard Ghosts were entered. One of them won its class, and evidently the powers-that-be at Rolls-Royce were so sure that it would win that they delayed the official opening of the factory until after the competition. The man they invited to perform the opening ceremony was John Montagu and in this move the shrewd hand of Claude Johnson, ever adept at associating Rolls-Royce cars with the upper crust, can again be detected, although John's cousin Lord Herbert Scott may have been responsible. Lord Herbert had been Field Marshal Earl Roberts' aide-de-camp during the Boer War, but at the time John introduced him to Claude Johnson he was an impoverished ex-Guards officer. Johnson made him London sales manager and a director of Rolls-Royce in January 1907. He became Chairman in 1936 and died in 1944.

The opening ceremony at Derby on 9 July 1908 was the kind of well-organized and widely-publicized affair that Johnson arranged so well. John

Montagu symbolically set the new factory in production by switching on the electricity, and in a speech full of praise for Johnson 'the man of business', Rolls 'the most skilled driver' and Royce 'the mechanical genius' he commented: 'There is one reason why I think the Rolls-Royce is the best car in the world and that is because I have just ordered one myself'.

Almost hidden behind one of Rolls-Royce's many trophies, John opens the company's factory at Derby. Charles Rolls is sitting at the far right of the table. The car behind him is the famous Silver Ghost.

The timing of his announcement was impeccable. Intentionally or otherwise the impression John left with his audience and those who read the next day's newspapers was that he had only recently decided to become a Rolls-Royce owner, although in actual fact he had been running his 'Light' Twenty for about two years. But the new factory and the decision to build only Silver Ghosts was in a sense a new beginning for the company and the 40/50 car was to become the first classic Rolls-Royce.

John's Silver Ghost was no 'ordinary' Ghost, if such a word can be applied to such a celebrated marque. Indeed, it is debatable whether it should be called either by its official name, the Rolls-Royce 40/50 or by the popular name derived from the aluminium and silver car that made those relentless journeys between England and Scotland a year earlier. Before moving to Derby, Henry Royce had been experimenting with a new and more powerful six cylinder engine, different in several respects to those installed in the

40/50. For instance, overhead inlet valves instead of side valves were fitted. Claude Johnson wanted the two Ghosts entered in the 1908 Scottish trials to have exceptional hill climbing abilities and so they were powered by Royce's new engine, which developed 70 hp.

It is generally believed that only four of these Type 70 cars were built: two (named White Knave and Silver Rogue) for the trials, one for Charles Rolls' personal use and the fourth for H.C. ('Fatty') Neill, the racing driver. But there was a fifth Type 70, chassis number 60751, built for John Montagu and named Dragonfly. He must have been pleased with it. For the rest of his life his principal car was always a Rolls. All of them played an important part in his personal life but one in particular, the Silver Ghost, chassis number 1404, that he bought in December 1910, played a leading role in what has become the most romantic of the many legends that add a touch of fantasy to the Rolls-Royce story. This legend, unlike some others, is founded on fact.

John Montagu's Dragonfly – no ordinary Rolls-Royce.

The principal characters in this particular episode of motoring folklore are John's artist, Charles Sykes and his private secretary Eleanor Thornton. Claude Johnson occupies the centre of the stage for part of the time and at others is watching from the wings.

By 1909, although still *The Car Illustrated*'s chief illustrator, Sykes had established himself as an artistic all-rounder, talented in commercial art, cartoons, paintings, pastels and sculptures. Never a motoring enthusiast, he nevertheless became a superb motoring artist; John's Rolls-Royces obviously fascinated him and one of his early efforts shows Dragonfly (minus a few technical features that Sykes somehow failed to notice) effortlessly climbing a hill on what looks suspiciously like the road to Beaulieu. The publicity value of artistic impressions of Silver Ghosts in their natural habitat was soon appreciated by Claude Johnson and he asked Sykes to produce a series of paintings for Rolls-Royce's brochures. 'Arrival at the Opera' and 'Arrival at the Meet' were typical of Sykes' subject matter and in most cases he also executed contrasting paintings, showing how lords and ladies made their arrivals and departures in horse-drawn carriages a hundred and one years earlier.

Johnson's efforts to place Rolls-Royce on an artistic as well as engineering pinnacle received a setback when a craze for car mascots developed and silly things like golliwogs and toy policemen were to be seen mounted incongruously on the radiator caps of even the most expensive cars, Rolls-Royces being no exception. These adornments definitely lowered the tone of what had, for several years, been advertised as The Best Car in the World, so Johnson countered the craze in late 1910 by commissioning Sykes to design a suitably distinguished mascot exclusively for Rolls-Royce owners. Sykes' response was the familiar Flying Lady statuette, mounted above the radiator grille and in a letter to John Montagu, Johnson explained that it was intended to convey the spirit of the Rolls-Royce: 'Speed with silence, absence of vibration, the mysterious harnessing of great energy, a beautiful, moving, living organism of superb grace'.

Sykes, continued Johnson, had in mind 'the spirit of ecstasy, who has selected road travel as her supreme delight and has alighted on the prow of a Rolls-Royce car to revel in the freshness of the air and the musical sound of her fluttering draperies. She is expressing her keen enjoyment, with her arms outstretched and her sight fixed upon the distance.'

Spirit of Ecstasy was to become the official name for the figurehead but when it was assigned to Rolls-Royce in March 1911 it was called Spirit of Speed. Interestingly, Sykes had given this title to a a painting, reproduced on the front cover of *The Car Illustrated*'s Christmas 1906 issue, which depicted a winged chariot being driven through the night sky by a half-naked female holding a flaming torch. The painting, the Flying Lady and various other sculptures created by Sykes during the years he worked for Montagu and Johnson depict nude or lightly clad women in various poses, and there is no doubt that Eleanor Thornton was his model on many occasions. Was the creation of Spirit of Ecstasy one of them?

John's Spirit of Ecstasy statuette.

Eleanor Thornton as an artist's model.

Miss Thornton led a double life. During the day she worked in John's West End office. In the evening she returned to live with her sister Rose at The Pheasantry, which was becoming the centre of an artists' colony in King's Road, Chelsea. Here, the Joubert family of artists and craftsmen had built a number of apartments and studios, occupied by a constantly shifting Bohemian population — an environment that says much about Eleanor's way of life.

Charles Sykes' daughter, Mrs Jo Phillips, knew Eleanor as 'Auntie Thorn', and said of her: 'She hated clothes. She needed to live with people who were free in their ideas. She loved life. She definitely had quite an influence on my father's work.' The hatred of clothes refers to Eleanor's lack of inhibition when posing naked or diaphanously draped for Sykes' creations, one of which, a statuette of Phryne, the celebrated courtesan of ancient Athens, was exhibited at the Royal Academy. At other times Eleanor evidently took a close interest in clothes; photographs taken in John's office and various studios show her to have been a handsome and fashionably dressed Edwardian lady, strikingly attractive when wearing the elaborate hats of the period.

Because there is no documentary proof, it will never be established for certain whether Eleanor was the model for the Flying Lady — although the Montagu family, and some of those who have studied the story of Rolls-Royce, are convinced that she was. Mrs Phillips is less sure, pointing out that no one could have adopted the statuette's pose for long enough to allow an artist to make a sketch, let alone a sculpture. But she acknowledges that Sykes would probably have had a particular face and figure in mind and that, as one of his favourite models, Eleanor may have been his principal inspiration.

Certainly there is plenty of circumstantial evidence to support those who believe that it is Eleanor Thornton who is immortalized in the Flying Lady. The statuette's head, for instance, bears a strong resemblance to that on a motor boat racing trophy that Sykes designed in 1913 and which, in Jo Phillips' opinion, is an 'absolute portrait' of Eleanor.

Reggie Ingram, John Montagu's doctor, understood that she had been the model for the Flying Lady and once remarked: 'They shouldn't have put Eleanor's head on it'. Gordon Hayter, a friend of John and a writer for *The Car Illustrated*, also believed that Eleanor was Sykes' model. He knew both the Thornton girls around the time Sykes created the statuette, went to their parties at The Pheasantry, and married Rose Thornton a few years later. He therefore heard all about Eleanor's modelling activities from the sisters' friends, from Rose, and perhaps from Eleanor herself. When Rose died in 1945 Mr Hayter inherited several of Sykes' works from her, most of which had originally belonged to Eleanor. These included sketches of Eleanor, a woodland scene signed 'Charles Sykes to Thorny' and a solid silver Flying

Eleanor Thornton on John's 1910 Silver Ghost.

Lady. This statuette had once adorned the Thornton girls' apartment at The Pheasantry; it was bequeathed to Mr Hayter's second wife when he died in 1958 but was stolen during a burglary several years later and has never been recovered.

Claude Johnson's influence on Sykes' choice of a model for Rolls-Royce's mascot must also be considered. Eleanor had been his secretary at the Automobile Club until they went their separate ways in 1902. He would have followed her later career with interest and would certainly have known about her talents as a model. When commissioning Sykes, Johnson may well have put in a word for Eleanor Thornton when Sykes told him the kind of mascot he proposed to design.

Finally there is the evidence offered by a series of photographs in the Montagu archives, showing Eleanor on the running board of his 1910 Silver Ghost. In one picture the photographer has carefully ensured that both the Flying Lady and Miss Thornton are included in the shot, almost as if to say 'This is the mascot and here is the lady who inspired it'. One element of the Flying Lady legend maintains that Sykes was inspired to create the statuette after riding in John Montagu's Rolls-Royce, an experience that left him captivated with the car's smoothness and silence at high speed. The Rolls in question is most likely to have been the 1910 Silver Ghost, which John was proudly showing off to his friends at about the time Sykes was wrestling with

Eleanor Thornton (left) and Charles Sykes (centre) on a woodland road, circa 1911.

the task of producing a suitable mascot for future generations of Rolls-Royces. If one particular ride in a Rolls did spark off Sykes' artistic spirit, it is tempting to presume that the photograph that gives pride of place on the Silver Ghost to a smiling Eleanor Thornton and a shining new Spirit of Ecstasy was taken sometime in the early spring of 1911, to ensure that later generations would know whose face and figure inspired Sykes whilst he was making what proved to be his most lasting contribution to motoring art.

As if to reinforce that conclusion there is another photograph in the Montagu collection showing Eleanor Thornton and Charles Sykes on a woodland road, in company with Sykes' wife Jessica and their artist friend Joseph Longhurst. This picture too appears to have been taken in the early spring and since Eleanor is wearing the same clothes as in the photographs showing her on the 1910 Ghost, it may have been taken on the same day, the occasion perhaps being the first outing for Rolls-Royce's new mascot.

Because of the 20 mph speed limit the early Silver Ghosts were unable officially to demonstrate their full capabilities on public roads. So Charles Sykes' impression of the swiftness and silence of John's new car may have been gained on a lonely stretch of road, away from the speed traps that the Police were so fond of setting on highways where motorists were in the habit of 'scorching' along, or on the new privately owned motor racing circuit at Brooklands, H. F. Locke King's country estate at Weybridge, Surrey. Here several Rolls-Royces were put through their paces in a number of impressive speed and endurance trials. Two of the Type 70s, White Knave and Silver Rogue, acquitted themselves admirably at Brooklands in 1908 at over 65 mph, and in 1911 an improved version of the 40/50 managed 78.26 mph, after being driven from London to Edinburgh locked in top gear. It averaged 24 miles to the gallon whilst doing so; such frugality would today be welcomed by many owners of luxury cars. The new 40/50 outclassed a Napier which had covered the same ground some weeks earlier and a 'London to Edinburgh' Silver Ghost — widely regarded as the best version ever — then went into series production. John bought one and it became the third of the five Ghosts he was to own.

Brooklands was more to John than simply the place where his favourite cars were tested. He was associated with the promotion of the circuit from its inception and was Vice-President of its governing body, the Brooklands Automobile Racing Club, serving on a committee that included such luminaries as Prince Francis of Teck, the dukes of Beaufort and Westminster, their lordships Dudley, Churchill, Sefton, Essex, Tollemache and (inevitably) Northcliffe — and Mr E. de Rodakowski. The need for a private motor racing circuit had been apparent since 1903, when the series of fatal accidents that

This picture of one of John's Rolls-Royce Silver Ghosts exemplifies the excellent condition in which he kept all his motor cars in India during World War I.

marred the Paris-Madrid Race made it obvious that public opinion would never countenance road racing on English highways. Sometime in the early summer of 1906 John Montagu and Mr and Mrs Locke King were Lord Northcliffe's luncheon guests at Sutton Place, and when Northcliffe complained that the reason why British cars failed to win international honours was because there was nowhere for them to be tested at high speed, Locke King wasted no time in drawing up plans for a three-mile circuit on his estate.

In July 1906 John published an exclusive report on 'Mr Locke King's private motor car racecourse' in *The Car Illustrated* and the speed with which private enterprise was able and allowed to work in those days is reflected by the fact that construction began in September. On 9 March 1907 the committee met to plan the first race meeting — postponing this until 6 July because atrocious weather in January and February had made it impossible for the course to be opened in May as originally planned.

Later Locke King was to say that but for John Montagu's encouragement at the time the idea of Brooklands was first discussed at Sutton Place, and the publicity *The Car Illustrated* gave to the project, he would never have persevered and overcome the many difficulties he faced whilst building his racetrack.

John supported Brooklands throughout the years in which it became established as an international motoring venue. The main event of the afternoon at the opening meeting was a 30 mile race for the First Montagu Cup, won by Jack Hutton in a Mercedes. In 1908 John donated another trophy, designed by Charles Sykes; Frank Newton, driving a Napier, was the winner. In 1909 the Third Montagu Cup was won by H. P. Egleston in a Bianchi.

At the opening of Brooklands in 1907. Left to right: Cecil Edge, John Montagu, Montague S. Napier and S. F. Edge.

Today Brooklands is only a fading memory of the sights, sounds and smells of the pioneering days of motor-circuit racing, although the remains of some of the steep, curved embankments on which the world's greatest drivers risked their reputations and their lives are still in existence. A part of the banking is scheduled as an ancient monument as are some of the buildings. It is hoped that a Museum of Brooklands will open within the next few years,

Jack Hutton, winner of the Montagu Cup at Brooklands' first race meeting.

where the enthusiast can again see just some of the cars and motorcycles that once thrilled the Surrey crowds. The iron gates that stood at the entrance to the Locke King estate had until recently been kept at Beaulieu, but they have now been returned to their rightful home.

At the time Brooklands and the Rolls-Royce Silver Ghost were merely ideas, John Montagu was forecasting that one day Europe would become a vast holiday area for motorists. In the autumn of 1908 he set off on a motoring tour of France during which he was to become convinced of the future of another novel form of transport, the aeroplane. For John, that trip to witness some of Wilbur Wright's first flights in Europe was a revelation. But for one of his companions the fascination of flight was to prove fatal.

12

First Flight —
and a Snub for the Kaiser

The military training ground at Auvours, 130 miles south-west of Paris, was one of France's most fashionable resorts in October 1908. Wealthy and influential people from all over Europe gathered there to watch, in awe and amazement, the antics of 41-year-old former bicycle mechanic Wilbur Wright as day after day he flew higher and further than anyone had ever gone before in a heavier-than-air machine. It was nearly five years since Wilbur and his younger brother Orville had demonstrated their first aeroplane at Kitty Hawk, North Carolina; now they were hoping that in France, acknowledged as the world's leader in aeronautics, they would receive the support and encouragement that their invention had so far failed to win in their home country.

Wilbur arrived in Paris in May 1908, several months after his Type A aeroplane had been shipped to Le Havre. With the help of his agent, Hart O. Berg, he arrived to reassemble the machine at Leon Bollée's car factory at Le Mans. The nearby race course at Hunaudières provided a convenient site for test flights and on 8 August Wright began a long series of demonstrations. Because of their controlled swoops and turns these flights surpassed anything that France's pioneer pilots had achieved; but at least France had been trying. Britain at this time was about as backward in the development of 'aerial locomotion', as aviation was then called, as she had been in the development of automobilism.

At the time that Wilbur Wright was proving to Europe that aeroplanes should be taken seriously, would-be British aircraft constructors approached their Government for financial support, only to be rebuffed by the Under-Secretary of State for War, who told them: 'We do not consider that aeroplanes will be of any possible use for war purposes'. The French Army thought otherwise and having seen what was happening at Hunaudières, invited Wright to show off his Type A machine to the military authorities at Camp d'Auvours, where flights lasting up to an hour and covering distances of 40 miles became commonplace. Wright's performances at Auvours were, if anything, an even greater attraction than those he had given at the race course, especially when he started taking sightseers and journalists for short flights. He was to be based at the Army camp until the end of 1908 but it was during October that a group of Englishmen, among them John Montagu and Charles Rolls, made their way to Auvours to see what all the excitement was about.

Montagu and Rolls had been staying in Paris, where they were the only British representatives at the first International Road Congress. The event was, in John's words, 'the first concerted effort of the civilized countries of the world to debate questions concerning the making and maintenance of roads'. Civilized or not, Britain did not yet have a national highways authority — the Road Board was not formed until 1910 — and was therefore unable to send an official delegation. Montagu and Rolls attended as representatives of the Automobile Club. In what proved to be his last important appearance in the world of motoring Rolls presented a paper on 'The Effect of Road Surfaces on Vehicles', whilst John adhered to one of his favourite themes with a dissertation entitled 'The Value of Good Roads'.

The congress over, John set off on what was to be the first of many motoring holidays in France, during which he and Lady Montagu and their daughters were invariably accompanied by a group of close friends. On this occasion their party included Sir Charles and Lady Seely and Archibald Marshall, a writer who achieved modest literary fame as a contributor to *Punch*. From 1909 onwards it was John's latest Rolls-Royce that carried him and his companions on their annual and sometimes bi-annual journeys through France, but in October 1908 Dragonfly was still being built. Instead he used, for at least part of his holiday, a Daimler powered by a new Silent Knight engine, a so-called valveless design which ran quietly and smoothly and proved that Daimler was still a threat to the Silver Ghost and its derivatives that were now among the chief contenders in the luxury car market.

During his holiday John encountered Rolls-Royce's Silver Rogue and arranged an experiment to try to determine whether the Rolls or the Daimler provided the smoothest ride. The two cars followed one another at 40 miles an hour whilst John and his friends photographed the Rolls from the Daimler and the Daimler from the Rolls. The pictures came out reasonably sharp, proving that the cars had not shaken the camera unduly but John would not be drawn into stating any firm preference, saying 'I leave it to the two excellent firms to decide whether the photographs reflect greater credit on the car in which the photographer was travelling or the car which was following'.

The Rolls and the Daimler may have been constant companions through-out John's holiday, rather than passing strangers. Certainly the Montagus, the Seelys and Archie Marshall would have been rather cramped had they all had to share the Daimler. Marshall himself left an account in which he spoke of John taking two cars. It is possible that Silver Rogue was the second car; if so, its driver was probably Charles Rolls, who would surely have taken one of his latest cars to France that autumn in order to show it off to the world's road experts in Paris.

Be that as it may, Rolls and Montagu both went to Auvours when the congress ended, beginning a journey that was to chart the future course of their careers. For Rolls powered flight, as demonstrated by Wilbur Wright, was a completely absorbing challenge and from then onwards he took less and less interest in the motor business that he and Henry Royce had formed four years earlier. For John Montagu, Wright's flights were confirmation that a new form of travel and a new threat to Britain's security had arrived. He had already foreseen this some years earlier, when Rolls and his friends at the Aero Club were casting themselves adrift over London in their gas-filled balloons — mere toys when compared with aeroplanes. Now, in October 1908, John realized that it was more important than ever that Britain should waste no time in becoming an air power.

On 8 October Rolls was one of the first four Englishmen to fly in an aeroplane, the others being Griffith Brewer and Frank Hedges Butler of the Aero Club and Major B.F.S. Baden-Powell, President of the Royal Aeronautical Society. In those days there were no aviation magazines and *The Car Illustrated* was one of the few periodicals that treated aeronautics seriously. Rolls and Baden-Powell had been acting as John's air correspondents for some years and it was for *The Car Illustrated* that Rolls wrote an exclusive account of his first flight. 'We tore along at 40 miles an hour and soon came to the first corner', he wrote, treating flying like a motor race. John was not present to see the fun but arrived on 16 October, joining such other notables as Sir Hiram Maxim, of machine gun fame, with whom he served on the council of the Aero Club.

What is puzzling about John's visit to Auvours is that for some reason he did not have an opportunity to fly with Wilbur Wright. Since so many other interested onlookers at around this time were invited aloft it is odd that John, who had as strong a claim as any to a place in the passenger seat, remained a spectator. It may have been that Wright was not giving joy rides that day; his engine was not running smoothly and the three flights John saw lasted only a few minutes. Even so they left a lasting impression. Several years later he recalled that 'it was as if the leaves of the Book of Prophecy had been opened to me'. In an account written only a day or two after leaving Auvours he said:

At last, after countless ages, man can progress through the air like a bird. One feels that one is witnessing a new epoch in the world's history. In a few years there will be thousands of fliers. Just ponder over the possibilities of this victory over the air. Will armies flee and be discomfited? How will the mastery of the sea be affected? Shall we see Armageddon or the Millenium?

By coincidence, on the day on which John was watching Wilbur Wright fly in France, the very first aeroplane flight in Britain was being made by the flamboyant 'Colonel' Cody, an American, who managed to remain airborne over Laffan's Plain, Farnborough, for 27 seconds during a demonstration staged for the Army Balloon Corps. This marked the beginning of proper aviation in Britain and it came not a moment too soon for John Montagu. The 'Book of Prophecy' may have been opened to him at Auvours but back in 1903, the year in which the Wrights first flew at Kitty Hawk, he had written: 'All nations will strive for the command of the air. Armies will not then be of much avail and the command of the sea will be a thing of the past.'

In 1905, aware that words alone would not be sufficient encouragement to budding airmen, he offered a site overlooking the Solent shore, on the edge of his estate, to any aeronauts 'who might wish to carry out tests and build a shed to house their machines'. Crashes, or 'falls' as John called them, would be of little consequence, he said, because the site was bordered by shallow water and soft mud. There were no takers but John revived the idea a year later by offering land at Beaulieu, rent free, to the winner of the newly announced *Daily Mail* Air Race, the land to be used for aeroplane experiments. The race was the idea of Lord Northcliffe, who put up a prize of £10,000 for the first airman to fly from London to Manchester in less than 24 hours. John added £1000 to Northcliffe's bounty plus a 500 guinea trophy and the plot of land. In order to reward a 'good try' he also announced that he would pay £5 a mile for every mile covered by the airman flying the longest distance, even if he failed to reach Manchester. Nearly four years passed before the prizes were claimed; the winner, Louis Paulham, did not need John's land but he accepted his money.

As for John's dream of making Beaulieu a cradle of British aviation, this partly came true after the race when two pioneer aviators, W. D. McArdle and Armstrong Drexel, opened a flying school on the heath south-west of the village, from where they flew Blériot monoplanes. In the First World War their aerodrome was taken over by the Royal Flying Corps and it was from here that John probably made his first flight in an aeroplane.* He left no account of this experience but his daughter Elizabeth remembers flying from

---

* A picture of the aerodrome's hangars silouetted against the New Forest skyline survives among John Montagu's papers at Beaulieu. The only physical relic of the station is its officers' mess, now East Boldre village hall, on the eastern edge of the heath. A mile to the west can be seen the remains of the runways of an aerodrome used by RAF Coastal Command, the USAAF and the Airborne Forces Experimental Establishment in the Second World War.

the heath sometime during the First World War. It was her first flight and she made it whilst sitting on a passenger's lap. Although she cannot remember who that passenger was, she agrees that it was most likely her father; if so, it was probably his first flight too.

It was to take the threat of war to concentrate the minds of Britain's politicians on the nation's vulnerability to air attack and the lack of any means of retaliation, in the form of warplanes or anti-aircraft guns. Meanwhile, whilst doing his best to encourage private aviators by offering them prizes and flying fields and praising their activities in *The Car Illustrated*, John decided in the summer of 1908 — some weeks before his visit to Auvours — to attempt to shake the Government out of its complacency by making a rare venture into the writing of fiction. His story, *The Mystery of Max*, was set some ten years into the future and opened with its central character, an inventor named Max Schmidt, embarking on a series of flights in an airship from a forest near Munich. In several sorties that bear a striking resemblance to those made by German airships in early 1915, Schmidt tested Britain's defences by reconnoitring the south coast near Dover and Ramsgate. Then, whilst the Cabinet was meeting at the War Office to decide whether to expand Britain's defences, Schmidt swooped over Whitehall and dropped a bomb, killing three Ministers and injuring four others, the Prime Minister escaping 'dazed and incoherent'.

The story, published in the Union Jack Club's magazine *Flag*, was an opening shot in John's campaign to persuade the Government to embark on a national air defence scheme — a campaign during which, at first, his was a very lonely voice. In March 1909 he initiated the first air debate ever held in Parliament, asking the Government whether it was aware of the progress made in military aeronautics by foreign governments and requesting a return showing the amount spent by the great powers on such operations the previous year. During the debate John commented on the Government's reaction to the story of Max Schmidt:

> The editor told me that the story was an excellent one but that the War Office did not like it. I asked why and he said that the authorities thought it would be quite impossible for any bombs ever to be dropped on the War Office. Besides, he added, you have killed the Secretary of State for War. I expressed my willingness to restore the Secretary of State to life and to be content with the Under-Secretary as a mangled corpse, but I said I could not remodel the story to such an extent as to deny the possibility of the dropping of bombs from an airship.

In the interval between the publication of John's story and the debate, the Government had at last taken their first step towards accepting the possibility of aerial bombardment by appointing a committee, chaired by Lord Esher, to examine the dangers that might face Britain as a result of recent developments in aviation. The committee was also instructed to consider what naval or military advantages Britain could derive by using aeroplanes or airships. By the end of 1909 Blériot had flown the English Channel and Germany had built a fleet of 20 airships, leaving only the most reactionary politicians in any doubt about aviation's military advantages; but at the time when John was asking his awkward questions in the House of Lords and indeed for some time afterwards, there was a marked reluctance or inability in Government circles to take on board the deaths, injuries and serious damage that air raids might inflict. There was, he complained, a natural dislike in Government offices of anything new and he reminded the House that when torpedoes, smokeless gunpowder, breech-loading rifles 'and other improvements in the art of war' were introduced, it was a long while before the War Office decided to adopt them. Reviewing the progress that had been made by rival powers, John said:

> Within a year or two Germany and France will have a considerable fleet of speedy dirigible balloons. They will be capable of carrying six or eight men or the equivalent weight of explosives. High explosives weighing 900 lb may do very serious damage. When it is remembered that the balloon can be arrested in flight and remain stationary over a given point while the explosive is dropped on that site — be it a Government office, railway bridge, bank or dockyard — it is obvious that airships may be very dangerous instruments indeed.

Some of Britain's military experts, said John, tended to 'pooh-pooh' the whole idea of air raids but he pointed out that London was only 320 miles from Emden and just 90 miles from Boulogne: short distances to airships capable of 30 miles an hour. 'The insularity of this country is not what it was', he warned.

If any of his listeners thought that airships intruding over England could easily be shot down, they were soon disillusioned. 'Most of our fortifications are protected against horizontal attack,' said John. 'Few are protected against overhead attack. Our dockyards are not so protected at all. One of the first things that ought to be done is that the great arsenals of this country should be so constructed that bombs dropped upon them should not explode the quantities of power held in reserve. Even if we took no active steps for using aeroplanes as regards attack it should be the duty of the Government to get a gun that is capable of firing at a high angle. A fixed gun is of no use against an aerial enemy. The gun of the future is one capable of being moved rapidly, so as to follow airships and harass and destroy them.'

John complained that, in 1908, Britain spent only £13,000 on airships and aeroplanes and in 1909 had allocated only £19,000, whereas France had spent more than £47,000 and Germany nearly £144,000. He can hardly have been reassured when the Lord Privy Seal, the Earl of Crewe, replied for the Government by saying that in actual fact Britain had spent only £5000 in 1908, making the increase to £19,000 in 1909 'a very considerable advance'. Lord Crewe admitted that the Treasury was not disposed towards spending large sums of money on aviation experiments, adding lamely: 'That is one of the disadvantages under which we labour from the form of parliamentary government under which we live. Other countries ... find it easier to spend large sums on matters of this kind'.

John followed up the Lords' debate with several important speeches on the same theme, including one to the National Defence Association in which he said:

> It is conceivable that the war airship would be able to produce results altogether unrealized today, such as panic of the wildest description in a crowded city, and the dislocation of the railway services and other means of locomotion, by destroying communication between the headquarters of the State and its servants and between the Capital and the provinces.

An air raid on the 'nerve centres' of London — Parliament, Whitehall, the General Post Office and the main telephone exchanges — would, he forecast, paralyse and demoralize the nation; an airship attack would be swift and devastating and therefore Britain should have its own airships in order to 'meet like with like'.

By the end of April 1909 something of a turning point in Britain's progress towards becoming a fully fledged air power was being reached, although this was due to the enthusiasm of private aviators, rather than any significant change in the Government's attitude. On 30 April, a few days after John's speech to the National Defence Association, J.T.C. Moore-Brabazon became the first Englishman to fly an aeroplane in England. Britain was at last moving in the same general direction as her Continental rivals. In early May Wilbur and Orville Wright spent a few days in London, on their way home after their long programme of demonstrations in France and Italy. Their highly publicized visit, which included a Royal Aeronautical Society banquet in their honour at the Ritz, at which John was one of the guests, did much to focus public attention on what was happening in the skies of Europe. A month later the first public meeting of the Aerial League of the British Empire was held at the Carlton Hotel in London.

The aim of the Aerial (later Air) League was to urge a reluctant Britain to become as superior in the air as it had been for centuries on the high seas. The League was essentially an educational and patriotic pressure group; just the kind of organization that appealed to John Montagu, who as one of its founder members and later as its President played a central part in formulating its policy. John appears to have been the author of the League's principles, which defined its role *vis-à-vis* those of the Royal Aero Club and the Royal Aeronautical Society. This document, approved and signed by Colonel H.S. Massy, the League's first President, is among the Montagu Papers at Beaulieu; it is dated 3 May 1909, the day on which the Wright brothers were fêted at the Ritz.

During the preliminaries that led up to the League's highly successful inaugural meeting at the Carlton, the Lord Mayor of London organized a meeting in support of the League at the Mansion House. His motive was to alert his citizens to the airborne dangers London might soon have to face. Hiram Maxim and Admiral Sir Percy Scott were among those who took part in the meeting; Vice-Admiral Prince Louis of Battenberg, Lord Curzon and Winston Churchill sent messages of support. At the end of a long debate John proposed a resolution which summed up his fears and those of many of his contemporaries:

> That this meeting views with considerable anxiety the rapid development of the science and practice of aerial navigation by other nations and deplores the backwardness and apathy shown by this country regarding this new means of communication, which is of vital importance from a commercial as well as national defence point of view.

The motion was carried unanimously.

During the years immediately preceding the declaration of the First World War, John became increasingly worried by political developments at home and overseas. It is difficult to say which was of greater concern to him: Germany's growing superiority as an air power or the leftward trend in British politics. The Liberal Government was now laying the foundations of the Welfare State but the predominantly Tory House of Lords had rejected the 1909 Finance Bill in which the Chancellor of the Exchequer, David Lloyd George, had sought to raise an extra £16 million in taxes from the wealthy to finance, among other things, old age pensions and a national health service. At this time the hereditary Lords still had the power to prevent any Bill passed by the democratically elected House of Commons from becoming law. Their rejection of Lloyd George's 'People's Budget' forced the Prime Minister, Herbert Asquith, to call a general election in January 1910 so that the country could decide how much power the House of Lords should enjoy. The Liberals won, and a significant feature of the poll was the sizeable number of Labour MPs, 40 in all, who were returned. They, naturally, could be relied upon to support social reforms. After the election the Lords passed Lloyd George's budget, and whilst this was to pay for some projects which John doubtless supported — such as the rebuilding of the

Navy and the reorganization of the Army — Labour's emergence as a political force dismayed him. Soon after the election he wrote to Lord Northcliffe:

> I am thinking of going out to Nova Scotia in May and I want to know if you could help me with regard to what I want. I am thinking of purchasing a few thousand acres there and building a small house as a sort of assurance against coming bad times in this country. Would your company sell me 5,000 or 10,000 acres at a fair price or, if not, give me a long lease, including any fishing or sporting rights? I should like to be near the sea and to have some fishing on a river and some possibility of big game as well. I have no desire to live in a country that will be ruled either by Wilhelm II or Keir Hardie and I think it wise to make provision elsewhere.

Northcliffe was at this time developing his vast pulp and paper mill empire in Newfoundland. He was also recovering from one of the mental breakdowns that were to afflict him for the rest of his life. His reply, if he ever sent one, has not survived, nor did John proceed with his idea of emigrating to Nova Scotia to escape from German imperialism or British socialism. He did however visit Canada and the USA two years later to inspect their roads and motor industry, returning unimpressed by the former but full of praise for a man he met in Detroit, Henry Ford. 'Wake up and make a good and cheap car for the man of moderate means', John told British motor manufacturers when he returned, having seen Model T Fords coming off the assembly lines in Detroit at the rate of 1440 a week.

Whether it was the Kaiser or Keir Hardie who, in 1910, had the better prospect of ruling Britain is debatable; clearly they were equally obnoxious in John's eyes and although he is unlikely to have met Hardie, he had been host to Wilhelm II at Beaulieu, when he had the doubtful privilege of gaining a personal impression of the German Emperor's arrogance and egotism.

The occasion was one of Wilhelm's periodic visits to England during the years in which he was trying to win friends and influence people, with the aim of preventing Germany from becoming isolated among the power blocs of Europe. Wilhelm stayed at Highcliffe Castle, on the Hampshire coast, in December 1907 and decided at short notice to visit nearby Beaulieu. Montagu and the Kaiser did have one thing in common: an interest in motoring; during the previous two years Wilhelm had bought no less than seventeen cars. Perhaps it was his uncle, King Edward, who suggested that he should call on Britain's leading motoring spokesman. Whoever it was who initiated the meeting, Montagu barely had time to return to Palace House from London in time to greet the Kaiser, and he committed what the Emperor considered to be a social gaffe by wearing casual clothes. A photograph taken at the entrance to Palace House clearly shows a stern Kaiser standing squarely

Teutonic high dudgeon at Palace House. John (left) with the Kaiser and his aide Count Wolff-Metternich.

on a newly unrolled red carpet, with a serge-suited and bowler-hatted John Montagu standing at his side. Whilst clearly not sufficiently insulted to lose an opportunity to be photographed, Wilhelm left Beaulieu in Teutonic high dudgeon in one of the four Daimlers that had been provided for his party. True to form he turned the occasion into a diplomatic incident by complaining to King Edward about Montagu's mode of dress; presumably he had expected his host to greet him in military uniform. A few days later the

Foreign Office asked John for his comments; he replied by saying that since in the past he had worn similar attire whilst receiving the King of England, what was acceptable to Edward VII was surely appropriate for Wilhelm II?

No more was said about the incident and any rift there may have been between the Montagus of Beaulieu and the Hohenzollerns of Prussia was forgotten by the summer of 1911 when Wilhelm's younger brother, Prince Henry, was John's guest at a garden party during the Prince Henry Tour, an Anglo-German motoring rally which started in Hamburg and ended at Windsor. The bombastic Prince Henry was no nicer to know than his brother but during the tour to which he lent his name — with the laudable object of promoting goodwill between the motorists of the two nations — he was charm personified, earning lavish if obsequious praise from *The Car Illustrated*'s reporter, Charles Freeston.

The Prince landed at Hythe Pier, on Southampton Water, after an 18-hour crossing from Bremerhaven. John was there to meet him in his 1910 Silver Ghost, which proudly sported the new Spirit of Ecstasy mascot and another, more functional, novelty in the shape of Auster patent windshields, which had been fitted to protect the Prince and Princess from wind, dust and showers whilst John drove them through the Forest for tea at Beaulieu with the other members of the German motorcade.

In retrospect the Prince Henry Tour can be seen as a curious affair. There, on the trim lawns of Palace House, stood John Montagu, welcoming the Kaiser's brother and a throng of German motorists to the roads of England, whilst not far from his thoughts was the likelihood of a less welcome incursion of airborne Germans into the skies above Southampton Docks and perhaps the very heart of London.

To most people that summer, aeroplanes were a fragile threat. Charles Rolls' fatal crash at Bournemouth the previous July, during an air display that John Montagu had helped organize, appeared to confirm that aerial locomotion held more hazards for those who took to the air than those who remained on the ground. What was overlooked in the aftermath of that tragedy was that although Rolls' flimsy biplane succumbed with cruel and rapid ease to a structural failure, he had, just four weeks earlier, been the first man to fly across the Channel and back, non stop. It was proof to John Montagu, if such were needed, that aeroplanes as well as airships would soon be capable of flying from one country to another with impunity and of dropping something far more lethal than the bundle of letters, addressed to the French Aero Club, that Rolls had tossed out of his cockpit whilst over France.

In April 1913, when time for any effective anti-aircraft counter-measures to be taken was quickly running short, John had one of his last opportunities in peacetime to reiterate his warning that Britain was ill-prepared for air warfare. He did so in a typically controversial manner by stating publicly that

Prince and Princess Henry arriving at Palace House in John's 1910 Silver Ghost. From an advertisement for Auster windshields.

the War Office possessed only 46 aeroplanes, not 101 as had been claimed by the War Minister, Colonel J.E.B. Seely (the future Lord Mottistone). His claim earned him a reprimand from Seely, who summoned him to the War Office where he was shown official documents and assured by Colonel (later General) Sir David Henderson, who was then in charge of the administration of the Royal Flying Corps, that the Army really did have 101 aeroplanes and in a matter of weeks would have another 50.

The assurances John was given in 1913 were no more comforting than those he had received from Lord Crewe during the air debate in 1909. John thought that the War Office should acquire 500 aeroplanes and 750 pilots to match the aerial armadas that had already been assembled in Germany and France but in a letter to Seely, subsequently read to the House of Commons, John retracted his statement, saying:

> I am now fully convinced that the number of aeroplanes you have publicly stated represents those really available. I regret that I gave publicity to erroneous figures.

Seely said that he hoped the letter would put an end to reflections on his good faith and that of his officers and he thanked John for the 'characteristically prompt, frank and straightforward' way in which he had apologized.

What John did not learn until long after the outbreak of the First World War was that, at the time of this controversy, the War Office may have possessed 101 aeroplanes but only about 50 of them were operational. As John revealed when he resurrected the argument during a wartime air inquiry, he had in 1913 been concerned about the number of aeroplanes actually ready to go to war and had, therefore, been essentially correct when he disputed Seely's figures. The incident seemed to confirm in John's mind the muddled way in which Britain was coming to terms with a new challenge to its security. Subsequent events showed that he had every reason to be concerned.

13

On the North-West Frontier

John Montagu had retired from the Hampshire Territorials in 1912 with the rank of colonel. By then he had served as an officer in the militia for twenty-six years, taking command of the 4th Hants in 1904 and the 7th Hants a few years later. Although due to retire in 1908 he had stayed on for another four years, helping Hampshire's part-time soldiers organize themselves into the Territorial units that replaced the old Volunteer battalions when R.B.H. Haldane introduced his Army reforms. During the weeks preceding the declaration of war on 4 August Montagu had been following his usual routine — speaking in the Lords, editing *The Car Illustrated* and writing articles on motoring. In June he and Lady Montagu had celebrated their Silver Wedding and his 48th birthday. They were approaching what might have been a comfortable, uneventful, middle-aged period of their lives, had not Gavrilo Prinzip's aim at Sarajevo on 28 June hit its target.

In August 1914, at the time when in the words of Britain's Foreign Secretary, Sir Edward Grey, the lamps were going out all over Europe, Britain struggled to muster an expeditionary force of 100,000 soldiers to go to the aid of France and Belgium. Many of those called up as army reservists, and obliged to report forthwith to their units, were members of London's Metropolitan Police.

To take their place Sir Edward Henry, Commissioner of Police at the Home Office, was instructed to raise a force of special constables. John Montagu was one of many retired Army officers for whom the emergencies of war soon resulted in a recall to duty. On 6 August he arrived at Scotland Yard to take up the position of Director of Organization, Special Constabulary. The first 'Specials' were enrolled on 10 August and within a week the force reached its full strength of 20,000 men, all of whom had to be sworn in before a magistrate and issued with armlets, whistles and truncheons. They were then sent to guard reservoirs, power stations and other installations regarded as possible scenes of sabotage or civil disorder. Years earlier John had advocated the use of motor transport for military purposes in wartime and although it may not have been quite what he had in mind, he took charge of a kind of Dad's Army of 200 motorists and a thousand motorcyclists, who

John as an officer in the Hampshire militia (above and right)

placed themselves and their vehicles at the Special Constabulary's disposal. John also persuaded a group of his friends to offer their motor launches to the common cause; a flotilla of fifteen boats was mustered to patrol the London reaches of the Thames.

However much he may have enjoyed the responsibility of organizing the special constables and his fleets of motor cars and launches, John is unlikely to have relished the prospect of a long stint at Scotland Yard at a time when his friends in the Hampshire Territorials, with whom he had trained for such a day as this until only two years earlier, were encamped on Salisbury Plain waiting to hear what their role in the war would be. So it would have been with some relief that he learned, seven weeks after his appointment at Scotland Yard, that he had been gazetted to take command of one of the Hampshire Regiment's reserve battalions.

The 7th Hants, commanded by John Montagu, was one of four battalions that formed the Hampshire Territorial Brigade and like most part-time units it was intended purely for home defence. For this reason it had to make do with second-best arms and equipment. The policy was changed early in the war, when it became obvious that there would be very little work for the Territorials to do at home in view of the fact that the superior strength of the Royal Navy made it unlikely that Germany would attempt to invade Britain. At the same time a dangerous power vacuum was being created in India as a result of the drafting of nearly 290,000 Regular and native soldiers to Europe and elsewhere. The Territorials were now asked to take their place in India. The Hampshire Brigade returned to its summer camp at Bulford, near Salisbury, on 9 August, having temporarily guarded Portsmouth pending the arrival there of a Special Reserve force. All four battalions — the 4th, 5th, 6th and 7th — were immediately invited to volunteer for service overseas. They accepted almost to a man. Each battalion was divided into two, their 600 strong 'foreign service' units embarking for India on 9 October whilst their reserves — later named the 2nd/4th, 2nd/5th, 2nd/6th and 2nd/7th battalions — were billeted in and around various Hampshire towns, where they operated as 'home service units'.

On 26 September, when the imminent departure of the 'foreign service' battalions was announced, John Montagu took command of the 2nd/7th at Bournemouth. His main responsibility was to guard the coast between Poole Harbour and Hurst Castle near Lymington — a shore he knew intimately — but during this time his officers were busy recruiting the young men of the New Forest and the surrounding district. Several of John's own employees joined the battalion, and local legend maintains that he offered each Beaulieu recruit a plot of land and a cow as a reward for enlisting. No one could confirm this story nearly seventy years later, but three ex-privates of 'Montagu's Army' — R. A. Broomfield, Teddy Kitcher and Bob Stickland —

could still vividly recall their basic training with the 2nd/7th, and the adventures and hardships they shared when the time came for the battalion to forsake the balmy breezes of the Hampshire coast for more arduous duties on the other side of the world.

In less than two months John had brought his battalion, which was only 300 strong in late September, up to 'India Establishment' and when, as the 2nd Wessex Division, the battalions eventually sailed for India, the 2nd/7th was the only one that had managed to reach its full strength of 800 men without drawing on other units.

John's passage to India was a slow and at times uncomfortable experience. The strain of commanding his battalion and preparing it for foreign service had left him tired and unwell and he felt badly in need of a complete rest when, on Saturday 12 December, he boarded the troopship *Dunera* at Southampton. For the duration of the voyage that began that evening he was in command of a 240-strong contingent of New Zealanders, the 150 gunners of the Wessex Battery of the RFA and a unit of the Royal Flying Corps, as well as his own battalion. He soon found that *Dunera* — 20 years old, slow, dirty and badly equipped — was barely suitable for the 6200 mile voyage. Overcrowding was the main problem, with 1200 men crowding into quarters designed for about 750. In his first letter home John told his family about the deprivations he and his men suffered as their ship lumbered down the English Channel and across the Bay of Biscay:

> Our first night was a rather dreadful business as most of our men were entirely new to seafaring and were dreadfully sick. The sanitary arrangements are very bad and the hospital was about two inches deep with seawater swirling around the men's cots on the lower tier, due chiefly to the scuppers not working properly. The latrine accommodation is also insufficient. We have considerable difficulties to deal with but the men have been very good and have borne things patiently.

Matters were not helped by the tedious progress made by *Dunera* and the five other ships in her convoy, which was escorted by the cruiser HMS *Talbot*. At first they could manage only 6 knots, making the journey to their first port of call, Gibraltar, seem endless. 'The vessels behind us are not able to keep proper station,' John complained, 'nor, apparently, able to keep up.'

Despite this unpromising start he managed to sleep well and shake off his illness, and after a few days he and his fellow officers succeeded in making conditions tolerable for their men, whose own health soon benefited from the Mediterranean sunshine. At 9 am on Tuesday 22 December *Dunera* docked at Alexandria. Anxious to get his men ashore for a few hours after so long at sea John arranged for his battalion and the Wessex Battery to parade through the city. Four days earlier Egypt had been declared a British Protectorate and

John's procession seems to have had as great an effect on local morale as it had on that of his troops. This time he had more cheerful news for his family:

> We could not allow the men to go off individually as many of them might have come to harm, so with the band playing and with about a thousand men we set out to astonish the inhabitants. Many of the streets we passed through had never seen a regiment in full marching order. We certainly had a very good reception. It is clear that the British Protectorate is going to be popular. On our way back to the ship we went through some of the second-class streets and it was wonderful to see the interest the population took in British soldiers. As everybody knows the Oriental understands a display of power and in its small way our march did a good deal to make the Protectorate a reality to at least the more ignorant of the population.

John (on horseback, left) and his battalion at Alexandria.

As a seasoned traveller John was accustomed to living on ships and visiting foreign cities but for the young men of Hampshire, most of whom had never before travelled very far from their homes, the transition from the New Forest to the Nile delta in the space of a fortnight must have been quite a shock. Many of them would have been intensely homesick, especially on Christmas Day, when *Dunera* arrived at Port Said. In the afternoon John held a church service and in the evening the soldiers sang carols to the accompaniment of the battalion band. Their ship was to have taken on coal that day but was at the end of a long queue of vessels, which meant she had to wait until

Boxing Day. *Dunera* then made her way into the Suez Canal and towards evening Montagu went on deck to admire a spectacular sunset above the desert. Gradually the stars came out and all the ships in the canal switched on their searchlights. It was a sight that fascinated and pleased John Montagu. He was all in favour of searchlights on ships and after the *Titanic* disaster in 1912 had written to *The Times* saying how curious it was that fast liners did not use powerful searchlights at night in order to avoid icebergs and other hazards. En route to Suez he was pleased to see 'great beams of light visible miles ahead, sometimes coming towards us, sometimes receding'. By this means, he noted, pilots could see each bank and any vessels that happened to pass. *Dunera*'s searchlight was less than reliable; its generator failed and the ship was delayed whilst the light was rerigged. There was another delay a day later when *Dunera* had to wait off Suez from early morning until mid-afternoon to take on fresh water. Then, heading into a damp, hot wind coming up the Gulf of Suez, *Dunera* began the last leg of her voyage.

Bombay was sighted soon after dawn on Thursday 7 January but it was many hours before John and his battalion finished boarding the special train waiting for them in a shed alongside *Dunera*'s dock. The 800 men and their baggage took a long time to make the transfer from ship to shore to railway and it was after midnight when the train of 26 coaches, drawn by several engines, pulled out of Bombay and began its 197-mile haul to Secunderabad, where the battalion was to be stationed at Meadows Barracks, in the Trimulgherry Entrenchment, for two years before being sent to various other garrisons in India. As a student of road and rail locomotion John was perplexed by the cumbersome train that had been provided for his battalion and wondered why it had not been divided into two, shorter, trains. As he feared, the close-coupled juggernaut was capable of only halting progress and it took 42 hours to traverse the bare and arid terrain south-east of Bombay and climb the 2000 feet to India's central plateau. Feeding arrangements were also badly organized and some of the soldiers had to wait 17 hours for their first meal.

Soon after arriving at Secunderabad, John's unit, until then called the 7th (Reserve) Battalion, was renamed the 2nd/7th; adjacent barracks housed the 2nd/5th Bn, the Wessex Brigade of Artillery, the 7th Hussars and some native regiments. The reason for the establishment of such a large and predominantly white force at Secunderabad was that the Nizam of Hyderabad, the chief Muslim ruler in India, was entitled to such a presence under his treaty rights. John was intrigued by this and wrote:

I believe we are here more to protect the Nizam from his own people than with any idea of discouraging a rising against us. Everyone here thinks there is not much danger at present and that India has never been so quiet.

The natives in this part of the world are a rather degenerate lot and not to be compared with the finer races to the north. Nor is the Nizam much respected locally, as his morals are not above reproach.

In this, his first letter home after arriving in India, John admitted that he had no idea what duties were planned for his battalion; they expected to stay at their barracks until the rainy season, then move to summer quarters in the hills but there were also rumours that they would soon be sent north. Feeling isolated from the mainstream of the war, Montagu concluded his letter rather plaintively:

We hope our friends in England are not forgetting us and we hope they realize that in many ways it is less interesting to come to India to serve our country than if we had gone to France.

The battalion was to remain at Secunderabad until March 1916 but probably within a few weeks of arriving there Montagu came to the conclusion that, fond of the job as he was, the duties of a commanding officer of a battalion that had no immediate prospect of active service would in no way make full use of his ability to plan, organize and persuade the powers-that-be to change their way of thinking and adopt new ideas. At the beginning of the war John had been in his element — organizing the Special Constabulary and his volunteer motorists, and then bringing his battalion up to full strength for foreign service. From what we know of him it is difficult to imagine him relishing the responsibilities of day-to-day management once a show was on the road. If that assessment is correct, then the invitation he received from Lord Willingdon, Governor of Bombay, to take part in an expedition to the Khyber Pass in March 1915 would have been a welcome diversion and a timely opportunity to gain first-hand knowledge of what he regarded as one of India's most urgent problems: a shortage of motorized transport.

Accompanied by Lady Willingdon and Sir George Roos-Keppel, Chief Commissioner for the North-West Frontier, the Lords Montagu and Willingdon and their aides left Peshawar, ten miles from the Khyber Pass, at 7.30 one morning in four cars. One of them, which John himself drove, brought back pleasant memories for it was a 1906 Daimler, similar to the one in which he had been successful in the Herkomer trials nearly nine years earlier. At the fort of Lundi Khotal the party enjoyed a full English breakfast and then abandoned their cars, riding nine miles on horseback to the summit of Spinna-Zukha where 'all Afghanistan and the kingdom of the earth was at our feet'. John also observed that only a few distinguished white travellers, including 'a Viceroy or two' and the Crown Prince of Germany, had seen this stunning view. Wilhelm, he commented, came here 'base and spylike, to receive our hospitality and report on our readiness or unreadiness to fight here or elsewhere'.

On their way back to Peshawar some 'ruffianly looking prisoners' were brought for trial before Roos-Keppel, who was regarded as a demigod by the restless tribesmen of the frontier. The men had been caught shooting at local villagers and attempting to steal their women and cattle. John described the impromptu trial:

> The prisoners looked frightened but murder and sudden death are concomitants of daily existence hereabouts and on the frontier they expect to be shot or hanged before sundown. As the Willingdons were there (she pleaded for them) special consideration was shown and they are to be let off easy to frizzle at 130° in the shade and 150° in the sun in Peshawar gaol for a summer or two. They say that shooting is the better fate and I can well believe it.

Two days later John went on another expedition, this time into the Malakand Pass; in the account he wrote of this journey he gave a hint of the kind of job he hoped would soon be found for him in India:

> In Peshawar the roses, millions of them, are coming out, just when I have to go back to my red-hot hell. But the staff billet may yet come, I fancy. Viceroys generally carry through what they want and the Viceroy wants armoured motor cars to be ready for the Sikh rising, if it comes.

The Viceroy of India at that time was John's friend Lord Hardinge of Penshurst. Later in the war, when the Montagus found themselves unable to afford to run Palace House on John's Army salary, his wife and younger daughter Elizabeth lived for a while on Hardinge's estate in Kent. In 1912 Hardinge had been seriously wounded in a bomb attack and at the time he and John met in India in 1915, Lady Hardinge, who had escaped injury, had recently died from prolonged shock. Despite this experience Hardinge persisted in his efforts to establish friendly relations with the people of India; when the war in Europe broke out he had sufficient faith in their loyalty to the Crown to agree to the massive military exodus that for a time left India barely capable of defending herself. In his memoirs Hardinge wrote: 'It was a big risk but I trusted the people of India in the great emergency that had arisen, and I told them so, and my confidence was not misplaced.'

It was indeed a big risk. The vast numbers of officers and men who served in India until late 1914 were needed to maintain internal security and keep the peace on the 2000-mile long North-West Frontier. They were armed with outdated rifles and relied on mules and horses for transport. Motor cars, lorries and artillery were rare; aeroplanes were non-existent. The regiments and their equipment were adequate for their limited purposes but when one unit after another began to leave India it became obvious that those who remained needed greater mobility and fire power if they were to operate as a credible pacifying force. In a word, the Army left holding the fort of India had to become mechanized and it was to this end that on 7 April 1915 John Montagu went to Simla, the Indian Government's summer headquarters in the foothills of the Himalayas, to join the Army General Staff as Inspector of Motor Vehicles. He had won his 'staff billet'. His title was something of a misnomer; John was to spend as much time procuring and organizing motor vehicles and aeroplanes as inspecting them and on 8 April he set off on a fact-finding tour with two objectives — to review the efficiency of the few armoured car units that were already in service and to find suitable sites for aerodromes on the North-West Frontier.

He visited 12 of the 14 garrisons and forts where armoured cars were based and was far from impressed with what he saw. He knew before he set out that there were only three or four armoured cars at each base (and a total of only 40 or so in the entire sub-continent) and he was sadly disappointed by their condition, armament and personnel. At Lucknow the cars had no machine guns and were operated by untrained crews. At Bombay the armour plating on the cars prevented them from being steered safely; the gun platforms wobbled at the slightest movement. At Kohat he found that the petrol tank in one car was placed directly above the engine, so that the slightest leak would cause an explosion. Faults like these abounded, largely because the cars had been purchased very hurriedly between January and March 1915. Too many different types had been acquired, John reported, and most of them were totally unsuited to the Indian climate and frontier roads. The diversity of types meant that neither their spare parts nor their crews were interchangeable. John recommended the adoption of a standard type of armoured car and the introduction of a uniform system for training personnel for armoured car units; some stations had two or three cars but no crews at all. Schemes for manning the cars and providing garages and stores for them were also recommended.

In his report on aerodromes John suggested 14 sites between Chakdara and Tank and came out strongly in favour of operating bombers and reconnaissance planes all along the frontier. 'The moral effect of aeroplanes and the dropping of bombs on hostile lashkars and villages would probably be very great,' he reported. The effectiveness of bombs dropped from aeroplanes was proved later, during the Third Afghan War, when Amir Amanulla Khan declared a holy war against the British. 'Stringbag' bombers from frontier airfields soon brought the war to an end, killing 30 people in Dakka and then administering a *coup de grâce* by destroying the tomb of the Amir's father in Jalalabad and that of his great-grandfather in Kabul.

Having outlined India's need for more and better armoured cars and a chain of air bases, John turned his attention to ways and means of supplying the troops with provisions and ammunition. He discovered that a division in the field needs 40 tons of stores a day, which had to be carried by 672 pack mules, 112 mule carts or 246 camels. They formed a convoy up to a mile and a quarter long, covered only ten miles in a day and cost between 500 and a thousand rupees for every 40 miles travelled. On the other hand, John calculated, 20 2-ton lorries could carry 40 tons of stores between 60 and a hundred miles in a day, in a convoy less than a quarter of a mile long (making it less vulnerable to attack) at a cost of 420 rupees for every 40 miles. The reduction in personnel that his scheme could achieve was equally remarkable; the mule trains needed 267 handlers, whereas a lorry convoy would need only 40 men. 'On these grounds,' he advised, 'the Government of India should consider before long the extension of mechanical transport all over India for Army purposes.'

There were at this time fewer than 12 Army lorries in the whole of India but as John himself stressed, it would put the cart before the horse to embark on his plan to make more use of armoured cars, lorries and aeroplanes until the roads were capable of carrying extra and heavier traffic. There were a few metalled highways — the one in the Malakand Pass, for example — but many of India's hill roads were crudely surfaced by the time-honoured method of lighting fires on the naked rocks and splitting them into fragments by dousing them with water. John drew attention to the deficiencies of India's roads in a report on the state of the Grand Trunk Road from Delhi to Peshawar, a vital link in the event of a war on the frontier. The road was dotted with such hazards as inadequate bridges and stretches surfaced with heavy sand which were impassable to motor vehicles, even in dry weather. John advised that the central government should take over the provincial governments' responsibilities for maintaining roads of national importance; that the roads and bridges serving the North-West Frontier should be strengthened; and that minimum standards of construction should be laid down for all India's main roads. Finally he proposed that alternative road bridges should be built wherever rivers were crossed by bridges carrying both rail and road traffic, since the destruction of bridges like these by warring tribesmen would make it impossible for troops in some areas to be resupplied or reinforced.

In these first reports as Inspector of Motor Vehicles Montagu was preaching to the converted. Lord Hardinge was already aware of the Army's need for motor transport; the problem was to persuade the British Government to release, for service in India, machines that were needed on the Western Front. So on 15 July 1915 John was instructed to return to London to plead India's case at the War Office. He departed on 22 July. Four days later the first results of his efforts during the previous few months were seen at

Peshawar, with the formation of the first properly organized armoured motor car unit in India. This was No. 1 AMU, comprising three Rolls-Royce armoured cars. A tattered exercise book containing photographs and a handwritten account of the unit's engagements survives to this day at King's College, London and in a foreword the unit's CO, Captain A.J. Clifton, wrote:

> I presume to dedicate it to the master-mind who first conceived the possibilities of this arm in these regions and who, more than anyone else, is responsible for its introduction to this country: Colonel Lord Montagu of Beaulieu.

Whilst No. 1 AMU was training for skirmishes to come, John was on his way home with his 'shopping list' of urgent supplies. To avoid the passage across the Bay of Biscay he left his ship at Marseilles and travelled up through France, crossing from Boulogne to Folkestone on 11 August. It was on the Channel ferry that he had a fortuitous meeting with David Henderson, the man who two years earlier had helped Colonel Seely answer John's allegation that the Army had fewer aeroplanes than it cared to admit. Henderson was the First World War's oldest airman; he had learned to fly in 1911, at the age of 49 and in December 1914 had taken command of the Royal Flying Corps in France. On 19 August he was succeeded by Hugh Trenchard and returned to the War Office as Head of Military Aeronautics. Henderson was just the man to help John, who later wrote to Lord Hardinge:

> I told him of our sore need for 'planes on the frontier. He was very sympathetic and told me to come and see him when I arrived in London. Evidently Henderson did not realize the importance of 'planes in India and I think I impressed this point upon him.

Before calling on Henderson, John went to see Austen Chamberlain, Secretary of State for India. 'I talked to him about Indian things in general, especially about the 'planes,' John told Hardinge. 'I am afraid I must have made myself somewhat of a bore.' Whether or not that was so, the message came across and when John had his meeting with Henderson he was offered much more than he expected — namely, a flight of four new B.E. aeroplanes, with pilots, for immediate use in Mesopotamia and eight aeroplanes (Avros and B.E.s) for delivery in September and October to the North-West Frontier. 'It is the best I can do at the moment,' John wrote. 'Before I leave England I hope to obtain for you another flight of four machines of the very latest type, for Henderson told me that he is turning out pilots at the rate of 70 a month and machines at about 30 a month.'

Hardinge passed on the news to Roos-Keppel, who wrote to congratulate John; 'If you carry through your scheme you will have done more for the

After a flight on the North-West Frontier.

pacification of the North-West Frontier and for the prevention of a possible Afghan War than anyone in the last 25 years.'

The war was postponed rather than prevented but it was thanks to John's efforts in London in August 1915 that planes were stationed on the frontier by the time it did occur.

Procuring motor transport and armoured cars proved more difficult because the motor industry was working flat out. However, John heard that there were some secondhand armoured Rolls-Royces to spare at the Admiralty, following the recent disbandment of the Royal Naval Armoured Car Division, whose 15 squadrons had been equipped with about 150 armoured cars, all built in a burst of enthusiasm between October 1914 and March 1915 at the behest of Winston Churchill, First Lord of the Admiralty.

John's old political chum Arthur Balfour had by August 1915 succeeded Churchill at the Admiralty and it was with undisguised glee that John wrote to Hardinge about the prospects of purchasing the Admiralty's armoured cars for India:

> Some of these are of the very latest pattern. Chamberlain seems to think we can get them at a greatly reduced price, in which case it would be most worthwhile for India to buy some of them as we shall never get anything better. I may tell you confidentially that Churchill seems to have made a great fool of himself in regard to these matters. He ordered cars most recklessly and enlisted men at up to eight shillings a day to work them. Now the whole of this naval squadron is practically useless owing to Balfour quite rightly confining the operations of the Navy to the sea.

Unfortunately Army units in the Middle East had a more convincing claim to the cars; India had to make do with those it already had and it was not until 1917 that reinforcements arrived, in the shape of 40 Jefferey Quad and six Rolls-Royce armoured cars.

John spent four months organizing the despatch of motor vehicles to India and Mesopotamia and for several weeks he studied mechanical transport operations on the Western Front. Then, having formulated a more comprehensive plan for the reorganization of Army communications and the deployment of aeroplanes in India, he appointed G. Foster Pedley as his agent in London and prepared to return to India. On 23 December he left London for the Kent coast, crossed the Channel and travelled on to Marseilles to join the P & O liner SS *Persia*. For the second year in succession John left his family just before Christmas in order to sail to India, but this time Cis had two reasons to be concerned as she bade her husband farewell. The first was that Eleanor Thornton was accompanying him for part of the voyage, ostensibly to help him complete the report that he intended to present to the authorities in Simla. Cis must have known by now that John and Eleanor had, by this time, been lovers for many years. Her second cause for concern was that Germany had now switched her U-boat offensive to the Mediterranean, placing ships such as *Persia* at great risk as they headed to and from the Suez Canal during their voyages between London and Bombay. Cis's attitude towards the relationship that John and Eleanor had formed during the thirteen years they had worked together can only be imagined: all that remains, to suggest how the three of them handled what must always have been a delicate situation, is an extraordinary letter from Eleanor to Lady Montagu written just after John announced that he soon intended to return to India and that Eleanor would accompany him for part of the journey. She began by discussing John's health:

> He still continues to do too many things, to be in three places at once. He will never rest and will talk at a tremendous rate, and hustle around on people who don't matter a fig. I have spent my life since schooldays trying to save him in little ways but it doesn't seem that I can do much. Even today, after he came back from a luncheon party where I could see he had tired himself by talking too much, I got him into an armchair and made him rest. About half an hour afterwards I heard his voice downstairs. I found him with his coat off, arguing at a terrific rate and quite overdoing himself on a matter that was as dead as a dodo. He has flown off to the War Office because someone happened to mention a possibility as to taking over the old flying ground at Beaulieu. He could have sent all the particulars by post but no, he must go and when he gets there he will doubtless find other things to get excited about. There is one thing; on the voyage out he cannot rush from one office to another, so the lord has perforce to go more slowly.

Both Cis and Eleanor had been concerned about John's health ever since he returned from India. One of the purposes of Eleanor's letter was to advise Cis of her efforts to persuade John to see a specialist. She concluded her letter with a comment that was soon to acquire vivid significance:

> It is awfully kind of you to give your sanction to my going as far as Port Said. I hate spending the money but you have the satisfaction of knowing that as far as human help can avail, he will be looked after. I do not think for one moment that there will be any trouble in the Med. but supposing ... well, then the lord will have an extra chance, for there will be my place in the boat for him, even if he has to be stunned to take it.

These thoughts cannot have been far from Eleanor's mind as she and John struggled to reach their lifeboat on the *Persia* after a violent explosion rocked the ship, splitting her deck open and filling the main saloon, where they were about to take lunch, with smoke, steam, fragments of broken crockery and the stench of guncotton and TNT.

14

'Poor little Whitethorn'

Before leaving to join the *Persia* John Montagu stayed with his sister, Lady Forster, in London. Whilst he was there, he received a long letter from his wife who was at Beaulieu:

My own darling. I quite expected that you might have to start this week, though of course I am a bit disappointed. Still, if it means that you may get back sooner then all is well. We have had such lovely times together lately and I hope and pray that you will come back safely. You will take all care, I know, and I promise to do the same. One must realize, I suppose, that we are going through what thousands of others are, though it doesn't make it any easier, but I am proud to know that you are so much wanted and that your services are appreciated. Also, I know that it really is the best thing for your health and that another spell of India (although you hate it) will probably set up your lungs for life. But you must be very careful of your dear old heart and not strain it in any way. We have come together through so much and I think you feel, in fact I know you do, the parting ... but please God when this is all over we shall both be very happy, knowing that you did your bit. I shall be proud, too, as I feel sure that that bit will not be a small one. It is always hard at first, isn't it, but mercifully one gets more or less accustomed in time to the condition though one does not mind less.

I am glad that Miss Thornton is going to Aden. She will be away for quite a long time.

I mean to run the household as cheaply as possible as I quite realize that things may be more difficult still in the future. Evidently Helen does not mean to come back yet.

This letter, like the one written by Eleanor to Cis a month earlier, gives an interesting insight into John's personal life. His daughter Elizabeth, though only six in 1915, remembers Eleanor as 'a very beautiful and charming person; as a child I took an instinctive liking to her'. She says that Eleanor was on friendly terms with her mother and was regarded with great affection by all the family. It is Elizabeth's belief that her mother became resigned, with no feelings of bitterness, to John's *affaire* and took the view that, if he had to take a mistress, then it was as well that he had chosen someone as sweet-natured as Eleanor Thornton, rather than someone who might eventually have turned against him and caused a scandal. Lady Montagu's letter perhaps suggests that she hoped that, one day, Montagu would leave Eleanor ('please God when this is all over we shall both be very happy'). It also reveals that the Montagus' daughter, Helen, who had left home to go on the stage, was still causing concern.

The only photograph of John and Eleanor Thornton together, taken shortly before their voyage on the Persia.

Lady Montagu's letter was among the papers that John took with him when he and Eleanor left London for France on Christmas Eve. They probably boarded *Persia* on Christmas Day, about 24 hours before she sailed from Marseilles. Even though it was wartime and a hazardous voyage lay ahead, the ship's company ensured that their passengers celebrated the occasion in fitting style. D. Coughlan, the Chief Steward, decorated the main saloon with flags and bunting but he annoyed some of his colleagues by cutting up a spare Red Ensign in order to make an Australian flag. At lunchtime A.J. Croxson, the chef, carved a boar's head; J. Chant, the baker, cut the iced cake that he had made; and W.R. Dowling, the 24-year-old head waiter and his staff were kept busy distributing wine and cigars. For Coughlan, Croxson, Chant and most of their assistants this was their last Christmas party but Dowling survived. Fifty years later, his memory of that day still clear, he described the emotions of the passengers and crew as they left Marseilles and headed for Malta:

> The festive mood of the passengers seemed to stay with them. What had they to worry about? Every day they were getting further from the war ... and it was a nice break to be away from our troubled country with its shortage of food and the hardships war can bring. For us in the crew, we were doing a job of work. We knew that we had to go back and that all the while we were away someone at home was wondering if we would come to any harm.

Some of the passengers who had travelled from London were under the impression that, having reached Marseilles, the most dangerous part of their voyage, in terms of the possibility of a U-boat attack, was over. But John was in a pessimistic mood. On Monday 27 December, as they approached Malta, Colonel E. St Aubyn, a fellow passenger, remarked: 'John, you seem depressed.' He replied: 'I am afraid I shall be until we get to Port Said.'

Persia's master, Commander William Henry Selby Hall, was also worried. Before leaving London he had been handed instructions on the precautions he should take en route and he was given further orders by the senior naval officers at Gibraltar, Marseilles and Malta. These instructions would have covered such matters as the necessity to destroy confidential documents if there was any danger of the ship being sunk or captured by an enemy raider, and the course to be taken between each port. Thus briefed and forewarned, Hall arranged for *Persia* to leave Malta at 10 pm on Tuesday, 28 December. By departing at this hour Hall was able to time the ship's progress so that it passed at night through the 120 mile wide area south of Crete where the chances of being attacked by a submarine were considered to be higher.

Wednesday, 29 December was uneventful. Only five passengers had joined the ship at Malta, whereas 52 had disembarked. There were now 186 passengers on board but with a crew of over 300 there were more than enough hands to run the ship and keep the passengers comfortable. With few newcomers to adjust to the ship's routine and make friends with those who had embarked from ports further west, life on *Persia* was for most of the day without excitement or incident. There was, though, a lifeboat drill to break the monotony. This was the second to be held since the ship had left Tilbury Docks, downriver from London, on 18 December and its purpose was to ensure that those who had joined the ship at Malta knew the proper emergency procedures. During the homeward run a few weeks earlier *Persia*'s Chief Officer, Gerald Clark, had been involved in an argument with some of the passengers when he ordered the deck awnings to be taken down so that they would not get in the way if the lifeboats had to be launched. The passengers insisted that the awnings should be replaced. This angered Clark, who thought that safety should come before comfort. On 29 December, however, he was pleased to note that the lifeboat drill was carried out correctly and he was also reassured by the fact that, because there were fewer passengers than usual on board, the 14 main lifeboats, suspended from davits on the boat deck, would be only half full in an emergency. These, plus *Persia*'s two accident boats (also on davits) and four more lifeboats on chocks on the fore and poop decks, were capable of holding 900 people. All the passengers had lifejackets, which were left on the floors of the cabins — not in racks — so as to be ready at a moment's notice. There were also nearly 200 lifebelts in boxes on the upper deck, plus 18 lifebuoys.

As they went about their duties or rested during the night of the 29th, Clark and his subordinates were satisfied that, so far as the provision of life-saving appliances was concerned, *Persia* was properly equipped for any emergency.

Clark was officer of the watch from 4 am on 30 December but although he officially went off duty at 8 am he remained on the bridge with Commander Hall, who had been on the alert all night whilst *Persia* steamed through the danger zone off Crete. It was a tense night: every unusual sound or unexplained light would immediately have been suspected as emanating from a surfacing U-boat. But as the sun rose higher Hall relaxed slightly. 'We are all right now', he told Clark, saying that his mind was easier and that he expected to reach Port Said by about 2 pm next day. Clark, too, considered that from what he knew about the submarine threat, the ship was now in safety. Below decks the mail officer started to get the mail bags ready for discharge. Throughout the ship, although there were still 24 hours to go before Port Said would be in sight, there was a general feeling of relief that *Persia* would soon be between the banks of the Suez Canal and beyond the reach of marauding U-boats. It was probably because some of the apprehension of the past few days was now lifting that the chain of command on *Persia* slackened momentarily and allowed a mistake to be made that hastened the ship's destruction.

It was another warm morning and the main saloon was becoming increasingly stuffy. To cope with conditions like this the saloon had large portholes but as these were near the waterline they were not opened in stormy weather. Today the weather was fine and the sea merely choppy. In peacetime the ports would have been opened without any hesitation but in the Mediterranean, in December 1915, open ports were unquestionably a needless risk. Millions of gallons of seawater could very quickly pour through them into a sinking, listing ship and rapidly reduce its buoyancy. Many of *Persia*'s passengers were either unaware of this risk or prepared to ignore it, and because the saloon had no electric fans or punkahs it was not long before one of the passengers asked head waiter Dowling: 'Cannot we have some of the ports open?'

Dowling replied: 'Without instructions I dare not open any ports'.

'Can you get permission?'

Other passengers joined in the clamour and to Dowling's surprise someone on the bridge gave permission for the ports to be opened.

Shortly before one o'clock, as *Persia* steamed 71 miles SE by S off Cape Martello, a prominent landmark on the southern coast of Crete, Dowling ordered the luncheon gong to be sounded and stood at the foot of the main companion to usher the passengers to their tables. John Montagu and Eleanor Thornton were shown to one on the port side of the saloon. Unknown to them and indeed to anyone on *Persia*, *Unterseeboot-38* of the Imperial German Navy was lurking just below the surface, probably no more than a 1000 yards away. As the waiters bustled around the saloon serving the first course, Kapitan-Leutnant Max Valentiner focused his periscope on the liner's hull, which was laying beam-on across his sights. A few seconds before ten minutes past one he ordered *U-38* to fire one of her 500mm torpedoes.

What happened next, happened quickly. Those who survived were to remember every second of the next five minutes for the rest of their lives.

Persia was attacked without warning. Only one man, Second Officer Harold Wood, had any inkling that the ship was in mortal danger, but by the time he became aware of this there was nothing he could do to alert the passengers and the ship's company.

Wood had taken over the watch from Gerald Clark but because of the choppy state of the sea he failed to see *U-38*'s periscope as the submarine stalked *Persia* and moved into position to attack. All that Wood saw, at nine minutes and fifty-nine seconds past one, was the track of the torpedo four points on the port bow; it was heading, so far as he could judge, for a point just below and behind the ship's aft funnel. One second later the torpedo speared into *Persia*'s hull and exploded. At that moment the first victims of the disaster — the 35 men in the engine room and stokehold — were killed, or so seriously injured that they were unable to clamber onto the deck and abandon ship.

When he spotted the torpedo Wood's immediate reaction was to try to give a series of blasts on the ship's steam whistle, to warn everyone to go to their lifeboat stations, but before he could do this there was a second explosion and the whistle went dead. Wood's fellow officers were by this time fully aware that the ship had been torpedoed, even though no one had been able to raise the alarm. They all thought that the second detonation was, in fact, a second torpedo. But Wood knew better. Having seen only one track, he knew that there had been only one torpedo and that after this had exploded one of the boilers had blown up. This accounted for the loss of steam to the whistle.

Wood reckoned that the torpedo had fractured the bulkhead separating No. 3 hold from the stokehold, an area opposite the ship's forward boiler rooms. Whilst no one who was anywhere near the torpedo's point of impact survived to say exactly where the ship was hit, Second Engineer Henry Eves, resting in his cabin after a spell on watch in the engine room, believed that it was the port forward boiler that blew up.

The loss of steam to the whistle may not have been a serious problem. Most people on board had heard and felt the explosions which, as Able Seaman Alfred Scrivener later recalled, shook the vessel from stem to stern and immediately caused it to list ten degrees to port. The list increased every second and the passengers and crew did not need a whistle to tell them that they had only a few minutes in which to fetch their lifejackets and go to their lifeboats. What was serious, so far as the operation of the ship's boilers was concerned, was that some of them — perhaps five out of a total of six — were still intact, since steam was still being delivered to the engines. Because of the deaths, injuries and damage that had been caused it was not possible to stop the engines and they continued to propel the ship along at about $16\frac{1}{4}$ knots. This and the worsening list caused complete chaos when attempts were made to lower the lifeboats. The situation became even more critical when, less than three minutes after the torpedo exploded, the main saloon slipped below the waterline, allowing torrents of water to gush through the open ports. Had the saloon remained watertight for even a minute longer, more of those who were below decks at the time of the explosions, or who went to their cabins to collect their lifejackets, would have had time to reach the promenade deck; it would also have been easier to launch the lifeboats.

Having failed to sound the alarm Harold Wood ran to the lower bridge where Commander Hall had been joined by Gerald Clark, who had been eating his lunch in his cabin on the bridge deck. Wood asked Hall if he could help him destroy the secret despatches the ship was carrying but Hall replied: 'No. I am attending to them myself. Get out the port boats as quickly as possible and look after your passengers.' Clark reinforced the master's orders.

The passengers were by now trying to look after themselves. The torpedo had exploded below and behind the area of the saloon where John Montagu and Eleanor Thornton were sitting; the shockwave sent crockery and cutlery clattering off the tables and the saloon was filled with the acrid odour of guncotton and TNT which wafted up through the floor. This had been split open by the force of the explosion. Elsewhere on the ship, steam and hot ashes erupted through jagged fractures, some of them two feet wide, that had appeared in the decks. John, whose earlier depression suggests that he had been dreading such a moment as this, hurried with the other passengers to collect and don his lifejacket. Even though the cabin allocations have not survived, it is highly probable that he did not have to go very far. Being aware of the advantages of travelling 'posh' (port out, starboard home) on voyages between England and India he would have booked first-class cabins for himself and Eleanor Thornton on the cooler, port side of the ship. Even though his closest friends were aware that he and Eleanor were lovers, propriety would have prevented their sharing a cabin. What can be assumed is that they chose cabins that were only a short distance apart.

Most of *Persia*'s first-class cabins were on the bridge deck but a few of the best cabins were on the promenade deck. As these were in a favoured position, being only a few feet from the deck chairs and ship's rail where passengers passed most of their time, it is possible that John and Eleanor occupied two of these during their voyage. With only 78 adult first-class passengers to accommodate from Marseilles eastwards, in a ship that had room for more than 300, *Persia* would have been able to offer a wide choice of cabins. Regardless of whether they chose cabins on the bridge deck or promenade deck, they are likely to have chosen to travel as close as possible to a point midway between the bow and stern, since the pitching motion of ships in rough seas is less pronounced here than elsewhere. So, by making a few reasonable assumptions, it is likely that John and Eleanor had first-class cabins on the port side of the ship somewhere in the region of the vessel's two funnels. This theory is supported by the fact that their lifeboat station, No. 6 on the port side, was almost exactly amidships. When working out their lifeboat plan at the beginning of the voyage Hall and his officers had taken care to allocate passengers to their nearest lifeboats wherever possible. So when John and Eleanor hurried to their cabins and then to their lifeboat station they may not have had far to go. The main saloon lay immediately forward of the ship's fore funnel, and was only one deck below the first-class cabins nearest the centre of the ship. If their cabins had been on the bridge deck they would have had to run up the main companionway and into the passageway along which the cabins were situated. Then they would have climbed another flight of stairs to reach the lifeboat stations, on the promenade deck. If they had had cabins on the promenade deck itself it would have taken them slightly longer to fetch their lifejackets, but in order to reach No. 6 lifeboat station they would only have had to walk out of their cabin doors directly onto the promenade deck.

S.S. Persia.

Unlike the majority of the passengers, John emerged on deck wearing a Gieve waistcoat, a popular garment among seafarers at that time because it was worn as an ordinary waistcoat and easily inflated to become more buoyant than a cork lifejacket. Whilst staying with Lady Forster in London, John had met his cousin, Admiral Mark Kerr, and at his behest purchased the waistcoat from Gieves' shop in Regent Street. It is not known whether he also bought one for Eleanor Thornton but he had every reason to do so. Her journey was likely to be even more dangerous than his, for after accompanying him as far as Aden (she had originally intended to leave the ship at Port Said) she would then have had the prospect of another long voyage back across the Mediterranean, in order to travel home. She therefore had twice as much chance as John of being the victim of a shipwreck.

There is little doubt that Eleanor was wearing a lifejacket of some kind as she accompanied Montagu to their lifeboat station. Gerald Clark and Harold Wood saw only one passenger — a lady carrying a baby — without a lifejacket, and Wood gave her his own before the ship sank.

By now attempts were being made to lower the port lifeboats but even though the passengers were behaving calmly, remembering their lifeboat drill the previous day, there was confusion on the promenade deck because the leftward tilt of the ship was swinging the lifeboats away from the deck rail. This made it impossible for them to be lowered and loaded properly. No. 6 lifeboat had in any case been blown to pieces by the force of the explosion but John and Eleanor do not seem to have been aware of this. They momentarily considered trying to find a place in one of the port boats but even if they had

Lifeboats under davits on the Persia's *port side, where the lifeboat allocated to John and Eleanor was blown to pieces.*

lingered at their lifeboat station for only a few seconds, they would have been horrified by the scene. Above them, on the boat deck, members of the crew were struggling to lower the boats from their davits; on the promenade deck, passengers who had not been trapped down below were leaning or leaping from the rail as they tried to board the few boats that could be lowered. By now Commander Hall and Gerald Clark had left the lower bridge and had just, or would soon, reach No. 4 lifeboat. Although they managed to lower the boat it was torn loose as soon as it touched the water, due to *Persia*'s fast forward speed, and then smashed or swamped, flinging its occupants into the sea.

Able Seaman Scrivener, who had been smoking on the forewell deck whilst waiting to relieve the wheelhand, should have helped launch No. 4 boat but by the time he had warned his fellow ABs of the danger they were in, and rushed up to the boat deck, No. 4 was being lowered. Instead he went to the next boat forward, No. 2. This was one of the accident boats, which was always ready to be launched in the event of an emergency, such as 'man overboard'. Together, Scrivener and Jack Pinner, the baggage master, lowered No. 2, which was swinging out of reach, by climbing up its davits and releasing its falls. *Persia* was now about to capsize and Scrivener and Pinner only had to allow their boat to drop six feet before it hit the water. They then unhooked the tackles, cut the painter and desperately rowed clear as *Persia*'s funnels, still belching smoke, lurched downwards until they were almost parallel with the water.

No. 2 boat escaped being smashed by the aft stack by only three feet and later picked up Gerald Clark and 20 other survivors, all blackened and almost suffocated by the dying gasps from *Persia*'s funnels. By this time Clark and Hall had parted company. The Chief Officer had been thrown into the water whilst trying to release the two inboard boats on chocks on the foredeck. Hall fell or jumped into the sea a little later; Harold Wood saw him swimming amidst *Persia*'s flotsam but he soon disappeared and was never seen again.

Only one other boat, No. 14, was lowered safely. No. 16 nearly got clear with several passengers but was pressed under water by her own davits as *Persia* turned turtle. No. 2, with Gerald Clark in command, became the leader of *Persia*'s rescue operations, linking up with No. 14 and two inboard boats that had somehow floated clear from the poop deck. One of these saved Harold Wood's life; he swam to it and picked up 43 survivors, including Dowling, who in turn saved a mother and her baby boy. Altogether the four boats rescued more than 150 survivors who were picked up 30 hours later by HMS *Mallow* and taken to Alexandria.

Although the efforts to abandon ship from the port rail ended in confusion, Commander Hall had had no alternative but to order Harold Wood to try to lower the port boats. With *Persia*'s leftward lurch becoming more and more pronounced he knew that it would be impossible to launch the starboard boats, since they would be swinging from their davits towards the ship and would easily jam in their falls or be dashed against the hull. Adhering to their lifeboat drill, some of the passengers had nevertheless gone to their lifeboat stations on the starboard promenade deck, but Hall soon appeared and ordered 'All women and children down to the port side'. 'Down' was the operative word; the deck was now rearing up to starboard at an alarming angle. The futility of trying to evacuate anyone into the starboard boats was obvious, as Harold Wood discovered. Having done what he could to ensure that the port boats were being released he hurried across to starboard, where he found W. J. Hickingbotham, the Third Engineer, trying to lower No. 15 boat, in which a number of people had taken refuge. The boat became wedged on the 'eyebrow' (steel framework) over one of the portholes and Wood shouted to its passengers to jump for their lives into the sea.

Meanwhile the women and children who had been ordered to the port deck joined the other passengers and crew members who had originally been allotted places in the starboard boats. Gerald Clark was surprised how few passengers there were on deck, and surmised that the rest were already trapped in their cabins. One survivor, perhaps unfairly, later criticized Hall for ordering the women and children off the starboard deck, claiming that they were consequently caught in 'an absolute deathtrap' when they found themselves unable to board the port boats. By the time they realized that there was little chance of any of the boats getting away it was too late for them to jump safely into the sea, or clamber up the now almost vertical deck in order to try once again to abandon ship from the starboard rail.

This, then, was the scene that confronted John Montagu and Eleanor Thornton when they reached the port deck. Desperate attempts were being made to lower the lifeboats. Those that were being launched were swinging several feet from the deck rail. And the deck itself was becoming too steep to provide a foothold. Unaware of Hall's order or Hickingbotham's problem with No. 15 boat, they had every reason to believe that they would have a better chance of surviving by making for the starboard rail.

They tried to reach it, but failed. As John stumbled up the deck, hauling Eleanor by the hand or arm, the ship began to sink rapidly, stern first. At the same time her list reached the critical angle at which it would inevitably capsize. A wall of water surged along the deck, sweeping John off his feet and into the sea. At this instant Eleanor was torn from his grasp. Moments later *Persia*'s funnels disappeared below the waves. The time was 1.15 pm. Only five minutes earlier Dowling and his assistants had been serving lunch in the main saloon. Now, more than 300 people were drowning as the ship rolled over and sank from sight.

Dowling was now swimming at a safe distance and as *Persia* began to disappear he had been fascinated to see baggage master Pinner skilfully use a boat hook to manoeuvre No. 2 boat out of a whirlpool that threatened to suck the boat into the now horizontal aft funnel. Dowling then watched *Persia* surrender to the sea as, with her stern now fully submerged, her bow reared steeply upwards before being dragged downwards into oblivion. To Dowling it appeared that the ship had sunk with scarcely a ripple but John Montagu found himself being sucked down in a violent vortex. He was struck several times by pieces of wreckage, injuring his head and left shoulder. After what seemed a very long time he found himself being blown upwards by air and steam escaping from the ship, his buoyancy increased immeasurably by his Gieve waistcoat which undoubtedly saved his life. Of Eleanor Thornton there was no sign. Although in all probability she was wearing a lifejacket or even a Gieve waistcoat, the most plausible explanation for her disappearance is that she was somehow trapped on *Persia*'s starboard deck as the ship capsized and sank. Had she floated clear of the wreckage and remained conscious she would have had every chance of being spotted by John Montagu or one of the other survivors, and pulled into a lifeboat. It seems that few of the passengers and ship's company who were able to abandon ship and shout for help failed to find a place in one of the lifeboats. *Persia*'s death toll consisted almost entirely of people who were unable to reach the promenade deck before the ship sank.

When John recovered his breath and his senses he found that he was one of many people who had managed to swim or float clear and were now struggling to find a boat or piece of wreckage to cling to. He swam to a nearby signal locker but found that this has been commandeered by the ship's surgeon, Dr Everett, who appeared to be stunned (and who later drowned). Montagu therefore made for an upturned, badly damaged lifeboat about 50 yards away and clambered astride its keel band, from where he took stock of his predicament.

His position was, to say the least, precarious. A large crowd of Lascar seamen was clinging to his boat — more than it could properly support — and so he yelled to a half-filled boat only a short distance away. This was one of the four that would soon be mustered by Gerald Clark. John's cries were ignored and the boat rowed away. With many people still floundering in the water, those in charge of the boat must have decided that John seemed safe, at least for the moment, and that less fortunate survivors in the water nearby deserved priority. From this moment he lost any chance of being among those who were later rescued by HMS *Mallow*. Instead he had to take his chance with the native seamen, who one by one became too weak to hold on, and were swept away. Soon only 20 of them were left.

It proved impossible for John Montagu and his companions to turn their heavy, waterlogged boat upright but luckily this problem was solved about an hour later, by a heavy wave. With some difficulty John and the Lascar sailors, together with two Goanese stewards and five Europeans who had now joined them, were able to heave themselves aboard. A quick inspection revealed that the boat was almost unseaworthy. There was a large hole in its bottom, its bow was split open, and some of the copper buoyancy tanks under the starboard seats had been punctured. As well as being in danger of sinking because of its structural damage, the slightest movement to starboard tended to make the boat capsize. This happened several times, and after repeatedly falling into the sea the passengers found it increasingly difficult to regain a hold on the boat and haul it upright.

There were, during those first few hours after the attack, more than 150 people in various states of distress anxiously awaiting rescue around 34°56′N, 25°06′E, where *Persia* had sunk. There was a Marconi operator among her crew, so she was obviously equipped with radio, but there is no evidence that she had time to transmit a distress signal before she went down. No one, therefore, knew of her plight and her survivors could only drift in their lifeboats and hope that they would be spotted by a friendly ship. Their anxiety was increased at about a quarter to four that afternoon when gunfire or an explosion echoed across the water. This, they learned later, was the sound of *U-38* claiming another victim, the British steamer *Clan Macfarlane*, which was also attacked without warning.

By sunset Gerald Clark's boats were to the east and almost out of sight of

John's fragile craft and it is likely that, by now, whoever had ignored his shouts for help had assumed that he had drowned or was now safely aboard one of the four boats. However, his plight was growing more serious by the hour. At nightfall there were only 19 men left in the boat — the natives, an Italian passenger, a Scotsman named Alexander Clark, a steward named Martin, and John Montagu. A heavy swell developed during the night, swamping and overturning the boat again and again; on more than one occasion, Clark and Martin saved John's life by helping him back into the boat. At around 8 pm their hopes were raised when a steamer passed about a mile to the south with all her saloon lights ablaze. John and his companions shouted for help whilst, to the east, one of Gerald Clark's boats fired two red flares but the steamer failed to stop. It probably saw the flares but suspected that they were a decoy set up by a U-boat. Stories of enemy submarines fooling ships into stopping to pick up bogus survivors of shipwrecks, or lurking in the vicinity of genuine lifeboats in order to attack ships coming to their help, were rife at this time.

Later in the night, as John dozed, a Lascar seaman twice tried to edge him into the sea. Eight of the natives died of exhaustion. Their bodies were thrown overboard, although Montagu sat on one of them for an hour or two in order to raise himself above the water, which was almost up to his waist. Three hours after dawn next morning — New Year's Eve — the 11 men who had survived the night had their hopes of rescue dashed yet again as a westbound two-funnelled steamer passed three miles to the south. Their improvised signal, a torn flag tied to an oar, was not noticed and for the rest of the day they continued to drift aimlessly. At noon one of the natives found a tin of biscuits, which although tainted with sea water provided Montagu and his companions with their first refreshment for nearly 24 hours. John had had only a cup of tea and a biscuit since dinner on 29 December.

The last sunset of 1915 was the last he thought he would ever see, for by then everyone in the boat had virtually given up hope. John voiced his fears to Alexander Clark who answered: 'I'm afraid our number is up'. The Italian had by now yielded to the temptation to drink sea water and in his consequent delirium capsized the boat again. Once more it was righted but the remaining biscuits and a tin of flares they had intended to use during the night were lost. With no food or flares and a deranged passenger on their hands, their chances were slim indeed; yet paradoxically for John and his companions, and for the passengers and crew in Gerald Clark's boats over the horizon, *Persia's* survivors were all about to be saved in simultaneous but totally separate rescue operations.

Two hours before sunset Clark had left his small fleet and rowed off in the direction of Port Said in No. 2 boat. He was able to attract the attention of HMS *Mallow* and direct the ship back to the area where he had left the other three boats.

Meanwhile, many miles to the east, John Montagu, Martin and Alexander Clark had seen a light rise above the eastern horizon. At first they assumed that it was a star but later they suspected that it was a masthead light. This was confirmed when they saw the sidelights of a ship heading more or less directly towards them. With no flares to attract attention, John and his friends could only shout. Luckily Donald MacClean, who was officer of the watch on the Blue Funnel liner *Ningchow*, had exceptionally keen hearing and having heard what he at first thought was a seabird's cry — an unlikely sound after nightfall — he alerted his master, Commander Allan. Fearing a submarine ruse, Allan nevertheless ordered his ship to turn and investigate. Later, John wrote the story he never thought he would live to tell; that of his rescue:

> I began to rally my fellow sufferers and the idea came to me to make them shout 'Hitherao' (Hindustani for 'Come here') because I knew that no German in a decoy boat — and there were very many of them in those seas — would cry out in Hindustani. Just as *Ningchow* seemed to be going to run us down she stopped. After nearly an hour of cruising around us the great 7000 ton ship came near, towering above us. I was able, by shouting directions such as 'Go ahead and port your helm', to get the vessel so close that a rope was thrown to us and at last we were pulled up one by one. When I saw the last of my companions hauled on board and felt the bowline tauten around my shoulders I looked down on the eggshell to which we had clung and began to realize the miracle which had saved us. Even as one looked, the cockleshell grated against the steel side of the ship and broke in two.

The loss of *Persia* had been made public in London at 11 am on Saturday, 1 January in a Lloyd's telegram which stated: 'Most of the passengers and crew lost. Four boats got clear.' Early that afternoon P & O announced that the occupants of the boats had been rescued and this was followed, next day, by a statement containing a provisional list of 158 survivors who by then had arrived at Alexandria. Most people read about the attack and the loss of more than 300 of her passengers and crew in *The Times* on the morning of Monday, 3 January. John's name, of course, was not in the list of survivors since at this time no newspaper knew that a fifth lifeboat had escaped and that John was in it. When *The Times* went to press John was still on *Ningchow*, heading for Malta. His friends and family spent an anxious weekend waiting for more news of the disaster, hoping — with little cause for optimism — that he and Eleanor Thornton were safe. But at least one person, the Vicar of Beaulieu, Mr Powles, was convinced that John had survived. Mr Powles said that whilst walking near the village he had seen an apparition of John

Montagu. Because this appeared in front of him he knew that John was alive; had the vision appeared behind him, it would have meant that John was dead.

At Ditton Park, Rose Thornton had seen, or would soon see, an omen of a different kind. Returning to Garden Cottage, a tiny house that she and Eleanor shared at Ditton Park, she was horrified to find that her neighbour, Mr Stephens, the estate's gardener, had decorated a portrait of Eleanor with sprigs of yew and holly. In those days it was considered unlucky to bring yew indoors.

John and his ten fellow survivors arrived at Malta in the early morning of Monday 3 January and for the next two weeks he stayed with the Governor, Field Marshal Lord Methuen. During this time he had the salutary experience of reading his own obituaries in various papers. *The Times* gave a full scale resumé of his career and then said:

> In the next few days anglers will write of John as an angler; shooting men will tell of his prowess; authorities on explosives will treat of his expert knowledge gained as a working director of a powder company; naturalists will describe his intimate knowledge of flora and fauna; motorists will narrate the great part he played in introducing the automobile and airplane; and believers in the future of high speed hydroplanes of the good work he did in aiding the progress of the boats he deemed to be the future enemy of the submarine — the submarine which, alas, was to end a remarkable and useful life. He leaves a host of friends, ermined and overalled, in the world of politics, engineering, sport and labour. He will be long missed and his murder not forgotten in the hour of reckoning.

The obituary was unsigned but the family knew that the writer was none other than Lord Northcliffe who fourteen years earlier had helped John embark on his career in journalism.

To John the real tragedy of the *Persia* incident was the death of Eleanor Thornton and his sorrow must have been compounded by the fact that, because few knew about their *affaire*, he felt unable to assuage his grief in the one way that would have helped him come to terms with his loss — by writing about her and telling the world about his feelings when he surfaced from the sinking ship and found that they had been parted. There was, it is true, nothing that he could have done to prevent her from being swept from his grasp as they were bowled over by the wave of water that surged across the deck when the ship started to sink; nor was there any way in which he could search for her afterwards. But was her journey really necessary? Ostensibly she had intended to accompany him as far as Aden so as to help him finish the report he was taking to Simla. Yet John had been back in England, gathering information for this report, for four months. And Eleanor knew, on 23 November (the day she wrote to Lady Montagu about the voyage) or even earlier, that she would be going with him. The length and complexity of

John's report is not known, since it went down with the *Persia*, but his papers indicate that it was completed by 30 December. Was it really necessary for the report to be finished on the ship, or had it in actual fact already been completed before John and Eleanor left London for Marseilles? The answers to those questions will never be known, but it does seem likely that the real reason why Eleanor insisted on accompanying her lover was that she wanted to be with him throughout the most dangerous part of his journey to India — *Persia*'s passage across the Mediterranean.

When talking and writing about the *Persia* disaster, John said very little about Eleanor Thornton's fate and could only bring himself to make such comments as: 'Poor Thorn, it was awful.' But among the hundreds of messages and letters he received congratulating him on his escape (including one from King George V) were some from a few friends and relatives who felt able to commiserate on the subject that was foremost in his mind. One relation wrote:

> You have also a loss to bear of a great and noble friendship which you can always be proud you inspired, for Miss Thornton had a heart and nature of gold.

In a few instances John did privately reveal his feelings. In reply to a note from Lord Northcliffe he wrote:

> You will know as a fellow human what is my grief at the loss of Thorn, who for fifteen years was all in all to me and who was the most devoted and lovable woman God ever made. As for myself I had a hard time but lived through it by the grace of God — for a good purpose I hope.

It was, though, John's closest friend, Tommy Troubridge, who wrote the briefest but most poignant condolence of all:

> Poor little Whitethorn: I am so sorry.

After he returned to England in mid January 1916, John had a plaque erected in Eleanor Thornton's memory in Beaulieu parish church and loaned the waistcoat that had saved his life to Gieves, where it was put on display to raise funds for the Red Cross. Predictably, he wrote to P & O's Chairman, Lord Inchcape, on the question of safeguarding the passengers of liners sailing in waters patrolled by enemy submarines. Inchcape replied by saying that if *Persia* had managed to stay upright and afloat for ten minutes instead of five, everyone on board except those in the engine room would probably have been rescued. There was no court of inquiry into the incident. Statements were taken from some of the officers and hands when they returned to England, and Harold Wood said that if the ship had remained afloat for a few more minutes, nearly everybody on board would have been saved. But one of the most important aspects of the whole affair — the fact that the ports in the main saloon were opened a few hours before *Persia* was attacked — was evidently not mentioned. Forty-nine years later the boy — now in his early fifties — who had been rescued by Dowling wrote to tell him that his mother had died. This moved Dowling to write an account of his experiences on *Persia*, in which he related the conversation with the passengers that had resulted in the ports being opened.

John seems to have nursed a lingering hope that Eleanor Thornton had somehow survived and managed to reach Crete, Cyprus, Cyrenaica, the Greek Islands or Egypt. In the summer of 1918 he wrote to the British authorities there but received the same answers from all of them. One official commented:

> That Miss Thornton could have arrived alive on these shores and no news be had of her is quite impossible and to admit the contrary would be to encourage hopes which are certainly illusory.

Eleanor Thornton died at about 1.15 pm on Thursday 30 December 1915, aged 35, although it was nearly three years before John Montagu accepted that fact. But their *affaire* retained its most important secret for another 50 years, when there was an extraordinary sequel to the story of the lady who inspired the creator of The Spirit of Ecstasy.

15

War in the Air

On returning to England, John Montagu received a hero's welcome from his tenants at Beaulieu and was made a Companion of the Order of the Star of India by King George V. He intended to convalesce for a few weeks and set off for India again in March, possibly in company with the new Viceroy, Lord Chelmsford, who succeeded Lord Hardinge.

On 8 February John dined with Lord Kitchener and Lord Chelmsford and learned that Major General Sir George Kirkpatrick was to be the new Chief of Staff in India. Next day, picking up the threads after his enforced absence, John resumed his efforts to obtain mechanical transport for India and began corresponding with Kirkpatrick, Roos Keppel and Hardinge. It was only a matter of days before Austen Chamberlain, Secretary of State for India and his Military Secretary, General Sir Edmund Barrow, decided that John should remain in London until the autumn. As John explained in one of his letters to India:

> They say that aeroplanes and motor lorries are beyond their ken and they want me to help them through the coming months.

By this time India was beginning to benefit from John's attempts to give her depleted forces greater mobility and fire-power, in the form of lorries, cars and aeroplanes. Deliveries of aircraft had not proceeded quite as quickly as John had expected when he wrote to Hardinge shortly after meeting David Henderson in August 1915, but on 6 February a second flight left England for the North-West Frontier; by now both the organization of India's military motor transport and the supply of new vehicles were also improving. Hardinge had already thanked John for what he had achieved in 1915. Responding to his account of Chamberlain's attempts to purchase ex-Admiralty armoured cars, Hardinge had said that he hoped his Commander in Chief would 'try to acquire some of those cars which Winston Churchill so recklessly bought'. Motor lorries and No. 1 AMU's armoured cars had been used successfully in operations against the Mohmands in the autumn, and Hardinge was looking forward to the further mechanization of the Army in India during 1916, although as one of his letters to John reveals he was dismayed at the way in which politics in Britain were hampering the military effort:

> It is depressing to hear of all the fighting and quarrelling that goes on at home amongst those whose whole energies ought to be applied to the successful prosecution of the war and not diverted from that object by petty jealousies. Unfortunately party politics and trades unionism still seem to rule the day, patriotism being only a secondary consideration.

Despite all this Montagu enjoyed increasing success as he pleaded India's case with the military authorities and visited motor manufacturers to specify, test and order what became known as Indian standard lorries. These had numerous features in common, including their carrying capacity, tyres and engine power — all of which made transport operations simpler to organize. The early summer of 1916 was to see the transformation of India's military transport. Until the spring there was only one mechanical transport company there — No. 1 Indian MTC — and this had a rather motley collection of lorries. Then, in May, four Army Service Corps motor companies arrived. One of these consisted of a convoy of 50 ambulances supported by four lorries, four cars and seven motorcycles. This convoy was probably the one that John demonstrated to King George V and Queen Mary at Buckingham Palace on 22 March 1916. Four months earlier John had been one of the supporters of 'Cinema Day', an occasion on which the Kinematograph Trade Ambulance Fund persuaded 2500 picture palaces to donate an entire day's takings to pay for the construction by the Star Engineering Works at Wolverhampton, of an entire convoy of ambulances for the Army. The event raised £37,000; the target had been £30,000. The ambulances subsequently served in Mesopotamia. (A film showing the ambulances being built and handed-over has been donated to the Imperial War Museum by the present Lord Montagu.)

The other motor transport units that arrived in India in May 1916 were supply columns, proving that John Montagu's arguments for using lorries instead of mules had been accepted. A total of 79 3-ton Albion lorries and one hundred other vehicles arrived that month, with 11 officers and 583 other ranks. One of the supply columns, No. 694 Company, went out without any vehicles but in a matter of months was equipped with 60 light Star lorries suitable for crossing bridge boats and traversing kutcha roads and sand. Later in the war the number of Indian companies operating lorries in India was increased to five and there were also various formations on active service in adjacent countries. For the Indian units John procured standard lorries from Leyland and Thornycroft and these types were also beginning to replace the ASC's Albions when the war ended.

Whilst at the India Office John also found time to re-write the report he had

To solve his personal transport problems John took his own Rolls-Royce to India. He is seen here with an aide and his chauffeur Teddy Stephens. Note the car's mascot, Whisper, created for John by Charles Sykes, designer of the Spirit of Ecstasy, the official Rolls-Royce mascot.

lost on *Persia*. In this he repeated his familiar pleas for motor transport and aircraft and put forward suggestions for supplying the troops with what, at that time, were still military novelties, including searchlights and night sights for the artillery; wireless wagons for the infantry; mobile electric generators for the Royal Engineers and underground oil tanks for the motor transport companies. With a population of 315 million to govern and three-quarters of a million armed tribesmen on the frontiers to control, India's regiments urgently needed 'the best mechanical transport, to make every one of its soldiers equal to as many foes as possible'. In his report John also emphasized some of the fundamental problems facing the British Army:

> One of the most important lessons of the present war is that mechanical equipment counts more than ever before in battle. By means of superior equipment an army can hold at bay a largely superior force however brave and well led that force may be. The truth of this is attested by the fact that the Allies have been copying constantly the superior mechanical devices of the German Army after an interval of a few weeks or months. The result has been that we have always been behindhand in almost every kind of mechanical warfare and have suffered accordingly. The reason for this, apart from our natural aversion for anything new or scientific, seems to be that there has been in our military administration at home and abroad no

proper department whose duty it was to concentrate upon the invention, examination and construction of mechanical devices of all kinds for the use of armies in the field. The mechanical devices in use have been left to fall casually into the hands of various departments, some of which are traditionally jealous of each other.

This lack of co-ordinated consideration and effort should not be allowed to exist in the future ... warfare will become more and more scientific both on land, in the water and in the air. Battles fought between nations in the future will be won by the most scientifically equipped and small numbers will, notwithstanding numerical differences, ultimately win the fight or be able to produce a state of stagnation in attack which must eventually lead to a drawn war.

All this led up to a proposal for the formation of a mechanical equipment department in India, with a corresponding department in London whose function would be to keep India aware of all the latest improvements that were being used by the European armies. As it happened it was the parlous state of Britain's air services in France and the resumption of Zeppelin raids on England that were to occupy John's mind for much of 1916 and prompt him to follow up his prewar demand for a national air defence scheme with a call for the formation of an air ministry.

In 1912 the War Office had accepted that aviation was likely to have a role in future warfare and had established the Royal Flying Corps. At that time aeroplanes and airships were looked upon as reconnaissance machines rather than weapons, so it seemed logical to divide the corps into military and naval wings, assigned to the Army and the Royal Navy, and allow them to develop and purchase their own types of aircraft without being obliged to co-ordinate their activities. No one with any influence on the Government seems to have realized that this division of responsibility would lead to bitter inter-service rivalry and jealousy over the procurement of aircraft, or that it would make it virtually impossible for the two services to work together when the time came to wage the aerial battles that John Montagu, and those who supported him, had foreseen.

By the end of 1915 British air policy was in tatters. The slow and stable aeroplanes the RFC had developed for reconnaissance work on the Western Front had proved to be hopelessly ill-equipped to defend themselves during the dog fights that inevitably sprang up over the enemy lines; nor were they successful when they tried to carry the fight beyond the lines and attack the German positions. The RFC thus lost command of the air in France and Flanders. Now, short of aircraft and experienced pilots, it could not respond to demands, led by John Montagu, for the creation of a strategic bombing force capable of penetrating into Germany. At home the Admiralty was in charge of anti-aircraft defence but was finding it hard to deter Zeppelins from their night raids; 70 people were killed in the Midlands on the night of 30 January 1916 alone.

This, then, was the background against which the Government made its first attempt to co-ordinate its air services. On 15 February Asquith and his war cabinet decided to set up a joint naval and military war air committee under the chairmanship of Lord Derby, the man who had masterminded Lord Kitchener's recruiting campaign. Also on the Derby Committee were Murray Sueter, Rear Admiral Vaughan Lee and Squadron Commander W. Briggs from the Admiralty, and David Henderson and Lieutenant-Colonel E. L. Ellington from the War Office. This committee was instructed to co-ordinate the design and supply of *materiél* to the air services and prevent clashing or overlapping demands being made on manufacturing resources. In the month that elapsed between the decision to form the committee and the date of its first meeting, John Montagu initiated the House of Lords' first major wartime air debate.

The debate stemmed from a question in which John asked the Government whether, in view of the 'great and growing importance of aviation in modern warfare, both by land and sea, and the need for special attention and effort to be concentrated upon it, they would create a special Ministry to deal with the whole question'. There was, he said, no possibility of Britain regaining supremacy in the air until the existing arrangements for equipping the air services were altered. He added:

> It is to the air service that we must look in the future for the real defence of the country and in my view one of the logical outcomes of the war is that the greater part of future warfare will be in the air. We want more powerful aeroplanes at the front and better anti-aircraft guns and airships at home. We should do to the enemy what they have done to us. They attacked our manufacturing districts and the only way to reply is to bomb and destroy the enemy hangars and manufacturing districts. The German fleet may come out when the weather suits the Zeppelins and the task of our fleet would be rendered much more difficult. Zeppelins are a greater danger and no official statements saying that little damage has been done will alter that fact. We must overcome the menace by carrying the war into the enemy's camp. Let it not be said with shame that in our generation we did not trouble to guard in the air what our forefathers had won on the sea.

Although ideally he wanted to see the creation of a Ministry of Aviation or Air Ministry, with all the powers of a department of State, John said that if that was not possible then at least a Board of Aviation should be established, under the chairmanship of a member of the war council, with Admiralty and War Office representatives and 'a commercial man'. The Board that John had in mind was essentially one similar in composition to the Derby Committee but with greater authority — including that of being able to initiate a strategic bombing campaign. But the Government would have none of it. Lord Lansdowne, Minister without Portfolio, admitted that there were serious shortcomings in the air services due to 'the stupendous and wholly unexpected effort' they had had to make, but he believed the services should always be ancillary to the Army and Royal Navy. Lansdowne said he hoped that Lord Derby's 'very strong committee' would suffice. John, summing up his case at the end of the debate, said he hoped the Government would 'magnify the functions of the committee' until it became something like the Board of Aviation he had advocated.

The Government's response to John's question was disappointing but widespread public support was given to his proposals, especially in Lord Northcliffe's newspapers. After the debate one or two newspapers suggested that, if an Air Ministry were to be established, then John Montagu should be appointed Air Minister. The *Daily Mirror* commented: 'It would be difficult to find a more capable administrator.'

As a result of the House of Lords debate, Asquith asked John to become a member of Lord Derby's Committee. In his letter of acceptance John said: 'I do this because I am assured by Lord Derby that the committee is considered to be the nucleus of a Board of Aviation with wider powers and greater responsibilities to be formed in the near future. If the committee were merely to remain an interdepartmental committee I would not like to leave the very important work I am doing now for India, but I feel it my duty to do so if the committee is likely to grow into a really responsible body which can really assist and influence the development of military and naval aviation throughout the Empire.'

John attended his first committee meeting on 20 March and was immediately disillusioned. Whatever hopes may have been held out to him by Lord Derby were soon dashed. He immediately had to reconsider his acceptance of Asquith's invitation and had a long conversation the following afternoon with his old political friend Walter Long, who had recently returned to the Local Government Board. John then wrote to Lord Derby and outlined his doubts about the committee's prospects of being allowed to initiate significant changes in air policy:

> I told Walter Long about our committee, that I felt that it had nothing like sufficient power and that we should be able to come to few conclusions on things that matter while the representatives of the Admiralty and War Office were there as members of the committee and could resist proposals made by you or myself . . . So far as I can see the committee has done very little except put an end to some abuses in regard to factories . . . and the reallotment of a number of engines between the departments. Beyond this I do not see that the committee can do much more on its present basis. At

the present moment we are regarded, quite wrongly, as being largely responsible for aerial offence and defence. Although this is a totally erroneous impression it will stick to us whatever you or I say and if there are any more serious raids we shall be blamed, although we have nothing to do with it. If our committee is merely departmental and advisory in small ways, you and I are both wasting our time.

As well as lacking executive powers the Derby Committee was handicapped by the fact that although David Henderson was a member of the Army Council and could speak for the War Office, Vaughan Lee was not a member of the Board of Admiralty and therefore could not make any important decisions or recommendations without first referring to the Board. John suggested that the committee should be reconstituted to supervise air policy and research as well as the design and supply of aircraft and equipment. He also proposed that it should consist solely of himself, Lord Derby and Admiral Sir Hedworth Meux (then Commander-in-Chief Portsmouth), with military and naval representatives and a member of the General Staff attending merely to give advice. In a memorandum to Asquith, written within days of the committee meeting on 20 March, John proposed specific subjects on which the committee should offer advice direct to the Cabinet and the Imperial defence committee, including the lighting of cities during air raids (John favoured a total blackout instead of the partial switching off of lights then practised), the use of searchlights and guns near large towns (he thought they should draw back and form an 'outer circle' so as to fend off aircraft before they reached their target), the provision of more aerodromes for the RFC, the use of underground hangars, and the adequacy (or otherwise) of the air services' construction programmes.

By the end of March Lord Derby was also having doubts about the effectiveness of his committee and he agreed that it could not function usefully unless it had executive powers. These were not forthcoming and on 3 April he and John resigned. In his letter of resignation Derby referred to a 'fundamental disagreement' between the Admiralty and the War Office and complained that the committee's terms of reference were so narrow that decisions on question of policy could not be reached. John reminded Asquith that he had joined the committee because he hoped it would become a board that would take over the administration of the air services:

My experience on the committee convinced me that there is no chance of this reform being effected by means of this committee... Nothing short of the establishment of a proper administrative department under a Minister with full powers can remedy the present defects and lay the foundations for improvement.

With a later letter to Asquith, John enclosed his detailed proposals for a Board of Aviation and stated:

There are undoubted scandals — duplicated duties such as inspection, contracts, etc. — over which the two great services quarrel like cats. A board might save much money and time here.

The inevitable disbandment of the Derby Committee after Derby and John resigned could hardly have come at a worse time in terms of its effect on public confidence in the way the Government was conducting the war. John had warned Derby that the committee would be blamed if there were any more serious air raids and although, fortuitously, there were none during the committee's brief existence, the Zeppelins returned on three consecutive nights as soon as the committee broke up. The new anti-aircraft scheme introduced in February was soon to bring about some improvements in aerial defence, even though the airship campaign continued for another two years, but in April 1916 the public was not to know this and could only assume that the raids were about to be resumed on the same scale and with as much success, from Germany's point of view, as before. Consequently John attracted sympathetic audiences when he embarked on a series of speaking engagements aimed at winning support for the proposals that he had just put to Asquith. There were, though, pockets of resistance to his ideas. Unlike the Northcliffe press, one Birmingham newspaper considered him to be a 'skilled amateur, as opposed to the naval and military experts' and said he was 'one of those men who sulk when they cannot get their own particular way'. The choice, to the Birmingham commentator, was 'between Balfour (the First Lord of the Admiralty) and Beaulieu' and John's proposed Board of Aviation was seen as a threat to the existence of the entire Admiralty. Many shared that view or had other reasons for opposing John and although in May 1916 the Government established an Air Board under the chairmanship of Lord Curzon, the powers of the new body were not significantly wider than those of the Derby Committee.

Curzon's Board first met on 22 May. The following day John initiated another debate in the Lords by calling on the House to resolve that the development of aviation for war purposes could no longer be carried out efficiently under the existing system of divided control and responsibility, and that the time had come to concentrate the supply of men and material under a single control, whilst leaving the executive control of air operations in the hands of the Army and the Admiralty. John had put down this motion two weeks earlier and at that time he must have been hoping for an early debate in which, in view of the Derby Committee débâcle, their Lordships would have approved his resolution. This would have put the Government under great pressure to form a proper Air Ministry. However John's resolution was pre-empted by the Cabinet's decision, taken on 11 May, to set up the Air Board. This was made responsible for organizing supplies of materials to the air services and preventing competition, but John warned the House that it would run into difficulties because it had no authority to lay down the policies on which orders for supplies would be based. He said:

> Eventually a fully-fledged Air Ministry must come out of this. I think it will come sooner than most people think and it will come partly owing to the efforts of myself and people who think like me. It will also come from the inevitable pressure of circumstances, because the more you see of the war the more you realize that it is the combats in the air and what aircraft can do that may decide it.

The people who thought like John Montagu had no success that day. Successive speakers, including Lord Curzon, opposed his motion and John saw no point in forcing a division. A week later John, who attended a few of the Air Board's meetings, sent Curzon some detailed suggestions on how the supply of pilots, aeroplanes and engines to the air services could be increased. He proposed that the production of aero-engine components should be sub-contracted to motor car manufacturers and that extra aeroplanes for the RFC and RNAS should be built in the USA and Canada. He also aired, once again, his belief in strategic bombing: 'A few missiles dropped into Essen or on the Rhine bridges would probably be of more value than thousands of shells fired at the front at targets of little military value.' Whilst the Air Board achieved more than the Derby Committee, it soon ran into difficulties when the Admiralty asked for, and received, without the Air Board's approval, an allocation of £3 million from the Treasury with which to buy aeroplanes and engines. Curzon protested in strong terms to the Cabinet. Balfour, for the Admiralty, replied that the matter was none of the Air Board's business; the Admiralty alone was responsible for the RNAS and was not obliged to carry out its orders 'in subordination to another department'. Problems of the kind that John had warned about on 23 May were beginning to materialize, but before this particular row rekindled the still-smouldering controversy over the way Britain's air services were run, an incident occurred that again drew John on to the centre of the stage on which the confusing progress of British aviation was being enacted. This time it was not the inter-service rivalry over the ordering of aeroplanes and engines that came under fire — at least, not directly — but the administration of the Royal Flying Corps and the Royal Aircraft Factory at Farnborough, where the Army's aircraft were developed and built. The incident in question was the loss of Royal Aircraft Factory Aeroplane No. 1A and its pilot and passenger (an Army officer) in circumstances that were not fully explained until sixty-two years later.

On 27 June 1916 John Montagu went to the House of Lords to ask what was perhaps the most awkward of all the questions he posed to the Government during the war.

'My Lords', he said, 'I rise to ask His Majesty's Government whether they can give any information to the House as to the start, flight and landing of a certain F.E.2D aeroplane which left Farnborough on 31 May.'

His question was intended not to embarrass the Government (although it undoubtedly did so) but to bring into the open the reasons why the first F.E.2D built for RFC squadron service, equipped with additional armament and powered by one of the first aeroengines to be manufactured by Rolls-Royce, had been inadvertently delivered, not to the RFC at St Omer, but to the German Army at Lille! Coming so soon before the Battle of the Somme this incident gave away all the secrets of Britain's latest aeroplane at a time when it was vital for the RFC to regain supremacy over the battlefields. It was thanks to a tip-off from Claude Johnson, Chief Executive at Rolls-Royce, that John tried to discover what had happened.

Johnson had regarded the outbreak of the war as a disaster for Rolls-Royce, whose sole business at that time was building luxury motor cars. As expected the market for these collapsed completely and it was some time before he and Henry Royce realized that their company had a future — as a manufacturer of aero-engines. Initially they built an engine designed by a French company, Renault, but characteristically Royce decided he could improve on this, and by the end of 1915 his famous twelve cylinder 250 hp Eagle engine was in production for the Admiralty, whose Commander Briggs — John Montagu's future colleague on the Derby Committee — was largely responsible for encouraging and supporting Rolls-Royce during the company's first ventures into what was an entirely new field. Because the Admiralty and the War Office acted independently when ordering aero-engines, Rolls-Royce became one of the first victims of the clashing and overlapping demands on manufacturing resources that Lord Derby tried in vain to prevent. Having originally turned down a tender from Rolls-Royce to build one hundred six cylinder engines designed by the Royal Aircraft Factory, the War Office changed its mind several months later and ordered the engines. In the meantime Rolls-Royce had accepted its first order from the Admiralty for Eagle engines, 25 in all. This meant that the company would have to tool-up to make the Eagle engines, then adapt its machines at great cost in order to make the RAF engines. Anxious to ensure continuity of production of Eagle engines, further orders for which were expected, Rolls-Royce asked the Admiralty to persuade the War Office to have its engines built elsewhere. The War Office refused to do so and Rolls-Royce had to fulfil both orders in succession. This increased the cost of production and caused delays whilst the machines were re-tooled.

It must have been because of anomalies like this that, on 26 June, Johnson sent John Montagu a letter which, he said, had been written by 'a well-known member of the RFC' and was 'undoubtedly authentic'. The original recipient of the letter in question was probably Sir Edward Goulding, a director and future Chairman of Rolls-Royce. In passing it to John, Claude Johnson said he hoped he would read it in the House of Lords but added: 'You had better *not* mention Sir Edward's name nor ours.' Johnson had every reason to request anonymity; as the following extract reveals, it contained some grave allegations:

> The War Office asked for two F.E. pilots, the machines being F.Es in which the engines were placed, to fly them overseas. Owing to an error in the delivery of the message it was understood that the pilots were to fly ordinary F.Es with the result that in one case an inexperienced pilot was sent. I saw the pilot who complained that he was not an experienced F.E. pilot, also that he had never been overseas and was not sure of the way. The authorities there who heard all this took no notice … and told him to take the machine … later a report came through that an F.E. had crossed the lines … and disappeared in the direction of Lille. That evening the German wireless communiqué stated that an F.E. had landed intact southwest of Lille, the pilot having lost his way. Thus it will be seen that within three hours of its having turned out of the factory, our newest and latest machine was handed over to the Huns.

The F.E. aeroplane had been designed by Geoffrey de Havilland and the F.E.2D, which was the penultimate version, was important not only because it was better equipped for aerial combat than its predecessors but also because it introduced the Eagle engine into RFC service.

Although nearly all the hundreds of Eagles ordered in 1915 and early 1916 were built to Admiralty contracts the RFC managed to acquire some engines from the first batch of 25. In his letter to Lord Derby in March 1916, Montagu said that one of the few things the Derby Committee had managed to do was to reallocate a number of engines between departments; the Eagles that were delivered to Farnborough in the early summer of 1916 were almost certainly the ones that John Montagu had referred to. When the controversy over the loss of the F.E.2D erupted, John learned from Claude Johnson that the engine installed in the aeroplane was Eagle engine No. 7 and it was probably this incident that led to the publication, in Germany, of a complete technical description of the engine at a time when it was still Top Secret in Britain. When he sought an explanation for the aeroplane's loss, John was not to know the extent to which the Germans would exploit the incident, but he was aware that the introduction of the F.E.2D would not now have the advantage of being a surprise to the enemy. He quoted the letter from the 'well-known member of the RFC' in full when he spoke to the House of Lords and he put three additional questions direct to Lord Curzon, who as

Lord Privy Seal and Chairman of the Air Board, answered for the Government. John asked him who was responsible for entrusting the F.E.2D to an inexperienced pilot; whether it was true that other pilots with no experience of the Western Front had been ordered to fly there on previous occasions; and whether the Government would ensure that mistakes of this kind did not occur again.

Curzon said he would do his best to answer John's original question but was unable to answer the others in any detail. 'The noble Lord is obviously fully acquainted with all the details,' he said. 'Indeed, it is clear that he knows more about it than I do.' The F.E.2D's pilot and his passenger were now prisoners of war, he went on. He believed that the pilot was inexperienced but it would not be wise to insist that only pilots familiar with the route should deliver aeroplanes across the Channel. Experienced pilots were at that time better employed on the front than in ferrying machines to France. Pilots from both sides had lost their way over the battlefields and landed by mistake in enemy territory. This was one of the risks that had to be faced in aerial warfare.

Curzon had a point. The great offensive on the Somme — which was to become Europe's biggest disaster since the Black Death — was due to begin in a matter of weeks and all experienced pilots were needed at the front. If the lost aeroplane had not been the first of a new type John would probably have let the matter rest. He subsequently learned that the pilot, Lt Littlewood, had not been awarded his 'wings' until 13 May, had been equipped with 'incorrect' maps (according to a letter Littlewood wrote from captivity to his father) and had been forced to land when his engine 'gave up the ghost' after his aircraft was hit by anti-aircraft shells whilst he was flying unwittingly over enemy territory. There was, though, no question — at least in the opinion of Littlewood's father — that Littlewood had complained to the authorities before his flight; he had in actual fact been selected to fly the F.E.2D to France.

It seemed to John that both the RFC and the Royal Aircraft Factory had bungled the whole business. He therefore wrote an account of what was known of the incident for the magazine *Science Progress* and although he never received full answers to his questions, his efforts to find out who was responsible for sending Littlewood to France did result in the affair being examined by the judicial committee that had been set up under the chairmanship of Mr Justice Bailhache to inquire into allegations of maladministration in the flying corps. An RFC officer stationed at Farnborough told the committee that someone at the War Office, whose name he had forgotten, had telephoned to say that Littlewood was to take the F.E.2D to France. The mysterious 'someone', who never owned up, was told that Littlewood had never flown this version of the aeroplane before but the reply from the War Office was that he was capable of doing so. The Bailhache Committee reported that it had not been able to discover how Littlewood was chosen for the job, and that was the last word on the subject until 1978 when a fascinating account of the flight and capture of RAF Aeroplane No. 1A, written by Littlewood's passenger, Captain Douglas Lyall Grant, on 2 June 1916, was published for the first time in a collection of extracts from PoW diaries.*

The Bailhache Committee, which took evidence on 22 days between May and August 1916, was appointed on 10 May and was the Government's response to criticisms of inefficiency in the RFC and concern over the corps' loss of air supremacy in France. John Montagu was the RFC's chief critic in the Lords, whilst similar calls for reform were voiced in the Commons by Colonel Walter Faber and Noel Pemberton Billing. Committees were endemic at this time. Curzon's Air Board was about to try to succeed where the Derby Committee had failed, a month earlier, to coordinate the supply of equipment to the air services, whilst Charles Parsons was about to head an enquiry into alleged bad management at the Royal Aircraft Factory. Later in the summer John was to find that some of the matters that came within the terms of reference of the Bailhache Committee, to which he was invited to give evidence, overlapped those that were supposed to be the concern of Parsons' Committee but initially at least he had no difficulty in presenting Bailhache and his colleagues with detailed criticisms of the way in which the RFC had been unprepared for war. He set out his views in two long memoranda, which he submitted on 26 May. In one of these he was able to state, for the public record, that he had after all been essentially correct when in 1913 he had alleged that the War Office had only 46 aeroplanes and not 101 as had been claimed.

'We had great difficulty in persuading the Government to advance the flying wing', John told Mr Justice Bailhache. 'It seemed as if they had gone to sleep.'

One of Bailhache's colleagues, Mr Balfour Browne, asked: 'Were the reasons for not going forward political?'

John Montagu: 'I would not say, but they did nothing. I gave them many warnings but my warnings fell on deaf ears. The airship policy was constantly changing. Sir David Henderson was convinced that the rigid type of airship would not develop. He has been proved wrong.'

John went on to criticize the Government for expanding the Royal Aircraft factory into a large aircraft manufacturing concern, when it should have remained as a research and experimental establishment (a role to which it later reverted). He said that it was his 'general impression' that the factory

---

* *Black Bread and Barbed Wire*. Edited by Michael Moynihan; published by Leo Cooper.

was regarded as a competitor by privately owned manufacturers and that they viewed the factory with suspicion and dislike. He added that they were unwilling to give evidence to the committee because they were afraid of losing contracts or being victimized. He also claimed that designs belonging to private manufacturers had been submitted to the factory — his inference being that the War Office was thereby giving the factory a commercial advantage over private industry.

In making these allegations John left himself open to a probing cross-examination from David Henderson, who was present at the hearing to defend the RFC. John had said that he deplored private industry's distrust of the aircraft factory. 'So do I', commented Henderson, 'and also the people who foster it'. He seemed to imply that John was one of those doing the fostering.

Henderson then asked John to produce evidence that private designs were submitted to the factory.

Montagu: 'The manufacturer always says that he has submitted his design'.

Henderson: 'To whom?'

Montagu: 'To you. Will you give me your word of honour that a design has never been taken to the factory?'

Henderson: 'I am asking you a question and you are giving evidence. Have you any evidence whatever that a private design has ever been submitted to the Royal Aircraft Factory?'

Montagu: 'That is a manufacturers' question. I cannot produce the manufacturers here'.

Henderson: 'That is a definite statement and I deny it. I say it is entirely without foundation. You have no evidence except your statement here'.

Montagu: 'No. That is my statement'.

Clearly, John failed to press home his allegations because he relied on 'general impressions' instead of coming to the hearing armed with specific evidence. Even though, as he said, private manufacturers would not have been willing to be identified because they feared victimization, he could have guaranteed them anonymity in exchange for hard facts. One of those who could perhaps have helped him was Claude Johnson, although it must be said that Rolls-Royce had no reason to quarrel with the Royal Aircraft Factory. The company was in any case more involved with the Admiralty at this time but it had been offered one of the factory's aero-engine designs, the RAF3, for development and completion — a case of the Government submitting one of its own designs to private industry, whereas John had complained that the traffic in plans was moving in the opposite direction. As it happened, Rolls-Royce decided to develop its own engine, the Eagle, instead of developing the RAF3, but the company's experience with the RAF3 shows that the War

Office's procedures did not necessarily always place private industry at a disadvantage.

At his next appearance before the Bailhache Committee, on 11 July, John persisted in criticizing the management of the aircraft factory even though by now Parsons had completed his inquiry. John announced that he intended to call two anonymous witnesses from the factory and ask them to give evidence of wastage of materials and manpower. The first witness, called Mr A, was asked whether he had noticed any wastage.

'Oh yes. A tremendous amount of scrapping. Quite excessive. It is reported — of course, I cannot prove it — that 27,000 pieces were scrapped in June.'

General Sir Horace Smith-Dorrien, who had commanded one of the BEF's corps in France in 1914, was a member of the committee and he asked Mr A whether the scrap consisted of finished work or parts that did not meet their specification.

Mr A: 'Some possibly are half finished'.

At this point the committee's Chairman seems to have lost patience with John over his line of questioning. He reminded him that the Parsons Committee had already inquired into the Royal Aircraft Factory and that the Bailhache Committee was concerned with design and manufacture at the factory, not its administration.

Montagu: 'That is one point I criticized very strongly and was asked to bring evidence about'.

Chairman: 'There has been an independent inquiry about that'.

Montagu: 'I am going to show by my witness that the inquiry did not learn the truth that they should have learnt'.

Chairman: 'We cannot inquire into an inquiry'.

Sir Charles Parsons was in fact a member of the Bailhache Committee and he said that the allegation that 27,000 parts had been scrapped meant nothing unless the total number of parts made in the month in question was known. Even in the best regulated workshops parts had to be scrapped because of workmen's carelessness. John pressed on.

'There have been several visits of committees to the factory and two visits by the King?' he asked.

Mr A: 'Yes. Special instructions were given on these occasions to keep the machines busy in all the shops. Parts of aeroplanes were fixed up to look real and soon after the King left some of the shops were as empty as they had been before he came'.

Montagu: 'In other words there was a great deal of window dressing.'

Mr A went on to say that men at the factory played cricket in working hours and that a quarter of them were 'duds', either because they were avoiding military service by working at the factory or because they were doing jobs for which they were not qualified. He added: 'I never saw a place with so many foremen. The general way of putting it is "One man, one foreman"'.

Mr Balfour Browne: 'We really cannot inquire into this'.

Montagu: 'Surely this sort of evidence affects the efficiency of engines and the quantity of output?'

John was allowed to proceed but after Mr A had given further evidence of time-wasting, needless scrapping and pilfering of materials, the Chairman ruled that the committee could not hear any more evidence of that kind.

Montagu: 'I think it is a pity that you do not want to hear corroborative evidence as to the special preparations for the visit of the King'.

Chairman: 'We do not want any more evidence'.

Montagu: 'May I take it you do not contest that point?'

Chairman: 'You can take only what I have said'.

Montagu: 'I have a witness here who ... can speak at first-hand on that point, showing that the factory was faked for the purpose. If the committee do not wish to hear him there is no more to be said. I have my own remedy to make it public through other channels.'

He did not need to do so. The Superintendent of the factory, Colonel Mervyn O'Gorman, explained that at the time the King visited the factory he was recovering from an accident and therefore special arrangements were made in the workshops so that he would not have to walk too far.

Again, John seems to have failed to prepare his case with sufficient thoroughness. As had happened during his earlier appearance before the committee, the establishment won the argument. When the committee published its final report in December 1916 it 'whitewashed' those who had been responsible for the RFC's set-backs and dismissed as 'frivolous' John's suggestion that private firms regarded the aircraft factory as a competitor. The committee did make the important recommendation that the responsibilities of equipping and commanding the RFC should be separated, since David Henderson could no longer be expected to do both jobs. It was also suggested that a single department should be formed to supply equipment to both air services. However the committee did not go so far as to advocate uniting the services into a single air force.

By the time the Bailhache Committee reported John Montagu had made his long-delayed return voyage to India, but not without delivering some final ripostes, in articles in *The Times* and in memoranda to the Government, on the need to amalgamate the air services. By now there had been a marked improvement in the RFC's performance on the Western Front and the corps now had about 600 aeroplanes — twice as many as in February 1916. John was now developing another argument in his demands for greater air power; he wanted the creation of an Air or Aviation Ministry to be followed by the formation of a third service. This would be an independent air force, called the Imperial Air Service, which would carry the aerial conflict into the heart of Germany and, after the war, help develop aviation throughout the British Empire.

John called for a force of 10,000 aeroplanes, 6000 of them to be bombers, to be assembled by the summer of 1917 to attack targets up to 200 miles behind the enemy's front line. He also wanted a permanent force of 20,000 aeroplanes to be created after the war to form an 'air cordon' around England for the purpose of deterring future enemies.

All this was, perhaps, rather too much to ask for but when John arrived in Simla he was heartened to learn that the Air Board had been reconstituted under Lord Cowdray as a department of state and given executive powers to control the design and supply of aircraft to the RFC and RNAS. The foundations of an Air Ministry were at last being laid.

16

The Montagu Doctrine

John Montagu's second attempt to return to India nearly came to the same fateful conclusion as his voyage of 11 months earlier. Mindful of his previous experience in the Mediterranean and aware that losses of Allied merchant ships had increased alarmingly throughout 1916, he wrote two letters before leaving London on 3 November. They were intended to put his mind at rest on two matters that were causing him some concern. The first letter contained explicit instructions on the arrangements his family should make for his funeral 'in the event of my death in this war or in any other way'. The second letter remained unopened for nearly 13 years and a secret for another 40, when its contents were revealed in extraordinary circumstances that will be described later.

Both letters show that John believed his chances of surviving another passage between Marseilles and Port Said were slim. His apprehension was heightened when his ship, whose passengers included 200 women and children, twice encountered enemy U-boats whilst heading for Malta. On both occasions their aim was inaccurate although in the more alarming of the two incidents a torpedo missed the ship by only 12 feet. John's arrival at Malta afforded him no respite from the fear and tension he and his fellow travellers had shared since leaving Marseilles, for they then learned that SS *Arabia* — SS *Persia*'s sister ship — had been sunk by a U-boat whilst steaming towards Malta from Port Said.

Nevertheless John reached the haven of the Suez Canal and eventually Bombay safely. By Christmas he had started his second tour of duty as Inspector of Motor Vehicles with the Military Works Branch of Army Headquarters. More and more motor vehicles were now arriving in India and although, even by the end of the war, there were never enough to satisfy all the roles and duties John had advocated, there were sufficient lorries in service by 1917 to create a shortage of skilled drivers. On John's recommendation India's first mechanical transport drivers' school was opened at Sohan, near Rawalpindi. Within a year this was turning out 300-400 drivers a month, most of whom were posted to MT companies in Mesopotamia where, as John was among the first to perceive, the military defeats of 1916 had largely been caused by a lack of motor transport.

The Sohan school was established by Col. John Hodgkinson of the 5th Cavalry and commanded by his twin brother Charles, a colonel in the 6th Cavalry. Later a second driving school was opened at Meerut, under John Hodgkinson. The Hodgkinsons were among the comparatively few senior officers who regarded John not as a crank but as a prophet, and supported his efforts to replace camels, mules and bullock carts with motor vehicles. Many veteran colonels of the supply and transport corps opposed John's ideas with all the indignation they could muster, realizing that the new motor companies could be administered by far fewer officers. To make matters worse, comfortable and undemanding postings to forage farms and the like were becoming a thing of the past now that the energy to move men and supplies up mountain passes was being derived from petrol instead of fodder. Charles and John Hodgkinson belonged to the minority who welcomed the Army's new mobility; their long friendship with John that was to lead them to spend their retirement in cottages on his estate at Beaulieu stemmed from the period when they took up their appointments at Sohan and Meerut.

During his second visit to India, John spent most of his time working on his scheme to introduce proper driving instruction into the Indian Army and on proposals for a training school for armoured car and motor machine gun personnel. He also toured the widely scattered MT units to make his annual report on their efficiency, and revisited the North-West Frontier to inspect the road construction work that was now in progress following recommendations he had made in 1915 to Maj. Gen. Williams, Director General of Military Works. Pleased with what he had seen, John returned to Army Headquarters in Delhi in February 1917 to complete his report but he then had to return to England somewhat earlier than he had intended, since on 7 March he received a telegram advising him that, under powers granted to it by the Defence of the Realm Act, the Admiralty intended to purchase one of the Montagu family's estates, Ditton Park.

John had fond memories of Ditton and of the visits he made to see his grandmother there whilst he was at school at nearby Eton. The moated mansion and its 200 acres of lush parkland had once belonged to the 2nd Baron Montagu of Boughton and was one of the properties that John inherited in 1905. But neither he nor Lady Montagu stayed there very often. They found the mock-Gothic house, with its 60 bedrooms, unmanageable and uncomfortable, and appear to have made several unsuccessful attempts to sell the place before the First World War. The Admiralty wanted Ditton Park in order to transfer its compass laboratory from Deptford, in South-east London, to the open countryside west of the capital, so that marine and aircraft compasses could be tested and developed in a 'magnetically clean' area far away from the electrical interference created by London's new electric trams and railways.

John was given a month in which to remove his chattels from Ditton and exchange contracts with the Admiralty, hence his somewhat hurried arrival in London in mid-April. He accomplished the move with the help of the Thornycroft company of Basingstoke, which was road-testing a number of lorries at this time and quite happy to allow them to transport John's furniture and family treasures from Ditton to Beaulieu. He received £20,000 for the house and grounds within the moat. Later the Admiralty purchased the rest of the park for another £20,000. Garden Cottage, the little house Eleanor Thornton had shared with her sister Rose, was not included in the deal; John leased it to Rose for £15 a year and she lived there with her husband Gordon Hayter (who had been one of Montagu's writers on *The Car Illustrated*) until she died in 1945. In the event, John need not have rushed back from India. The Admiralty postponed its move from Deptford until 1918 but this still left time for Ditton Park to contribute to the war effort, since it was there that the aperiodic compass was invented. Until then the limitations of existing air compasses had restricted the usefulness of aeroplanes as strategic weapons. The aperiodic compass contributed immeasurably to the development of the strategic bombers that John regarded as essential to Britain's air prowess. Ditton Park is still the Admiralty Compass Station.

John's return to England coincided with important developments in aviation. The first was the appearance over the Home Counties and London of a new German menace, the Gotha twin-engined bomber. Once again John found himself back in the centre of the constantly erupting controversy over Britain's inability to defend her own air space. The second, less contentious, development was the Government's far-sighted establishment of a committee, under Lord Northcliffe, to advise how civil aviation should be encouraged once the war was over. John joined the committee as the India Office's representative.

But the bombing became his first concern. As early as 1914 Germany had drawn up a plan to raid English cities and military sites using aeroplanes, not airships. That plan depended on the capture of airfields on the French coast within bombing range of England. When this failed, airship raids were launched from airfields on the German coast — frightening the civilian population of England even though, in military terms, the damage and injury caused by the raids was insignificant. By the spring of 1917 the anti-aircraft defences were coping quite well with the Zeppelin threat, but the situation changed dramatically in May when the Germans began to blitz England with their new Gothas, which unlike their earlier aeroplanes could reach England from airfields in Belgium.

The first raids killed nearly 100 people and injured 195 others in Sheerness and Folkestone but on 13 June a force of 14 Gothas made the first aeroplane raid on London. More than 160 people were killed and 432 injured in eastern areas of the capital, and the bombers managed to penetrate as far as Liverpool Street Station. This was too close to Whitehall for comfort. In 1909 John had warned that 'war airships' could dislocate railway services and whilst his other fear — 'panic of the wildest description' — did not materialize, there was such a public uproar that next day the Cabinet decided to double the number of RFC service squadrons. The idea of creating a strategic air force to bomb Germany was also, at last, given serious consideration.

The British took a long time to accept that, in total war, bombing an enemy's cities is a legitimate way to weaken its will and ability to continue the fight. The argument over whether it is morally right for warring nations to bomb each other's civilian populations continues to this day. John very quickly placed himself among the hawks, decrying those who complained that London was an undefended city and should not be regarded by Germany as a legitimate target. In yet another of the House of Lords' debates on air policy he enraged many of his fellow peers and a large section of the British public by saying:

> It is absolute humbug to talk about London being an undefended city. The Germans have a perfect right to raid London. It is defended by guns and squadrons of aeroplanes and it is the chief seat of energy for the war. We are only deluding ourselves when we talk of London being an undefended city and of no military importance and say that in attacking it the Germans are carrying out some act which is not worthy of a civilized nation.

John had preceded this statement by declaring that with the advent of the new German bombers the front line of the war now extended to anywhere within their range. He concluded his speech by calling on the Government to tell the civilian population that, because Britain was short of aeroplanes, it could not provide absolute protection against air raids. In what was now a war of nations, not armies alone, civilians in London — like those in France and Belgium — must now expect to bear casualties. Not surprisingly he took the opportunity to demand once again the creation of a supreme command for the air services, so that the war in the air could be prosecuted more effectively. All this, though, was generally ignored; what received all the attention was his comment: 'The Germans have a perfect right to raid London'. The reaction of the magazine *Flying* typified the uproar John's speech generated:

> Lord Montagu exonerates the Germans. He grants them full absolution. He gives them *carte blanche*. He hands them a blank cheque. The Montagu doctrine covers any and every form of indiscriminate bomb dropping. There is no limit whatever to the slaughter of civilians that may lawfully be carried out by squadrons of aircraft flying at a height which precludes the possibility of aiming at a military objective. Apparently the Montagu doctrine would justify the extermination of every man, woman and child

in London; for if it is justifiable to slay a hundred civilians it would be justifiable to slay a million or 5 million.

The row even brought John into conflict with his friend Lord Derby, now Secretary of State for War. During the Lords debate Derby was handed a note from the Opposition front bench demanding that John's speech be censored. Evidently, Derby agreed with the many members of both parties who felt that John had given valuable military information away by talking about the military importance of London and the difficulty of defending the city. Derby spoke privately to John after the debate and a few hours later John wrote to him to explain his position:

> Surely the Government realizes that the Germans know where every gun and searchlight is and every place of military importance or munitions factory in or near London? And should we not bomb Berlin (which is equally but not so well defended by guns etc.) if we could? And do you not think that our people would bear their casualties better if they were told the truth, that we cannot defend all our fronts at the moment because we are short of machines to do it?
>
> I have been and always shall be most careful to refrain even by implication from giving any information which could possibly help the hated Hun. But believe me, as an old friend who moves about more in unofficial circles than you do, that the public has nearly ceased to believe altogether in official statements on account of their ambiguous character ... Why not tell them when possible the real facts? They are not children and most of us realize that the Hun knows much more than the Government thinks he knows. Prevarication and suppression of news is futile and is already doing much to make this Government unpopular and diminish confidence in the executive — a most serious and growing feature in our public life. *

Derby was not persuaded. There was, he said, a great difference between telling the nation that the Government would do all it could to protect its citizens, even though there was only a limited number of aeroplanes available, and in saying that London was a legitimate target which the Government was incapable of protecting. He added:

> I am quite certain that within a week's time there will not be a German

---

* During 1917 John became a supporter of the new National Party, formed by Henry Paget-Croft and Lord Duncannon (the future Lord Bessborough). The party's aim was to urge the Government to take a firmer, more committed, approach to the war. John's support seems to have been confined to taking part in meetings of the party in October and November. His military duties overseas then prevented him from pursuing any ideas he may have had of becoming more closely involved in the party's affairs. By the time he returned to England in 1918 the party was moribund.

newspaper that will not quote your remarks as justifying what they had done and beg their Government to continue to bombard London.

As was usually the case John had the last word. The notion that Germany's strategic bombing policy would be influenced by newspaper reaction to his speech was, in his opinion, ludicrous. So was the idea that anything he had said about London's importance and its poor defences would be news to the Germans. Replying to Lord Derby he said:

> I do not think anything I or anyone else can say has the least effect on German military plans. They will continue to bomb London if it pays to do so. If it doesn't, they won't. The German newspapers for a long time past have constantly stated that London was bristling with anti-aircraft guns and that we were increasing our power of air defence month by month, which is perfectly true. What I said can be no news to them.
>
> Of course neither we nor the Germans have any right to kill non-combatants but in this war I cannot see that in bombardments of towns from the air any distinction can be made ... We have already bombarded Ostend and many places behind the enemy lines full of civilians, many of whom we have unfortunately killed. I am very sorry that I should have given you even the impression that anything I said would help the Hun. Personally I think the truth helps us, not them, and that the Government should try to tell the truth.

He could have added that, if the Government seriously believed that his speech would have serious consequences, it would have censored it, as demanded by the Opposition.

The controversy over the 'Montagu doctrine' had hardly abated when, on 7 July, London suffered its second aeroplane raid. This time 22 Gothas bombed various parts of the capital, causing 57 deaths and injuring nearly 200 people. As had been the case in June, nearly 100 British fighters tried with little success to intercept the bombers. This time there were signs of the wild panic John had foreseen seven years earlier. Rioters unleashed their anger on anything that had, or appeared to have, any connection with Germany. Shops whose owners' names ended in '-stein' or '-berg' were wrecked or looted and, according to some sources, dachshunds were kicked to death in the street.

The Government's next move was to divert two RFC squadrons to home defence and appoint Lt Gen.J.C.Smuts to report on the whole question of air warfare. One outcome of the Smuts report was the foundation of the Royal Air Force in 1918 but his immediate recommendation was that a new London Air Defence Area should be set up under Brig.Gen. 'Splash' Ashmore. This was equipped with sufficient firepower to break up bomber formations before they reached central London and was supported by fighter aeroplanes which now flew in formation (rather than singly as before) so that they could help split up the bombers and then set upon them individually. The scheme worked well enough to force Germany to abandon daylight raids but it was less successful when the Gothas started a series of night bombardments on London. The first of these left the shrapnel marks that can still be seen today on Cleopatra's Needle on the Thames Embankment.

By November the public was as concerned about the night raids as it had been about the earlier daylight raids. John tried to ventilate the problem in Parliament by giving notice to the House of Lords of his intention:

> To call attention to the recent air raids on London and other towns, and to ask whether without conveying information to the enemy the Government can make any statement as to steps they propose to take to defeat the enemy's aircraft and defend the capital.

It was a loaded question. The phrase 'without conveying information to the enemy' was doubtless included in deference to Lord Derby but this time the Government was determined to avoid the kind of row that had occurred after John's previous speech on the subject of air raids. Lord Curzon, Leader of the Lords, asked Montagu to withdraw his motion. He did so under protest, commenting: 'I am sorry the debate cannot take place as there is no doubt great public feeling on this question. I am sure that nothing would have been said which would have given any information to the enemy or been anything but helpful.'

Whilst saying no more in public, John did protest privately about his treatment. In a letter to Lord Curzon he said:

> I desire to place on record my opinion that the action of the Government in asking me to withdraw my motion as to air raids on London is unwise. So far the only Parliamentary debate has been that initiated by Mr Joynson Hicks and other members of the Parliamentary Air Committee in the House of Commons. The general impression among the people of London is that the Government has been lax in preparations to defend the capital and are disposed to be callous now as to what people are suffering ... I should have made a speech showing clearly how difficult it is to prevent raids reaching London and pointed out some new means of warning which would give confidence. The Government may, perhaps, regret eventually that the opportunity given by a friend who could have helped correct erroneous impressions was not taken advantage of. As you probably know the public has very little faith in official statements.
>
> I have no official position which limits my freedom of action but my objective was to help. My consent to withdraw on this occasion is only in regard to this particular motion.

John outlined the 'new means of warning' in a memo to Lord Cowdray,

President of the Air Board. During a visit to France and Italy in October he had seen such innovations as listening posts capable of estimating the direction and height of approaching bombers, 'circular barrages' of guns and searchlights around important buildings and anti-aircraft 'aprons' of wire supported by balloons. Although John was probably unaware of the fact, 'Splash' Ashmore was already working on plans for further improvements in ways of observing and reporting the movement of enemy bombers and bringing the ack-ack batteries and fighter squadrons into action. Radio and radar were to come later — in the case of radar, more than 20 years later — but the familiar control rooms of 1940 were already beginning to take shape.

The calmer currents of civil aviation provided John Montagu with a welcome refuge from the stormy arguments that raged throughout 1917 whenever the war in the air was discussed. On 31 May he attended his first meeting of the Air Board's new Civil Aerial Transport Committee, which was asked to suggest firstly how civil aviation should be developed and regulated when the war ended, and secondly how the airmen and aeroplanes of the RFC and RNAS could be employed in a civilian role. Lord Northcliffe was nominally the CATC's Chairman but he departed for the USA as head of a war mission soon after its first meeting, leaving the Under-Secretary of State for Air, Maj. J. L. Baird, in charge. It was a large committee, consisting of 40 members and 21 co-opted experts. In addition to representing the India Office, John served on a special sub-committee whose function was to look into the scientific and technical aspects of aeronautics. Here he studied air traffic control, the layout of landing grounds and other problems alongside such luminaries as Brig.Gen. Sefton Brancker (then the War Office's Deputy Director of Military Aeronautics), aeroplane designer Tommy Sopwith and H. G. Wells.

By May 1917 John had made many speeches and written numerous articles on the future of civil and military aviation. Committees, inquiries and campaigns were part of his daily routine and soon his position as Britain's most vociferous spokesman on air matters was to be consolidated by his election to the position of President of the Aerial (later Air) League of the British Empire. But if any one single event led to his appointment on the CATC it was probably the lecture he gave in January 1917 at the Imperial Gymkhana Club in Delhi on the subject of 'Aviation, Present and Future'. There he made the bold prophecy that within ten years India would become the destination for the first long-distance passenger and mail flights from England. The idea was greeted with polite jeers — an understandable reaction considering that there were as yet no long-range aeroplanes of any kind, civil or military. In his lecture John was probably the first person to propose publicly, in any detail, how such a service would operate. The distance, he remarked, was not great — a mere 3600 miles. Passengers would leave Peshawar at 7 am on a Monday morning, stop overnight at Gurieff (near the Caspian Sea) and Tarapol and arrive at Hendon aerodrome, in north London, at 6 o'clock on Wednesday evening. Alternatively passengers and mail could follow an 'all red' route from Karachi to England, flying for most of the time over British territory with overnight halts at Basrah, Alexandria, Malta and Gibraltar. The fare: £70 return.

As aids to navigation, John proposed that white circles should be painted on the ground at five mile intervals and miniature lighthouses set up every ten miles to shine brilliant beams of light into the air. Special lights would be set up to guide pilots as they descended to their landing grounds. It sounds slightly comical today but in the days before radio beacons and radar, marks and lights were the only fixed navigational aids available. In the early years of trans-continental aviation, pilots had to make do with very rudimentary help including, on the route to India, furrows ploughed in the desert. For their time, John's airway marks were sensible enough but his ideas for aerodrome layouts left a little to be desired. He proposed building hotels and other airport buildings in the middle of a mound which would become progressibly steeper from edge to centre. The idea was that aeroplanes would head for these mounds as they landed and be slowed down as they climbed the slope. The inherent dangers of such a system need not be described.

The Delhi lecture was the first of several imaginative and thought-provoking excursions into a subject which, to the audiences of that period, bordered on science fiction. The separation of air traffic into flight levels and air lanes, the identification of aeroplanes by means of letters denoting their country of registration, the issuing of pilots' licences, the preparation of weather forecasts and the use of prevailing winds to reduce flying times — all these and many other topics were discussed by John in some detail, both during and after the time he served on the CATC. In February 1918 the committee published a report which charted the future course of British civil aviation. The technical sub-committee on which John sat investigated the cost of operating a number of commercial routes, one of which — London to South Africa — was John's special responsibility. When, in the 1920s, regular flights on these routes began, the sub-committee's costings and other data proved to be substantially sound.

It was, however, as an advocate of an Imperial air service to India that John became famous and it is not surprising that Rudyard Kipling — his favourite author — was among those whose support he canvassed. On receiving a copy of John's proposals Kipling replied:

Guard them well, for these are an historical document and will be marked 1 : 1 in the archives of the ABC of the future. I have outlined your India route on my 24 in. globe where it looks very fine. The first Imperial air route laid down. Do you think that air traffic will excite the average Asiatic after the first year? The Arab doesn't fuss about 'planes in the desert and my own experience of the native of India is that once he has given a new thing a name he is as profoundly incurious as a metaphysician or a psychologist after he has labelled a new phenomenon. He will probably let it buzz about overhead without raising his eyes.

John attended his last CATC meeting on 16 November 1917. On that day he received a letter from Gieves Limited saying that his inflatable waistcoat had been severely tested and was in perfect condition. Equipped once more for the hazards of the high seas he embarked next day on his third wartime visit to India — sailing this time from Liverpool, since he had arranged to return to his duties via Canada, Hong Kong and Singapore. With the approval of Sefton Brancker and Lord Cowdray he intended to make a series of speeches to rally support for two ideas for which support was by now growing in Britain — the formation of an independent air force (which materialized as the Royal Air Force) and the establishment of an Imperial air service between Britain and her empire. He also intended to help recruit pilots from overseas for the RFC.

John arrived at St Johns, New Brunswick, on 1 December but before setting off on a speaking tour that was to take him to Canada's six principal cities, he visited New York. There, at the Hotel Chatham, on or about 8 December, he was reunited with his wayward 27-year-old daughter Helen, who had left home several years earlier to become a showgirl and an occasional (and reluctant) straight actress in New York. In 1916 Helen had married Arthur Clark-Kennedy. By the time of John's visit the marriage was already heading for divorce, but this had not diminished her zest for life nor interrupted her career. John had arrived in New York in military uniform and for this reason decided against meeting Helen at the theatre where she was appearing; no one at the stage door would believe that the dapper 51-year-old British Army officer had come to meet his daughter! Instead, he sat through the show and then sent a note backstage inviting Helen to come to his hotel for supper.

She arrived, dressed to kill, and asked the desk clerk to phone John in his room and tell him she had arrived. With a leer, the clerk called John and said: 'There's a lady here to see you, Lord Montagu. She *says* she is your daughter! Shall I send some champagne up too?'

About two months later, in mid-February 1918, John arrived back on the North-West Frontier. He now had a new title, Adviser on Mechanical Transport Services, which reflected the extent to which his duties had widened during the previous three years. In addition, the administration of India's military motor transport had been transferred from the Military

Collier's portrait of John Montagu.

Works Branch of Army Headquarters to the Quartermaster General's Branch. By this time there were 1620 Army motor vehicles in India and 3250 men were serving with the MT companies. The only area where there had been a major lack of progress, so far as the provision of motor vehicles was concerned, was in the 16 armoured car units, which still had less than 50 cars between them. Another 49, a gift from the Canadian Government, were on their way but only about 20 arrived. The rest were sunk by enemy action in the Mediterranean or diverted to the Army in Ireland.

John's visit to India in 1918 was, by and large, uneventful. He returned to the India Office in London in June, when he was made a temporary brigadier general, going back to India for his last spell of duty there in January 1919, when he made his last wartime visit to the North-West Frontier; since 1915 he had made no less than 14 complete tours of the Frontier from Karachi to Kashmir.

When he set off for home in April he left the country in a much more advanced state than it had been when he was appointed Inspector of Motor Vehicles in April 1915. The forces there now had 4000 motor vehicles, 70 armoured cars, 7000 MT personnel and 1000 miles of strategic roads over which to travel.* Whilst serving in India and at the India Office John received normal rates of pay, plus the standard Army of Occupation bonus of 42 shillings a week. In recognition of his services he was made a Knight Commander of the Indian Empire. On 1 November 1919 he returned to civilian life to face what was to be a period of great personal upheaval, followed by a resumption of his peacetime efforts to transform travel on wheels, wings and water.

---

* These included the metalled road through the Khyber Pass, featured as a background to the Hon. John Collier's portrait of John Montagu which is now on permanent view to the public at Palace House, Beaulieu.

17

The London-Liverpool Motorway

Cis Montagu had been in poor health for several years by the time John retired from the Army. A bout of rheumatic fever in childhood had left her with a weak heart and her many anxieties during 30 years of marriage, including John's *affaire* with Eleanor Thornton, his narrow escape from death aboard SS *Persia* and his long absences abroad must have taken their toll. John himself was not always as considerate and sympathetic as he should have been. Elizabeth recalls: 'He used to be irritated by my mother because she was not well enough to go out. I remember my mother being very distressed and I remember being very angry with my father. I think they were just not suited. They were poles apart.'

Cis died on 13 September 1919. Despite their basic incompatibility their marriage had been, to all outward appearances, a happy one, thanks to Cis's passive reaction to her husband's behaviour. John, surely, acknowledged that his success as a public figure owed much to her unselfish support. Her death, we must assume, caused him grief and perhaps remorse.

His life, though, resumed a course similar to that which he had followed before the war. Sometime in 1919 he had a brief and passionate *affaire* with Madge Limby, remembered by Elizabeth as a cool blonde in what, 25 years later, would have been called the Lauren Bacall mould. Madge Limby was one of the Beaulieu estate's most colourful personalities; she was at one time the proprietor of a tea-shop in the village but always in arrears with her rent and income-tax — despite the constant efforts of Mr Ashmead, the estate's accountant, to keep her finances in proper order. Madge Limby exploited her 'film star' looks a few years later when she acted as an extra in an early movie, *The Virgin Queen*, starring Lady Diana Cooper and Sir Guy Laking, filmed on location at Beaulieu. At the time of her *affaire* with John she was married to one of his Army friends, Major Limby; he was the first of her three husbands, the last being Col. John Hodgkinson.

Curiously, Major and Mrs Limby were two of John's three companions (the other was Archibald Marshall) when he set off from Beaulieu on 9 February 1920 to resume his pre-war habit of enjoying a winter holiday in the south of France. On this occasion he travelled in a style to which he was not accustomed. During his previous holidays he and his chauffeur Teddy Stephens had always taken turns behind the wheel of his latest Silver Ghost. This time, however, John was betwixt Rolls-Royces. He had taken his London-Edinburgh type to India during the war and sold it there. Now, in early 1920, the Barker-bodied open tourer that was to be his next Rolls-Royce had not yet been delivered. Instead, he and his companions somehow squeezed themselves into a four-seater Delage, although once they arrived in southern France the Limbys hired a Rolls.

John's destination was, as usual, Velascure by way of St. Raphael and on 13 February he pulled in at one of his favourite hotels, the Beau Rivage, intent on staying for a few days. Among the guests already in residence were Mrs Clara Alice Barrington-Crake and her effervescent 24-year-old daughter Pearl, who 60 years later recalled: 'We were sitting at our table when an Englishman came into the room. He was wearing an Old Etonian tie and a Royal Yacht Squadron tie-pin. He had been taking other guests for drives into the mountains and he asked my mother and me whether we would like to go for a drive.'

Soon after this little excursion, John's brief holiday came to an end and he motored over the Alps to Vienna to join his friend Sir Francis Dent of the South Eastern Railway at an international railway conference; he then went on to Budapest to stay with Sir Ernest Troubridge, head of the Inter-allied Commission of the Danube.

A few months later John visited the Barrington-Crakes at their home in London. It was presumed by his friends that he was attracted to his contemporary but to everyone's surprise he became engaged to the daughter, Pearl, in June and they were married at St. Margaret's, Westminster, on 10 August 1920. Among the wedding presents they received was a framed photograph of LSWR locomotive number 468 which John had driven between Bournemouth and London during the 1919 rail strike. The picture was a gift from a group of ASLEF members and came with an illuminated address expressing the enginemen's and firemen's appreciation for his many kindnesses over the years. Later the Bournemouth branch of ASLEF dissociated itself from the gift, writing to John to say: 'We never dreamt such a thing would be done in our name for, as you know, your action in the recent strike was not appreciated ... for a few men here to send this photo is such a high-handed action on their part and a libel on us as a body of men'. The letter was followed by an ASLEF delegation, which politely explained the union's point of view. John, always sympathetic to the railwaymen's cause and one of the few peers with a personal insight into their problems, listened patiently. The incident ended with both sides understanding the other's outlook and the delegation made a dignified departure.

John's second wife, Pearl.

John and Pearl after their wedding at St Margaret's, Westminster.

John and Pearl with Arthur Jacomb, who drove their honeymoon train.

In 1920 the brief post-war boom ended and unemployment started soaring towards the two million mark. All around there were signs of economic decline and decay — especially on the roads, which were still unprepared for the vast increase in motor traffic that even the diehards now knew to be inevitable. To some extent the war had benefited highway construction, for despite cut-backs in expenditure the Road Board had been authorized to build numerous roads for military use. After the war it was asked to prepare a £40 million roadworks programme to create jobs for ex-servicemen and others who were having difficulty in finding employment. In 1919, though, the Board, of which John had been a founder member, was absorbed into the new Ministry of Transport. He was then unable to exert his influence on general road policy from within, although he did become Chairman of the War Office's Joint Roads Committee, which dealt with war damage claims. He also remained on the committee of the Roads Improvement Association, a pressure group whose title fully explains its objectives.

John was deeply suspicious of the new Transport Ministry, arguing that it gave its Minister the absolute right to dictate what transport should use the roads and what should use the railways. He criticized the Minister, Sir Eric Geddes, for 'surrounding himself with railway officials' and renewed his campaign for the construction of better roads, which he regarded as being of greater potential value to the nation than railways. He argued that £50 million should be raised for new trunk roads by issuing a National Road Bond and by imposing tolls on road users.

John's early post-war speeches, lectures and articles on the need for new roads and the development of motor transport culminated in a series of articles on road reform which he was commissioned to write for *The Times* in 1921. He began by making a county-by-county tour of England, interviewing local surveyors and making copious notes, with Pearl's help, on the condition of the hundreds of miles of roads over which they travelled. Pearl's abiding memories of their journeys are of the potholes and ruts they had to negotiate in their Rolls-Royce Barker tourer and of the tasteless salads that were practically all that roadside hotels could offer for lunch. John's articles appeared in 12 consecutive issues of *The Times* at the beginning of the long, hot summer of 1921 and he concluded his final instalment with these words:

> Developments which are at present only dreamed of will be accomplished facts when our children grow up. Public services on the road by night and day and in every direction will develop in the next few years. Speeds and weights now thought dangerous or impracticable will then be the commonplace burdens of every road. The blood of traffic will course through the national arteries and veins with increasing force. The circulation must not be restricted ... we must make ready for the needs of

*In the 1920s, John resumed his motoring activities in the style to which he was accustomed.
He is seen here at the wheel of his Rolls-Royce outside Palace House.*

the future, for the value of road power to the nation will increase with
every succeeding year.

If John needed to re-establish himself after the war as Britain's leading
spokesman for roads and road transport, his articles in *The Times* had the
desired effect. Soon after they were published he became the paper's regular
transport correspondent, contributing articles on all aspects of motoring and
highway engineering. He wrote in similar vein for *Country Life* and the
Spectator and resumed his contributions to *The Car Illustrated*, which had run
into financial difficulties in 1916 and now belonged to publishers E. J. Burrow
Limited of Cheltenham, of which he was Chairman. John's freelance writing
activities were interrupted for three months in early 1922, when he and Pearl
spent a long holiday in India. During this time they met the Prince of Wales, a
young naval lieutenant by the name of Louis Mountbatten and his fiancée
Edwina Ashley. The Montagu and Ashley families had been friends and
neighbours for years, Broadlands being only about twenty miles from
Beaulieu. A year later John's friendship with Edwina's father, Col. Wilfrid
Ashley (the future Lord Mount Temple) would prove to be less useful than
he would have wished.

Whilst in India, John and Pearl drove for 1500 miles along roads that had been built in the frontier regions during his wartime service there. They had taken their Rolls-Royce to India, hoping to sell it there before returning to England, but they found that by now nearly every Maharaja owned one, so they had to bring the car back to England at considerable cost.

John resumed his journalistic work as soon as he arrived home and by April 1923 was advocating a radical solution to London's traffic congestion, in the shape of overhead roads from the London docks to Marble Arch and from the Surrey Docks to Battersea. It was a theme to which he returned again and again but his idea was 40 years ahead of its time. It was not until the 1960s that work began on the elevated motorway that links central London with its western approaches.

Overhead roads were a startling enough concept in 1923 but there was an even bigger surprise to come, foreshadowed by this announcement in the *Daily Mail* on 25 May:

A company has been formed, with Lord Montagu of Beaulieu as

John's concept of an overhead city road.

Chairman, to build and control a great motorway, about 226 miles long, from London to Birmingham, Manchester and Liverpool at an estimated cost of £15 million.

There is no universally acknowledged 'inventor' of the motorway, in the person of someone recognized as having been the first to put forward detailed proposals for the construction of roads specially designed for long-distance motor transport. But although the first motorways were not built until the early 1920s — in Germany, Italy and the USA — a number of pioneers were working more or less in unison in Britain soon after the turn of the century. Their ideas were confined to paper, since Britain's first motorway — the Preston by-pass section of the M6 — was not opened until 1958. But their schemes were remarkably advanced when it is remembered that they were working at the very beginning of the motor transport era. Their plans, when re-examined today, bear a remarkable resemblance to the roads that their successors eventually built.

John Montagu was one of those pioneers. In 1902 he had presented Claude Johnson, then still Secretary of the Automobile Club, with proposals for a new road from London to Brighton. This, he had suggested, should be solely for the use of motorists and cyclists. In a letter to the club's committee Johnson set out his and John's ideas in some detail, proposing among other things an 80 ft wide carriageway (with separate tracks for fast and slow traffic), flyovers above existing roads and wide deviations around towns so that the road could be built on cheap rural land. Johnson did not regard Brighton as the optimum destination but thought that the road should run from London to 'a port of military importance' because this would encourage the War Office to subsidize its construction. The port, said Johnson, should be on the English Channel so that the road could facilitate communications between London and Paris. He and John thought that the road could be closed occasionally to allow a Paris to London motor race to be staged on it.

Later Sir Douglas Fox, a civil engineer, carried out a survey for a motorway from London to Brighton; his scheme was prominently featured in *The Car Illustrated* and at about this time John also lent his editorial support to another engineer, B. H. Thwaite, who perhaps has more claim to the title 'the father of the motorway' than anyone. In the late 1890s Thwaite had conceived the idea of 'a special motor carway through England', paved with wood bedded in a concrete base, on which motor vehicles would be allowed to travel at unrestricted speeds. John helped Thwaite revive this project in 1903, publishing maps and plans for a four-lane highway running almost as straight as an arrow from a terminus at Edgware, north of London, to Birmingham. A month earlier John had published his own scheme for a

An artist's impression from The Car Illustrated, *showing one of the motorways advocated by John. Today, the M25 runs close to this very spot.*

motorway from London to the 'Garden City' that George Cadbury was planning to build in Hertfordshire. It is interesting to note that in those days John was totally committed to motorways but doubted whether — as Thwaite and his contemporaries believed — they could ever be built by private enterprise. When, 20 years later, John became directly involved in Britain's first serious attempt to build a motorway between London and Britain's main industrial centres, he wanted the venture to be backed with private capital, albeit with some financial support from the Government.

The scheme that later became known as 'Montagu's Motorway' originated in early 1923, when Whitley and Carkeet-James, a firm of civil engineers in Westminster, London, published proposals for a Northern and Western Motorway, to run from London to Liverpool via Birmingham and Manchester. A syndicate of promoters was formed in April for the purpose of obtaining Parliament's support for the road and in seeking a chairman and spokesman they could not have approached a more suitable candidate than John Montagu. By now he had done more, over a period of 20 years, to popularize motor transport than any other public figure. The construction of special roads for motor vehicles would have been a fitting, though belated, sequal to his success in helping the motor vehicle become a form of everyday transport. On 24 April he was given the task of producing a brochure for the syndicate and this became the first of a series of publications and articles in which he spelled out, to a perhaps astonished audience, how such a highway could transform communications over a region which, with a total population of more than 20 million, held the key to Britain's industrial future.

As John himself said, his syndicate's scheme for the motorway came nearly one hundred years after a heated controversy had waged in the Press and the committee rooms of Parliament over whether the promoters of the then-novel railways should be given powers to build 'the new roads on which the rails were to be laid'. Now, in 1923, there was likely to be similar excitement over whether — after years of conflict and congestion involving incompatible vehicles on inadequate roads — a purpose-built road, some 200 miles long, should be built to syphon fast, heavy motor traffic away from the highways and byways of the Midlands and the North and carry it quickly and economically from city to city. There had been a phenomenal growth of road traffic in Britain since the passing of the Motor Car Bill in 1903 and by 1923 there were one million motor vehicles in use; yet, said John, no new highways had been built anywhere in the country since the days of Telford and McAdam.

During May and June John used his Press contacts to put his motorway message across and pave the way for a private Bill, seeking powers to start building the road, that his syndicate intended to present to Parliament later in the year. The road would cost £15 million to construct, he said, and would directly or indirectly provide employment for 100,000 men over a period of two years. The motorway would go over or under canals, railways and existing roads along its route; no gradient would be steeper than 1 in 40 and no curve would have a radius of less than half a mile. Fast and slow lanes, built on a foundation of nine inches of reinforced concrete, would be provided and junctions (similar to today's familiar slip roads) would link the motorway with nearby large towns.

Initially John and his colleagues seemed confident that they would be able to finance the construction of the motorway largely from private capital, although by August they were talking of raising one third of the money privately and seeking the balance from the Road Fund or some other public kitty. Revenue was to be derived from the motorway by levying tolls of ½d. per ton mile, to be collected at toll gates at each end of the motorway and at intermediate junctions. Since he calculated that the motorway would reduce the cost of running heavy lorries over long distances by 1d. per ton mile, John believed that transport operators would have every incentive to use the new road. By routeing their vehicles along the motorway instead of existing main roads they would reduce their petrol consumption by 25 per cent and their maintenance costs by 50 per cent. Average daily mileages would be increased from 75 miles on ordinary roads to 150 on the motorway. The ½d. tolls, thought John, would be a small price to pay and he also proposed another source of revenue in the form of rents from factories he wanted to see built on frontages 150 yards deep alongside the motorway. This idea of 200 miles of 'ribbon development' was the only major flaw in an otherwise very practical scheme.

Another of John's proposed new roads, as imagined by one of his artists.

The promoters of what the *Evening Star* called 'nearly 200 miles of sheer joy for the motorist' held their second meeting on 9 May at their new office at Windsor House, Westminster, where a small staff had been recruited to deal with legal and engineering aspects of the scheme. Early on, the promoters had considered forming a company with a capital of £75,000 but this idea was soon abandoned and instead they operated as a syndicate, each promoter signing a form of guarantee. During its early weeks the project was managed by an emergency committee under John Montagu, which received weekly reports from its staff and advised the promoters — many of whom remained anonymous — of the progress that was being made. But by July John was presiding over a proper management committee on which the promoters were represented by such figures as Lt.Com. the Hon. Humphrey Legge (Lord Dartmouth's second son) and Lt.Col. the Hon. George Stanley (Lord Derby's brother). Evidently John had been busy rallying some fellow peers to the cause. At about this time Mr G. P. Blizard was retained to look after the syndicate's interests in Parliament, lobby MPs and prepare the ground for the introduction of the promoters' Motorways Bill. Since a similar Bill, seeking approval for an admittedly modest highway between Bournemouth and Swanage, was then being received favourably in Parliament, it seemed to John that at long last the political climate favoured the building of new roads, not only because they would improve communications between industrial centres but also because they would help reduce the very serious rise in unemployment that Britain was experiencing.

Astutely, John was to emphasize the job-creating potential of his motorway when the argument for better communications alone proved insufficient to persuade Government ministers to give the scheme their unanimous approval. But until the late summer of 1923 he seems to have had little or no idea of the political obstacles that lay ahead; certainly, when he discussed the scheme with the Prime Minister, Stanley Baldwin, he was left with the impression that Baldwin was attracted to the idea of the Northern and Western Motorway.

The meeting with Baldwin was arranged by John's friend, Wilfrid Ashley (Edwina's father), who was at this time a member of the Cabinet Committee on Unemployment and Parliamentary Secretary at the Ministry of Transport, a department whose future was very much in the balance, following various vicissitudes during its formative years. Its head, Sir John Baird, also held the position of First Commissioner of Works, leaving Ashley — who was not a particularly powerful politician — in day-to-day charge during what can now be seen as a crucial period for those who wanted Britain to follow the example of Germany and Italy and embark on a motorway construction programme. In July, when the motorway promoters started trying to exert pressure on the Government, John went to Ashley and, in what the latter called 'his usual vague way' said: 'I want to make a road. Will the Government help?'

Ashley, evidently taken aback, replied: 'What are your plans? When I know your proposals I can consider them'.

The meeting ended with John asking Ashley: 'Do, as an old friend, ask the PM to see me'. As Ashley later told John Davidson, Chancellor of the Duchy of Lancaster: 'I very stupidly did so, out of good nature and without thinking'.

Whilst his meeting with Baldwin was being arranged John had another interview with Ashley, who later complained to Davidson: 'He promised me plans etc., which so far I have never been able to extract from him and do not believe he has ever really worked out'.

Whether or not John was being as vague about the scheme as Ashley made out will never be known, but it is likely that at this stage of the project there was not enough information on paper to enable Government ministers to evaluate the scheme properly. Characteristically, John was probably trying to canvass support before the paperwork had been completed. It also seems that, before approaching Ashley, he had outlined his scheme to John Davidson, thus tangling the lines of communication between the promoters and the Government and creating what Ashley called 'dual conversations', during which John sought Davidson's support whilst at the same time trying to obtain Baldwin's approval via Ashley.

From this point Ashley tried to remain aloof from the scheme, for which in any case he did not have much sympathy. In August John had asked Davidson if he could see him on the 21st of that month and whether someone from the Ministry of Transport could be present at the discussion. Ashley, however, turned down the idea of such a meeting, telling Davidson:

> I am sure you will agree that we cannot both continue to see Montagu ... might I suggest that you should see Montagu ... without anyone from the Ministry of Transport (being present) ... hear what he has to say and then, when I have seen and studied his plans I can tell you what I think of his idea. In any case there is no hurry. Under no circumstances could he get to work before next summer so this scheme does not come into the picture for this winter's unemployment scheme.

In Ashley's view John's motorway was far from being a viable means of providing work for the unemployed but was instead delaying the start of various other road construction schemes. On 8 August, a few days before he complained to Davidson about John's tactics, Ashley had written to Sir Philip Lloyd-Greame, President of the Board of Trade and Chairman of the Cabinet's Unemployment Committee, to tell him that John's scheme had practically halted all other major road projects designed to relieve unemployment. This was because local authorities, who were obliged to contribute 50 per cent towards the cost of such projects, were hoping that private enterprise would in future finance new roads at no cost to local funds. By this time John and his colleagues had admitted that they would need to obtain about 60 per cent of their finance from the Treasury or the Road Fund but even so it appeared that, between them, the motorway promoters and the Government might share the cost of building new roads, without calling for any contributions from local ratepayers. Lancashire County Council, for one, had abandoned an ambitious road building project — the proposed new road between Liverpool, Salford and Bolton — because it appeared that, thanks to John's syndicate, others were about to build it for them, free.

Later he was able to announce that 60 out of the 65 local authorities and public bodies along the route of the Coventry to Manchester section of the proposed motorway had passed resolutions in favour of the scheme and that the remaining five were expected to follow suit. The fact that the scheme promised to relieve local unemployment and improve communications at no cost to the communities along the way obviously influenced the authorities when their support was sought.

Ashley's attitude, as expressed to Lloyd-Greame, was that if the motorway scheme was a sound business venture it should be carried out by private enterprise, but that if it was meant to provide work for the unemployed then it should be the responsibility of the Ministry of Transport, using Road Fund money or a Treasury grant. He was suspicious of a scheme that was being presented as one that was an attractive business venture to private enterprise but nevertheless one that deserved Government finance. Ashley told Lloyd-Greame:

> As you know we have already decided on big schemes for this winter but if I am to carry out the instructions of the Unemployment Committee and prepare more schemes for next winter I fear they will all come to nothing until this motorway scheme is got out of the way.

Despite Ashley's opposition to the scheme Lloyd-Greame supported it, provided that the promoters would put up one third of the cost without asking for a Government guarantee. On 9 August, in a letter to Davidson, Lloyd-Greame said that it would probably be much cheaper for the Government to guarantee the remaining two-thirds under the Trade Facilities Act than to go 50:50 with local authorities in order to build a motorway. The Act, introduced in 1921, empowered the Treasury to guarantee loans of up to £25 million to businesses which, because of the stringent credit controls in force at that time, were unable to borrow money for new ventures from normal sources. 'Moreover', added Lloyd-Greame, 'the Montagu road has the attraction of placing a large number of orders for steel and mechanical appliances.'

In his reply to Lloyd-Greame, Davidson said that having now had an opportunity to study the promoters' papers he too was 'very much attracted to the scheme'. Together, Davidson and Lloyd-Greame — and especially the latter — might have been able to win wider political support for the motorway but John's prospects of success were markedly reduced when, in mid-August, Lloyd-Greame resigned as Chairman of the Unemployment Committee in order to preside over the forthcoming Imperial Conference. His place was taken by Sir Laming Worthington-Evans, the Postmaster-General.

By this time the minds of ministers and their advisers were being exercised more by the effect the motorway was likely to have on unemployment than on the way in which it would improve communications and revitalize trade. Until now the minister responsible for employment — Sir Clement Anderson Montague-Barlow, Minister of Labour — had not made any significant contributions to the inter-departmental exchanges that John Montagu's proposals had provoked but on 17 August he had a long talk with Stanley Baldwin. The date of their meeting had been fixed about ten days earlier and Baldwin wanted to discuss all the Government's options for job creation during the coming winter. As the roads programme was certain to be raised, Montague-Barlow took pains to bring himself up to date with the Ministry of Transport's plans and ideas. The facts and figures he required were supplied by Sir Henry Maybury, Director-General of Roads, who was also by now able to tell him about John's motorway scheme. Montague-Barlow was therefore fairly well briefed when Baldwin raised the question of the motorway, the subject still being quite fresh in his mind since his meeting with John had taken place only three weeks earlier.

Baldwin told Montague-Barlow that he particularly wanted the motorway scheme to be considered but he soon found that his Labour Minister had serious reservations. There were, Montague-Barlow admitted, certain attractions. For example (as Lloyd-Graeme had told Davidson) it would be cheaper for the Government, under the Trade Facilities Act, to guarantee two thirds of the cost of a private enterprise motorway than to put up half the money for a road to be built by the State and the local authorities. John Montagu's motorway could also be built more quickly, since the Government would not have to go through the tiresome business of obtaining the consent of all the local authorities along the route. (Obviously, Montague-Barlow realized that the authorities would be unlikely to object to the scheme if they were not going to have to help finance it.)

Having outlined the arguments in favour of the motorway, Montague-Barlow gave Baldwin the reasons why he personally opposed it. He had, he said, originally favoured the scheme because of its financial attractions and the speed with which it could be implemented but was now against it for two reasons. First, there was much to be said against reverting to the system of tolls under which the turnpike roads of the 18th century had been built. Second, a fundamental question of principle was involved. Local authorities were in any case none too eager to contribute their 50 per cent towards the cost of building new roads; they would 'sit back and refuse to help any more road constructions' if the Government allowed private enterprise to build them and make a profit in the process. Here, Montague-Barlow was making the very point that Ashley had put to Lloyd-Greame; he even cited, as an example of the problems John Montagu's scheme was causing, the decision by Lancashire County Council to abandon its proposed road from Liverpool to Salford. Montague-Barlow went on to propose a new policy to Baldwin, whereby the Government would embark on a £30 million national road construction programme to which local authorities would be asked to contribute only 25 per cent, or even less, of the capital cost of new roads in their areas. He urged Baldwin for an early decision on the whole principle of allowing private enterprise to build public roads. 'Lord Montagu is very active,' he said, 'and this point should be decided at once.'

However, no immediate decision was reached and in September John and his syndicate published a draft of their Motorways Bill. This sought to give the Minister of Transport the power to approve applications from those wishing to construct motorways if, in his opinion, approval would be in the public interest. The Bill was accompanied by a memorandum extolling the financial benefits of the scheme to the nation as a whole and to individual transport operators. To support their argument that projected traffic growth justified the construction of the motorway the promoters quoted from an official census of traffic movements in the area through which the motorway would pass.

Publication of the Bill inevitably crystallized public opinion and support came from unexpected quarters. The Mayor and Corporation of Newcastle under Lyme asked if the motorway could be diverted to serve the Potteries district of Staffordshire. The promoters agreed and Mr J. Griffith, Newcastle's Town Clerk, joined the promoters' management committee. Josiah Wedgwood wrote to Baldwin, urging him to support the scheme and make his name immortal by 'Baldwinizing the roads of England'. Sir Samuel Hoare, Secretary of State for Air, told Baldwin that he was in favour of the scheme because the motorway's lights would guide aeroplanes flying at night to Birmingham, Manchester and Liverpool. John had earlier tempted Hoare by offering to look into the possibility of building two or three aerodromes alongside the motorway for the Air Ministry.

But despite this peripheral encouragement, opposition was hardening in the place where the scheme's future would be decided — the Unemployment Committee. On 23 August, six days after Montague-Barlow's crucial meeting with Baldwin — crucial because it was then that the first seeds of doubt were sown in the Prime Minister's mind — the committee had discussed the scheme for the first time. Montague-Barlow produced a memo outlining the points he had put to Baldwin during their discussion on the employment situation — including his arguments for and against the motorway — and the committee also took on board the Ministry of Transport's view that the scheme was hindering the progress of other road construction projects. The committee directed that an inter-departmental committee, comprising representatives of the Transport, Health and Labour Ministries, the Board of Trade and the Treasury, should be formed to evaluate Montagu's scheme and discuss the principle of building toll roads and report back at a later meeting. Sir Henry Maybury was appointed Chairman of the committee.

The committee's findings, which later became known as 'the Maybury report', were published on 1 October and discussed by the Unemployment

Committee four days later. The report proved to be a demolition job. Whilst taking the view most favourable to the motorway promoters on any doubtful point, estimating construction costs optimistically and accepting the promoters' own estimates of the volume of traffic likely to be attracted to the motorway, Maybury and his colleagues concluded that the volume of traffic using the motorway would be only a quarter of that required to ensure a $5\frac{1}{2}$ per cent annual return on the capital cost of the road. In other words, said Maybury, the road would not be a sound commercial investment. For this reason his committee thought it unnecessary to reach a decision on the principle of building toll roads; it asked the Unemployment Committee to pass its findings on to John Montagu.

The promoters responded by mounting a reasoned counter-attack on the Maybury report and on 11 October they published a memorandum which refuted Maybury's objections point by point. This was enough to keep the scheme alive both on the Unemployment Committee's agenda and in the minds of various ministers and officials whom John continued to lobby with unabated optimism. In mid-October, Col. J.T.C. Moore-Brabazon became Parliamentary Secretary at the Ministry of Transport, in succession to Wilfrid Ashley who had been appointed Under-Secretary of State for War. John probably regarded 'Brab', his former correspondent on *The Car Illustrated*, as a potential supporter of his cause but although he was later to be disillusioned, things got off to a fairly promising start when, as one of his first duties, Moore-Brabazon agreed to receive, in company with Worthington-Evans, a deputation from the motorway promoters on 17 October. This was headed by John and Sir Arthur Griffith-Boscawen, who had joined the syndicate's management committee as a consultant or adviser some weeks earlier, having been Minister of Health and Chairman of the Unemployment Committee as recently as March 1923.

Worthington-Evans took a generous view of the scheme. He had by now read the Maybury report and the promoters' reply to it, but he told the delegation that he did not want to discuss traffic densities and engineering costs on that occasion. If the promoters' figures were sound, he said, it would not be difficult to obtain approval for financial support from the committee that supervised the implementation of the Trade Facilities Act. What Worthington-Evans was anxious to find out that day was whether the promoters intended to form a company to build the motorway, and whether they intended to ask the Government to put up all or only part of the money they needed.

John and his colleagues had by now decided to continue to operate as a body of promoters rather than as a company, as originally proposed. They had also decided to seek some of their finance from funds available under the Trade Facilities Act. These points were explained by the syndicate's solicitor, Mr Dixon Davies but as Griffith-Boscawen pointed out, the promoters' immediate problem was to persuade Parliament to pass legislation that would facilitate the compulsory purchase of land on which the motorway was to be built and give the Government the authority to allow the promoters to start building the road. John had found that it would cost the promoters at least £40,000 to promote their private Bill through Parliament and that this would be a lengthy procedure. Instead, they wanted the Government to introduce a short Enabling Bill, amending the existing Light Railways Act to cover the construction of roads as well as railways. This, they thought, would enable work on the motorway to begin in March 1924.

Mr Brooke, an official from the Ministry of Transport, had accompanied Moore-Brabazon to the meeting. He pointed out that Parliament was at that time very reluctant to give up its power to authorize or reject major construction projects. Even if an Enabling Act were passed, approval of the necessary Statutory Order that would then have to be issued before the scheme could begin would be strenuously opposed by 'certain interested parties', meaning elements of the Labour Party and supporters of the railways.

John replied that he thought Labour members in the House of Commons would support the Bill and that the railway interests did not have much influence. Griffith-Boscawen then brought the discussion back to the promoters' intention to apply for financial support from the Trade Facilities Act Committtee. Would the committee undertake to guarantee the interest on part of the capital cost of the motorway if a Statutory Order were obtained? And was the Unemployment Committee likely to back the scheme, since without its support it was unlikely that the Trade Facilities Act Committee would approve the promoters' application?

Worthington-Evans advised the promoters to submit an application to the Trade Facilities Act Committee without delay, because their scheme was interfering with other important matters. He also undertook to tell the committee's Chairman, Sir Robert Kindersley, that the Unemployment Committee favoured any scheme that would provide employment although it was up to Kindersley and his colleagues to decide whether the financial and engineering aspects of the motorway scheme were sound. Pressed by the delegation to ask the Cabinet to find time for an Enabling Bill to be introduced, Worthington-Evans said he would do nothing of the sort until Kindersley's committee approved the scheme and recommended that it should receive Government backing.

John left the meeting with less than he had hoped for, and attempted to boost public support for the motorway by writing an article for the *Daily Mail* in which he reiterated the ways in which the scheme would relieve unemployment and revitalize the economy. 'But,' he added, 'we have not been able to persuade the Government to give us a definite promise of help. While committees sit and deliberate, time is slipping away. If the Government really wants to assist unemployment at once, there is no other scheme of such usefulness ready.'

For some weeks past Stanley Baldwin had been unable to take any further interest in the motorway; problems at the Imperial Conference had demanded his attention, especially the row over the Halibut Fisheries Treaty between Canada and the USA which had caused a crisis in Imperial relations. By 9 November, though, Baldwin had caught up with events at home, for when the Unemployment Committee met that day it heard that the Prime Minister had come to the conclusion that motorways should be built by the State, not by private enterprise. The committee also learned that no application for finance had been received by the Trade Facilities Act Committee (even though it was now three weeks since Worthington-Evans had urged Montagu to make such an application) and that in any case Kindersley now wanted the Government to reach a decision on the principle of private enterprise motorways *before* his committee considered any application. Some members of the Unemployment Committee then expressed the view that the Government could not decide on the question of principle unless Kindersley's committee investigated the financial and engineering aspects of the motorway! What later generations would recognize as a Catch 22 Situation was developing.

Baldwin's opposition to the scheme, as members of the Unemployment Committee must have known, was fostered by Montague-Barlow, at whose request the committee's meeting of 9 November was held. Before the meeting Montague-Barlow wrote to the Prime Minister deploring the Government's lack of progress in reducing unemployment and saying that he intended to ask the Unemployment Committee to reach decisions on various questions, the first being what he called 'The Montagu of Beaulieu road'. He told Baldwin:

> This involves the whole question of the road policy of the nation for the next 50 years ... this development should be a national development ... the broad, level motor roads which must be constructed throughout the country in the next few years should in my view be constructed by public authority and not by private enterprise ... I am not very keen on the Montagu proposals and I doubt if Trade Facilities will approve the scheme. The Montagu road would take the cream of the traffic of the country, as it runs down the centre of England. Public authorities ... will have to construct the new motor roads in the more remote and unpaying areas. If that is so, it is difficult to see why the cream of the traffic should be handed over to private enterprise.

Whilst taking note of Baldwin's views the Unemployment Committee doggedly and democratically adhered to its proper procedures, instructing

Worthington-Evans to urge Kindersley's committee to reach a conclusion about the motorway as quickly as possible. Kindersley and John Montagu had an informal discussion two weeks later but meanwhile, on 15 November, the promoters' Bill had been given its first reading in the House of Commons. Despite the daunting cost they had decided to proceed with this since there was obviously no prospect of the Government introducing an Enabling Bill. Cleverly, the promoters persuaded one of their Labour supporters, John Robert Clynes, Deputy Leader of the Labour Party, to present their Bill to the Commons. Thus, Parliament had the curious experience of listening to a Socialist politician attempting to win approval for private enterprise to construct a motorway that a Tory Prime Minister and many of his Cabinet colleagues thought should be built by the State.

Clynes said that the Bill had the support of all sides of the House, including the Labour Party but soon after it received its first reading its future and, indeed, that of the Government was overtaken by events stemming from the Imperial Conference. Urged at the Conference to end free trade and adopt a policy of Imperial Preference, Baldwin called a general election in December for what he hoped would be a mandate for measures that would end Britain's economic slump. Even though they won more seats than any other single party, the Conservatives lost their overall majority in the House of Commons and within a few weeks Baldwin was succeeded by Britain's first Socialist premier, Ramsay MacDonald. Indirectly the Imperial Conference had dealt two blows to John's motorway. First, Philip Lloyd-Greame became its Chairman and had to resign from heading the Unemployment Committee at the very time when his support for the motorway might have swayed the committee to support the scheme. His successor, Worthington-Evans, took a much more cautious line. Second, the election that followed the Imperial Conference caused Parliament's business in hand, including the Motorways Bill, to be abandoned.

In the dying weeks of Baldwin's first administration the promoters exhibited a model of their motorway at the International Commercial Vehicle Show in London. The Unemployment Committee met again, to find that John had still not submitted an application for finance to the Trade Facilities Act Committee. It was agreed that failure to do so by 31 December would leave the Unemployment Committee free to reach a decision about the motorway without waiting any longer. Then, on 18 December, the widely respected and influential commercial motor transport pioneer, Edward Shrapnell-Smith, President of the Commercial Motor Users Association, caused a minor sensation by writing to *The Times* expressing total opposition to the motorway. 'Any such motorway must within a few years become an abandoned and derelict property', he said. Thanks to improvements on the railways through-traffic by road was a 'diminishing quantity'. Money should be spent on new by-passes and on improving existing highways, not 'thrown away on motorways, which will certainly never be used by trade vehicles'.

Moore-Brabazon read the letter next morning and dashed off a note to Worthington-Evans:

> I think we can now put 'Closed' to the files dealing with the Montagu road scheme and might even add R.I.P. You have very likely seen Shrapnell-Smith's letter in *The Times* this morning ... Poor Montagu, rather a knock-out blow from the very section of the motoring world from which he expected to draw the more profitable portion of his traffic!

Evidently, Moore-Brabazon was not saddened by what was for all intents and purposes the end of the Montagu motorway. On 8 January the Baldwin Cabinet's Unemployment Committee held its last meeting and it was reported that, on the basis of the information presented to it the Trade Facilities Act Committee had decided that it could not recommend giving the motorway a State guarantee. The Unemployment Committee then told the Cabinet that there was no point in the Government giving the matter any further consideration. Moore-Brabazon was now able to write 'R.I.P.' on his files. John and his syndicate made another attempt to win Parliamentary support for their Motorways Bill in April 1924 but although the scheme rumbled on in the political backwaters throughout Ramsay MacDonald's return to power, the idea of private enterprise motorways was, by 1925, a lost cause.

Ironically, when the motor museum that commemorates John Montagu's life as a motoring pioneer was opened it was Moore-Brabazon — by this time Lord Brabazon of Tara — who helped perform the opening ceremony. The date was 22 April 1956. Thirty-two years had passed since Brabazon's colleagues on the Unemployment Committee had advised the Cabinet to waste no more time considering Montagu's motorway. Although, by 1956, many countries were traversed by motorways Britain still lagged behind. Another two years passed before the first section of Britain's motorway network was opened.

18

Last Decade

In the autumn of 1919, at the age of 53, John Montagu had to start rebuilding his life. If the loss, within a period of less than four years, of Eleanor and then his wife had left any emotional scars, these were soon healed by his marriage to Pearl and the birth, in October 1921, of their first daughter Anne (now Lady Chichester). Despite his wartime experiences John's reserves of nervous and physical energy remained undiminished. The zest with which he launched and sustained his campaign for the Northern and Western Motorway proved that he was far from being a spent force in the motor transport movement and although he no longer had his own publishing empire, his output of articles on motoring and other transport topics hardly faltered. Editors and publishers continued to accept almost everything he wrote, which was fortunate because he now relied heavily on his earnings as a freelance writer. After the war, as before, John found that nearly all his income from the Beaulieu Manor Estate had to be spent on repairing its buildings and maintaining its water supplies, drainage and other services. He seldom, if ever, profited from being Beaulieu's landlord; income from his investments and from the other properties he had inherited from his father undoubtedly assured his long-term financial future but he needed the fees he earned from his writing activities and lectures to cover his family's day-to-day expenses.

Although the years 1919-1929 were to be the last decade of his life they were enlivened by almost as many new schemes and responsibilities as earlier eras. As before, opposition or inertia in high places often prevented his pet projects from becoming reality, but once again his remarkable resilience to failure or the prospect of it carried him through. No sooner had one scheme died before another fired his imagination and his instinctive enthusiasm for any new form of transport or communication.

His reaction to the imminent collapse of his motorway scheme illustrates this facet of his character very well. His hopes that the Labour Government would include the Motorways Bill in its parliamentary programme were raised in April 1924 when the Bill was reintroduced in the House of Commons by Sir Leslie Scott and given an unopposed first reading. Despite the efforts of a deputation to John Clynes, now Lord Privy Seal and Deputy Leader of the House of Commons, the Government refused for several months to find time for the Bill to receive a second reading. When, at last, the Bill was included on the Commons' Order Paper, Parliament was about to be dissolved before the General Election of October 1924 (which the Socialists lost because of the notorious 'Zinovieff Letter' affair). The Motorways Bill was one of the casualties of the dissolution. By then, though, John was energetically advocating another transport revolution, for whilst the progress of the Motorways Bill was being impeded he had joined forces with Sir Samuel Instone, the shipowner and air travel pioneer, in an attempt to introduce a motorboat service on the River Thames.

Whilst the Thames is busy enough in summer, when hordes of tourists travel on the pleasure launches that ply to the Tower of London, Greenwich and Kew, the river has yet to be exploited as a commuter route through central London. Every day thousands of office workers struggle by car, bus and Underground to reach destinations that are within two or three hundred yards of the riverside — places like Whitehall, the Shell Centre, Temple, Fleet Street and the Cannon Street area of the City of London. John Montagu and Instone decided that the 18 miles of the Thames between Hammersmith in the west and Woolwich in the east offered a means of relieving London's roads and railways of much of their daily burden of commuters. In June 1924 they announced their plan for a Thames Express river service.

From the 1820s until the First World War there had been fairly continuous steamboat services up and down the river but these seldom paid their way. From June 1907 until October 1909 the London County Council operated 30 steamboats that called frequently at about 12 landing stages but the service lost more than £463,000 of ratepayers' money. This became one of the main issues in the fiercely contested LCC election in 1909, which resulted in the defeat of the ruling majority in the council chamber and the cessation of the steamboat service. Various proposals to resurrect the service were put forward in the ensuing years, without success. When Montagu and Instone conceived their scheme for a Thames Express they immediately realized that only diesel-engined launches could provide the kind of clean, fast and comfortable service that would attract enough passengers to make the venture profitable.

Their scheme involved running a fleet of 25 fast motorboats, each capable of carrying 300 passengers, at 15-minute intervals between 25 piers along London's waterfront. Montagu and Instone intended to form a private company to run the fleet, and reckoned that by charging a maximum fare of 1d. a mile the enterprise would make a profit. However, they wanted the LCC to build 12 new piers and meet the cost of maintaining these and 13 existing piers on the fleet's route, in return for a guaranteed annual toll of

£6000 if 5 million passengers used the service or £6600 if the number exceeded 5 million. Additional payments of $\frac{1}{4}$d. or $\frac{1}{2}$d. for every passenger were also offered in what amounted to a complicated estimate of revenues and costs.

Sadly the Thames Express, like the Northern and Western Motorway, foundered on financial obstacles. After studying conflicting estimates of toll yields and the cost of building and maintaining the piers the council decided, on 2 December 1924, that it would be prepared to build the piers only if this could be done without spending anything from the rates. John's express boat service was never launched. Sixty years later road traffic in central London is almost immobile during the rush hour, whilst the Thames flows serenely by, virtually deserted and ignored, still waiting for its full potential as a means of taking people to and from work, to be appreciated.

The year 1925 was, by John Montagu's standards, easy paced. Following the birth of their second daughter, Caroline, in February he and Pearl enjoyed their first long holiday abroad for three years when, at Baron Franckenstein's invitation, they visited Vienna. For John it was a working holiday, since he had been asked to prepare a report on road construction and maintenance for the Austrian Government. Afterwards he wrote a long article for *The Times* on touring in Austria; motoring on the Continent was becoming popular again and after John returned from Vienna he took delivery of the car that he and his family were to use for tours at home and abroad for the rest of his life. This was a Rolls-Royce Phantom I, chassis number 145MC — an early example of the legendary Silver Ghost's successor. So far as is known this Phantom is the sole survivor of the seven Rolls-Royce cars John owned at various times.* Sold after his death, it became a mobile canteen during the Second World War and when rediscovered by the present Lord Montagu it was hauling a gang mower around a school playing field in Somerset. It was restored by Leslie Willis and is now a much-admired exhibit at the National Motor Museum.

John's Phantom carried many important passengers and it would have been in this car that Queen Mary enjoyed a drive in the New Forest during at least one of the visits she made to Beaulieu. These took place during successive Cowes Weeks, and on each occasion John used his motor yacht *Cygnet* to bring the Queen to Buckler's Hard from the Royal Yacht *Victoria & Albert* anchored off Cowes. When *Cygnet* and the Royal Party arrived at the pier opposite the Master Builders House the Queen's equerry, Sir Harry Verney, invariably bounded up the gangplank and jumped strenuously upon it to make sure that it was safe. Queen Mary would then disembark and be entertained by John and Pearl Montagu for a few hours, taking tea at Palace House or the Master Builders House before returning to *Victoria & Albert*.

In January 1926 the Beaulieu Brotherhood, formed by John and Pearl to

John and Pearl with Queen Mary during one of her visits to Beaulieu.

strengthen the bonds of friendship between their family and close friends, held its first annual dinner. John, of course, was its 'Abbot' and its 'brothers' and 'sisters' included Pearl, Elizabeth and Helen Montagu, George Foster Pedley, Lord Forster, Sir James Kingston Fowler, Archibald Marshall and Sir Owen Seaman. Pearl's mother, Mrs Barrington-Crake, was elected 'Mother Superior'. It was Marshall, no doubt, who had introduced Seaman, editor of *Punch*, to John Montagu some years earlier and it was Seaman who penned the following lines, printed on the menu for one of the Brotherhood's feasts:

> The open road, the lore of forest's ways,
> Rules for pedestrians in the traffic's maze,
> The knack of driving engines well and truly,
> The North-West Frontier and the fowler's art —
> All these — and *Whitaker* — he has by heart,
> This Abbot (no, not celibate) of Beaulieu.

Then in May John's knack of driving engines was put to practical use when the railways were paralyzed by the General Strike. John quickly volunteered his services to the Southern Railway, which was trying to maintain a skeleton service between London and the south coast. First he drove the 10 am express from Portsmouth to Waterloo and then transferred to the Southampton line. On both routes his familiarity with the track and especially the complex long-distance signals around Clapham Junction, on the approach to Waterloo, were invaluable. Pearl would meet him at the Southampton terminus with a billy-can of tea and on one occasion they had lunch at the nearby South-Western Hotel; John in his oldest travel-stained clothes, Pearl pert and trim in one of her summer frocks. Hearing them address one another as 'Darling', someone at a nearby table remarked: 'What pretty wives these mechanics have nowadays'. At the end of one journey an elderly lady, observing the custom of those days of thanking the engine driver for a safe and punctual journey approached John and said: 'Well done, young man. I'm so glad you are defying your union!'

The General Strike proved to be the most arduous of John's engine driving exploits. In 1919 he had been assisted by an engine cleaner at the end of his day's work but he was not so fortunate in 1926. He had to clean and oil the engine himself and replace it in its shed before making his way home in his Rolls-Royce Phantom.

By now John had four daughters, Helen, Elizabeth, Anne and Caroline. Helen had shown no great interest in the management of Beaulieu and was now experiencing an unhappy marriage that would end in divorce. Because his stage-struck daughter had caused him so much concern, he had made every effort to dissuade Elizabeth from embarking on a similar career, to the

John Montagu, engine driver.

John Montagu, freelance journalist, at work in the Upper Drawing Room at Palace House.

extent that she had not been allowed to take part in school plays or to have her hair cut short. Instead, he encouraged her to buy a car with £100 left her by Lord Northcliffe (Lady Northcliffe was her godmother), and to become a qualified motor mechanic at the Mansions Motor School. A bright perceptive girl, he taught her much about the countryside and the good things of life. As she showed none of Helen's waywardness, he encouraged her to learn about the estate so that she would be capable of assuming her father's responsibilities if and when the time came for her to do so.

John was sixty and the desire to produce a male heir had become something of an obsession. Then on 20 October 1926, his and Pearl's third child was born at her mother's house in London, 29 South Street, and it was the longed-for son, christened Edward John Barrington. The godparents were the Duke of Buccleuch, the Earl of Sandwich and the sixteen-year-old Edward Cadogan. Today Edward Cadogan recalls John Montagu as 'a highly-strung man, with sandy hair and rather foxy features. He was a very kind person, very energetic, and had more knowledge on every subject than any man I have ever met'.

A few weeks after the birth of his son, John received an invitation from Sir Charles Greenway to visit Persia and Iraq. Greenway was one of the founders of the Anglo-Persian Oil Company (forerunner of BP) and ostensibly wanted John's advice on how to tackle certain motor transport problems involved in supplying the oilfields. But what he was really after was the support of this influential peer should any problems occur during the forthcoming renegotiations of the royalties paid to the Persian government under the concession that had been granted to Greenway's company in 1909. Pearl Montagu was also invited, although Greenway's son, who was to arrange the itinerary for the Montagus' journey, was somewhat alarmed when he realized that she had only recently been confined.

On 27 October he wrote these carefully chosen words to John Montagu:

> The conditions of travel over the desert route, though improved of late, are not yet by any means perfect and certainly this route could not be recommended as a comfortable or congenial one for ladies going to Persia, unless for the hardy ones who are prepared for an arduous motor journey and indifferent quarters. The accommodation and sleeping arrangements in the desert are not always of the most luxurious and the rather monotonous meals and other not always unavoidable phases of discomfort would, I feel, prove very irksome to many women — particularly any who may not be in a very robust state of health. Isolated tales of attack in the desert and the real or imaginary fear engendered thereby would probably prove disconcerting to some of the more nervous. I have thought it only fair to tell you the foregoing in case you might prefer that, in the circumstances, Lady Montagu should not accompany you.

John and his son Edward, the present 3rd Baron Montagu of Beaulieu.

The young Greenway had evidently not appreciated that Pearl was neither unused to arduous motor journeys nor likely to be deterred by the terrors, real or imagined, of the desert. In the middle of January 1927 John and Pearl set off overland for Marseilles sailing on SS *Narkunda* as far as Port Said and then travelling by train from Kantara to Jerusalem, where they spent a few days sightseeing as the guests of the British High Commissioner, Field Marshal Lord Plumer and Lady Plumer. Then, on 1 February, they began a six day 1000 mile journey across the desert to Baghdad via Haifa, Beirut, Damascus and Rutbah Wells.

Two cars were provided for the Montagus by Gerald Nairn's transport company and for most of the way they were followed by one of Nairn's new six-wheeled Thornycroft lorries carrying supplies for Imperial Airways, whose DH66 Hercules aeroplane (soon to be named *City of Delhi*) carrying Sir Samuel Hoare (Britain's Secretary of State for Air), Lady Hoare, Sir Sefton Brancker (Director of Civil Aviation) and Sir Geoffrey Salmond (AOC India) had on 8 January completed its pioneering flight from London to Delhi via Cairo and Rutbah Wells. In January 1917 John had delivered his famous lecture in which he prophesied that within ten years India would be the destination for the first long-distance passenger and mail flights from England. Now, in January 1927 it seemed that his dream had come true; and quite by coincidence he was about to motor across the desert on a route that would converge on and then run parallel with the furrow the RAF had ploughed in the sand to guide the pioneering flyers to Rutbah Wells. In the event problems of a political, not aeronautical, nature delayed the inauguration of a scheduled service to India. When Hoare and his party reached Baghdad word came from Tehran that Imperial Airways would not be allowed to fly down its chosen route along the northern coast of the Persian Gulf. Hoare found ways and means of completing his journey to India but it was another two years before the British Government was able to complete the negotiations with the various foreign countries over which Imperial Airways wanted to fly in order to operate regular passenger and mail flights. John, we can be sure, heard all about Hoare's problems at first hand, for on 6 February he and Pearl met Hoare and Sefton Brancker in Baghdad, during their return flight to England.

Next day John went to inspect the new oilfields around Kanikin, whilst Pearl stayed in Baghdad for a few days as a guest of the British High Commissioner, Sir Henry Dobbs. The Montagus then took a train to Basra to board a launch that took them to one of the ports on the Shatt-el-Arab, from where they motored inland alongside a 10-inch oil pipe to Arwaz and thence to Dar-i-Khazineh. This was their base for a tour of the oilfields of southern Persia, during which they saw what was then the most famous oil well in the world, F7, which had recently been sealed off after producing $6\frac{3}{4}$ million tons of oil in 16 years. Appropriately, John and Pearl left Persia on an oil tanker, *British Consul.* Because the ship was not a passenger carrying vessel they signed-on as a steward and stewardess but passed the time playing bridge with the captain and his officers before disembarking at Aden eight days later to join SS *Rawalpindi*, homeward bound from India. When they arrived at Marseilles on 12 March their chauffeur was waiting for them with their Rolls-Royce, ready to take them to the hotel at St Raphael where they had first met seven years earlier.

Iraq and Persia proved to be the last exotic lands to be visited by John and Pearl Montagu. He devoted the rest of 1927 to writing and speaking on familiar themes and spent much of the summer trying to persuade the Government to make the 65,000 acres of the New Forest a national park. This, he felt, would prevent its natural beauty from being spoiled by the indiscriminate felling of its oak, beech, ash and chestnut trees. John also fought in vain to deter the Forestry Commission from its policy of planting serried and monotonous ranks of fir trees, which to his mind irrevocably altered the character of the Forest. The legacy of that policy can be seen today in forests all over England; the New Forest has not escaped but as a founder member and President of the New Forest Association, John was one of the pioneer conservationists to whom much of the credit for the present condition of the Forest is due.

In 1928 the Montagus enjoyed another holiday in the south of France and in June their third daughter, Mary-Clare, was born. In other respects, though, it was a relatively quiet period in John's life and towards the end of the year ill-health necessitated a prolonged rest. It was a rare experience for him; with the exception of the weeks he spent recovering from his ordeal on SS *Persia* his activities had seldom been interrupted for long by illness or injury. This is not to say that he had no health problems; his asthmatic attacks were a recurrent affliction until, it seems, the last ten years of his life but he overcame these, usually by sheer will power. He also spoke of having 'heart trouble', although there is no evidence that he ever suffered a heart attack. But in October 1928 he underwent treatment in London for an enlarged prostate gland, a condition which soon began to have a debilitating effect on his health. In November his doctors decided that surgery would be necessary but he developed pleurisy in his left lung and the operation was postponed. He then returned to Beaulieu to spend Christmas with his family and write what were to be his last newspaper articles, commissioned by J. L. Garvin, editor of the *Observer.*

In the first of these articles, published on 13 January 1929, John called for an expansion of road construction work so as to create jobs for the unemployed — an echo of his previous pleas on this theme. His second article was a reasoned argument in favour of building a Channel Tunnel, coupled with a scheme for converting unprofitable railway lines into toll roads. Then, early in March, he went into a London hospital for a prostate operation. This was a success but, whilst recovering, John contracted pneumonia. A lung abscess then developed, necessitating another operation, after which he suffered a chest infection.

On 30 March 1929 John Montagu of Beaulieu, pioneer of travel by land, sea and air, died at the age of 62. It was Easter Saturday. London's railway stations were crowded with travellers setting off to spend the day or a long weekend at the seaside or in the country. Motorists heading for similar destinations were fuming as they inched their way along the narrow, congested roads that would eventually free them from the cares and confines of the city. To drivers stuck in traffic jams it seemed as if all Britain's 1½ million motor vehicles — of which more than one third were motor cars — were out and about that day. On the motor coach services not one seat remained unbooked, even though the number of coaches in service had been doubled and in some cases tripled to cope with the weekend demand. *The Times* reported: 'Every available motor coach has been pressed into use. The knowledge that by motor coach a seat was guaranteed was an additional inducement to many to travel by road rather than by train.' At sea the Cunard Steamship Line's *Mauretania* represented the ultimate in ocean travel, capable of crossing the Atlantic in little more than four days. Soon the Cunard fleet would consist of 18 luxury liners of 14,000 to 53,000 tons and plans to build two more — *Queen Mary* and *Queen Elizabeth* — of more than 80,000 tons would soon be announced. London's airport, at Croydon, was experiencing its busiest-ever Easter; nearly 100 airliners were due to leave the airport or land there during the holiday. One of them was Argosy G-EBLF *City of Glasgow*, which on the day John died took off from Croydon to inaugurate — at long last — Imperial Airways' through service to India. His dream had come true; of all the journeys by air that he would have liked to have been able to make, a through flight to India was the one that would have thrilled him most.

John Montagu left his estate in trust for his son Edward until 20 October 1951, his 25th birthday, when he became life tenant of the manor and estate of Beaulieu. One of the first tasks he set himself was to establish the motor museum that commemorates his father's efforts to place Britain among the world's leading motoring nations.

After John Montagu's death his family found one of the two letters he had written before sailing for India in November 1916. This was the letter that contained instructions for the arrangements that were to be made for his

funeral 'in the event of my death in this war or in any other way'. It read as
follows:

> I desire that if I die in the United Kingdom my body shall be buried in the
> simplest possible manner, in a coffin made of Beaulieu wood, in the family
> burying ground in Beaulieu Abbey. I also desire that the wearing of black
> as mourning shall be avoided by my friends and that the colours of purple
> or white shall be used by anyone wishing to show respect to my memory.
> And I desire that a simple tombstone memorial shall be erected over my
> grave, containing the following inscription:

> He loved Beaulieu, deeming his possession of it a sacred trust to be handed
> to his successors in like manner. He endeavoured to restore and beautify
> the Abbey in the same spirit, desiring that 'The Peace which passeth all
> understanding' should continue to be present therein.

On 3 April, after hundreds of relations, friends and tenants had filed past his
coffin in the upper drawing room of Palace House, his instructions were
obeyed. There was a simple funeral service in the Abbey Church and John
Montagu's body, in its coffin of Beaulieu oak, was interred in the family
burial ground in the Abbey cloisters.

Some days later Joan Eleanor Thornton, a 26-year-old school mistress,
was handed the other letter that John had written and sealed before his second
voyage to India in 1916. He had left instructions that this was not to be
delivered to Miss Thornton until after his death; its very existence was
known only to a close friend. This is what John had written to Joan Thornton
when the time came for him to leave England and join the ship that would
carry him within sight of the place where *Unterseeboot-38* had attacked SS
Persia 11 months earlier:

> My Darling Joan,
> If you ever have to open this letter it will probably be because I am no
> longer in this world to tell you what it contains myself. I intend to do this
> should I live but going out again as I am doing to India I know I am
> running risks and I may not return.
> So I tell you who I am; who you know as 'Uncle' now, and who you
> are, and why I love you so much, both for your own sake and for your
> mother's sake. I am your father whom you met at Windsor last summer.
> Do you remember that day in Windsor Park? How I enjoyed it!
> The story of my life I now give to you. About 1900 I first met your
> mother, three years before you were born. I fell in love with her at first
> sight but as I couldn't marry her I felt I must keep away from her as much
> as I could. However in the ordinary work of life I was a pioneer of
> motoring in those days and she secretary to Mr Claude Johnson, the
> Secretary of the Automobile Club.
> She began to like me and realize my feelings as well. Finally in 1902, in

February, she became my secretary and together we started *The Car* and put our whole energies into the new venture. Before long we discovered that we loved each other intensely and our mutual scruples vanished before our great love. From then until last December 30th when she was drowned and I eventually was rescued from the *Persia*, submarined in the Mediterranean near Crete, we never had anyone in our lives except us two.

Your mother was the most wonderful and lovable woman I have ever met. She showed me for 14 years a devotion which is beyond description and if she loved me as few women love, I equally loved her as few men love.

Our work, our lives, our ideals and most of our tastes became united in us. I can never tell you, least of all on paper, what we were to each other and how she saved my life before the *Persia* several times from heart trouble and I believe gave up her life for me at the end.

She avoided talking about you at all times, why I know not, but I feel sure loved you at the bottom of her heart. You are the oldest living link I have left with the noblest woman I ever knew. Will you try to love me or my memory?

Now as to your future, if I die. I have appointed three trustees, Dr Ingram, who you know; Walter Barrett my solicitor; and Mr Claude Johnson, who knew and appreciated your mother. They have been given funds by me to provide for you about £150 a year or about £3750 of capital. Your Aunt Pom will be your guardian and I know you will be good to her and do what she thinks best for you. Some day you will probably marry and your £150 a year will help you be free to marry a gentleman-like and good man who really loves you.

You should learn a trade, dear Joan, for it will be good for you to do this.

Some day, perhaps, I hope the same great joy produced by great love will come to you as it came to your mother and me. I should have married her if I had been able to or if anything had happened to my wife.

Darling Joan, you must never forget your mother or me or be ashamed of us. The world may be unkind to you and small-minded gossips may sneer but hold your head high and remember you came of noble origins on both sides, and your mother had fine old Spanish blood in her veins besides her English descent.

Perhaps someday you will see Beaulieu, my beloved Beaulieu, which she loved so much too. You will see in the church there is a bronze tablet I put up to her and my recovery from the sea when I was so nearly drowned. There at Beaulieu, especially on the river and sea outside, your mother and I spent many happy hours. Also we had gloriously happy trips to France. You will always remember that I loved you, darling, most deeply, and am always praying for you.

I know not what the future will bring for me but you will always be remembered as a gleam of sunshine to me, bereaved as I am.

Goodbye darling Joan.
God bless you always.
Your loving father,
Montagu of Beaulieu.

* As this book was about to go to press, Lord Montagu of Beaulieu was informed that the
chassis of his father's 1910 Rolls-Royce (see pp. 146, 147) had been discovered in Australia.

Epilogue

It was a letter that would have left Joan Thornton bewildered and heart-broken, had she been obliged to read it in the circumstances John Montagu had in mind when in November 1916 he had set off to begin what he feared would be another fateful voyage through the Mediterranean. Joan was then 13 years old and living with her foster parents, Sergeant and Mrs Arthur Ireson, at No.43 Rannoch Road, one of the side-streets between the River Thames and Fulham Palace Road in Hammersmith, west London. She had never met her mother and although by now Rose Thornton ('Aunt Pom') may have told her something about Eleanor Thornton's life and how she died, Joan had no idea who her father was. Nor is it likely that the Iresons knew the identity of her parents; the fostering arrangements were probably made by two of the trustees mentioned in John's letter — Reginald Ingram, his doctor and Walter Barrett, his solicitor. They would have been well aware of the need for discretion.

Happily, Joan was spared the shock of having to cope simultaneously with the revelation that John Montagu was her father and the news that he was dead. Coming so soon after the death of the mother she had never known, this would have been a distressing experience for one so young. By surviving his second encounter with the Kaiser's U-boats and other hazards of war, John was able for the next 13 years to develop a close relationship with Joan, during which she started to piece together the story of her mother's life and her tragic love affair.

Because the *affaire* lasted for more than thirteen years, close friends of John Montagu and Eleanor Thornton would have learned about it sooner or later, as would their colleagues on *The Car Illustrated*. As Elizabeth Montagu later discovered, Cis Montagu had also known of the *affaire* and become resigned to it. But *when* the *affaire* became known to these people is another matter. If John and Eleanor managed to keep it a secret for at least a few years, then the birth of their daughter fourteen months after they started *The Car Illustrated* might have been known only to a very few people indeed. Eleanor, admittedly, would have found it difficult to conceal her pregnancy from her friends and colleagues — unless she stopped working and lived in seclusion for several months — but it would have been possible to hide the fact that John Montagu was the father. It would have been equally easy for Eleanor at the end of her pregnancy to explain that she had had a miscarriage, or that the baby had died at birth. Whatever was known or not known about John's relationship with Eleanor during the early years of their *affaire*, and of Eleanor's pregnancy, the fact remains that the birth of Joan Thornton was never registered, even though the registration of births, marriages and deaths was then compulsory — as it still is today — under an Act of Parliament introduced in 1874. Registration, of course, requires that the name and occupation of the father must be given; furthermore, copies of birth certificates could then, as now, be obtained by any member of the public. John was anxious to keep the birth of his and Eleanor's daughter a secret in order to avoid incurring the wrath of the Buccleuch family; he therefore had to ensure that the birth was not registered. Whether, as part of his efforts to avoid a family row and scandal, he kept the secret from Cis Montagu as well is not known. It seems likely that at first he did, though he may have confessed in later years.

Even though Joan was denied a birth certificate she did at least know the date of her birth: 5 April 1903. Her place of birth, though, remained a mystery. Eleanor's recently widowed mother was living in Battersea at this time. Assuming she knew her daughter was pregnant, it would be logical to assume that she would have wanted to take care of her during her confinement. Margaret North, who had been Eleanor's and Rose's nanny, was now Mrs Thornton's companion and would have been the ideal person to help the family cope with the situation. But it seems there were compelling reasons against Eleanor having her baby at home — a desire to prevent the family's friends and neighbours from gossiping, perhaps, or concern about the effect Eleanor's predicament would have on Rose, then at the impressionable age of 15. Whatever the reason, it is almost certain that Joan was not born in Battersea but in Victoria. Reginald Ingram, John Montagu's doctor, had a practice there, at No. 149 Warwick Street, and Eleanor was a patient of his during her pregnancy. Indeed, she may even have stayed with the Ingrams, although Joan herself always thought she had been born at Artillery Mansions, a gloomy block of flats in Victoria Street, midway between Westminster Cathedral and Westminster Abbey.

Joan was never able to establish her birthplace for certain — the idea that it was Artillery Mansions probably came from Dr Ingram or (more likely) Rose Thornton and Margaret North, who remained close friends until the latter's death in 1944. There is no record of Eleanor Thornton ever having been a tenant at Artillery Mansions, but the building is certainly the kind of place where she could have lived quietly and anonymously for a while in 1903. Certainly, she had close links with Victoria for several years. She was a pupil at the Grey Coat girls' school, a minute's walk from Victoria Street; Dr Ingram practised in Victoria; and the Iresons lived in nearby Pimlico at the time they became Joan's foster parents, moving to Hammersmith ten years later.

Eleanor's feelings towards her baby daughter can only be imagined. She never saw her after the day she was born and, as John said, she avoided talking about her at all times. But despite this Joan enjoyed a happy and, in the circumstances, normal childhood, thanks to the Iresons. No doubt they received regular payments to cover Joan's keep and other expenses; these would have been a welcome supplement to Sgt. Ireson's Army pay and might have been the means by which they were able to afford to leave Pimlico and buy a home of their own in Hammersmith. Their mortgage payments were 28 shillings a week — not a modest sum in the years before the First World War. The Iresons became very fond of Joan and even intended that she should inherit their house, although in the event this scheme fell through because of legal difficulties.

John had no contact with Joan for the first 13 years of her life. He may have intended that this state of affairs should continue indefinitely but Eleanor Thornton's death in 1915 and his own narrow escape from drowning left him anxious to befriend their daughter and take a personal interest in her future. As a result, sometime in the summer of 1916, Joan was taken to Windsor Great Park — probably by Dr Ingram and Rose Thornton — to meet a man who was, so she was told, her uncle.

He was, of course, John Montagu and this unexpected meeting with someone who was then a complete stranger was to be the beginning of an exciting and perhaps unsettling period in her life — though she seems to have taken the meeting at Windsor, and everything that followed, in her stride. But for a few months after the meeting, so far as Joan was concerned, life returned to normal whilst John thought very seriously about her future. His concern was reflected in the poignant letter he wrote before he returned to India, but although this was to remain unread and, eventually, forgotten until his death in 1929, Joan regularly received other letters from him from late 1916 onwards. There were 80 in all, sent from London and distant parts of the world. They reveal John's affection for Joan and her mother. Above all they reveal how important his relationship with Eleanor had been to his personal happiness and his career during the most momentous years of his life, from the time he reformed the motoring movement and struggled for success as a publisher in the early 1900s until the time when, in 1915, he intensified his efforts to modernize military transport in India and obtain aeroplanes for service on the North-West Frontier.

Joan received her first letter from her father towards the end of November 1916. By then she knew that he was en route for India and in his letter he reported that he had reached Suez safely. No mention was made of the U-boat attack near Malta. A month later he wrote to say that he was back on duty on the North-West Frontier. John returned to England for several months in 1917 — the year of the great controversy over his declaration that 'the Germans have a perfect right to bomb London' — and when he next returned to India, this time via Canada and the Far East, he and Joan resumed their correspondence. Usually he would begin his letters with the greeting 'My dear little lady' or 'Darling little woman' and sign himself 'Your most affectionate Uncle M.' In 1917 and 1918, realizing that Joan was now growing up and taking an interest in world affairs, he slipped in some comments on the progress of the war, including this one on 15 December 1917:

> I don't like the look of things on the Western Front at all. I always thought that Haig and our own staff at home were too optimistic. We haven't got enough aircraft to worry the life out of the Hun.

As Joan approached school-leaving age John interspersed some paternal advice about her future among news of his travels and comments on military matters. 'Learn a little shorthand and typing', he said. On another occasion he advised her to learn French, German and Italian and said he hoped she would travel the world with him when she was older.

For about a year after their meeting at Windsor, Joan accepted the story that John was her uncle but eventually she became aware that he was her father. Years later, she could not recall any particular person telling her this, or any particular occasion when the truth emerged; the realization came gradually, without surprising or alarming her in any way and it happened at around the time when, at the age of 14, Joan was taken from the Iresons and given a new home with Dr and Mrs Alfred Keppel Barrett and their several daughters at No.5 Bedford Gardens, Kensington — some way up the social scale from Hammersmith. John Montagu made these arrangements with Dr Barrett — probably a brother or cousin of Walter Barrett — before embarking for Canada in November 1917. The prospect of another long sea voyage prompted him to introduce a note of concern in his farewell letter to Joan:

> I am not over happy at the prospect of the first 500 miles. If anything happens to me I have left instructions with your uncle, Walter Barrett, what to do for you. You know I love you very dearly and hope we shall both be the very best of intimate friends always.

As his ship approached St John's, New Brunswick, on 30 November he wrote:

> I am delighted you are with such nice people as the Barretts. Mrs Barrett seemed to me specially nice and will be quite a mother to you.

Joan's transition from humble Hammersmith to sophisticated Kensington eventually had a happy outcome but at first she missed the Iresons; they had cared for her as their own daughter and she thought they had been treated shabbily. John's motives were, of course, to provide Joan with a more suitable background from which to embark on the career of her choice. Her sadness at being parted from the couple who had been her parents in everything but name for as long as she could remember must have been reflected in her letters to her father, for on one occasion he replied with the comment: 'The Barretts are much more suitable as guardians and friends than the Iresons'. In the same letter, written a few days before Joan's 17th birthday, John said:

> Sometimes there are things a young girl can tell a loving and devoted man friend — old enough to be her father — which she can't so easily tell even to her girl friends or her foster mother. You know how fond I have grown of you and what an interest I take in your young life and your future. Tell me anything you like, dear girl, and at any time. Let me be your father confessor and real pal.

This was the closest John had yet come to telling Joan that he was her father and it must have confirmed her dawning belief that this was so.

When John became engaged to Pearl Barrington-Crake, Joan was among the first to be told. 'I know you will wish me joy, my dear Joan', he wrote. 'I haven't had a real home for many years. You know I have been a very lonely person for some time.' A few days after the wedding he wrote: 'My dear old thing. Yes, I am very happy at last and now know what a wife can do to make her husband happy and his home a real home.'

John Montagu's marriage and the responsibilities of raising another young family meant that he had less time to meet Joan than would have been the case had he remained a widower. However they continued to write often and meet occasionally and Joan was one of the first to receive news of each addition to the Montagu family. In December 1922 she received this letter from her father:

> My life now prevents me seeing as much of you as I should like but I know you don't forget me altogether and I often think how pleased your dear mother would have been had she lived to see you so happy and doing so well. It is seven years this coming December 30th when she was drowned in the *Persia* tragedy and I had the ordeal of surviving her.

The anniversary of Eleanor Thornton's death invariably provoked comments of this kind. In another letter — undated, but probably written on 31 December 1924 — John commented:

> It was this evening at 9 pm that I was picked up by the *Ningchow* after 32

hours in the water after the sinking of the *Persia* on 30 December 1915. Your dear mother was drowned when the ship went down and I always remember her specially at this time.

Joan's chosen career was that of a physical training teacher and in June 1924 John wrote to congratulate her on obtaining her first post — that of gym mistress at Streatham College for Girls. On 17 February 1925 he was able to pass on news from Reginald Ingram that she was to inherit the Iresons' house. Teasingly, he told her that she was to become 'the proprietor of land and houses, and a millionaire'. In the same letter he told Joan about the birth of his daughter Caroline ('though naturally I wished for a boy'). A few days later he wrote again, in response to a letter in which Joan had told him that she was thinking of buying a weekend cottage.

'I very much approve of your idea', he said, adding that she might instead consider buying an acre of land near a railway station accessible from Victoria, or anywhere else near London. The phenomenal growth of 'semi-detached London' — the leafy suburbs beyond the capital's Victorian perimeter — was about to begin and such an investment would have been a profitable one. 'When you have made further plans I might help you to a certain extent with the capital required and you can pay me back by instalments', John suggested.

In her next letter Joan congratulated her father on his 59th birthday, and he replied: 'It is really a great joy to me to feel you are happy and doing well. It was rather a struggle in the past at times to do what I wanted to do for you and your future, dear girl. If you marry happily some day, which I hope you will, I shall then be content about your future.'

John's letter of 17 February 1925 was not the first occasion on which he had confided his disappointment at not having a son. When Pearl Montagu had a miscarriage in 1923, Joan wrote to John to offer her condolences and was told: 'It has been a sad blow for I wanted a companion for little Anne, even if a girl. You know that Pearl is like life itself to me, only more so, and the danger to her — now mercifully past — was considerable. And it all seems so needless. While the curate's wife has 10 or 12 healthy children and lots of boys, fate seems against me having any.' It was another three years before he was able to write: 'I have now got a son and heir, born 5.30 this morning. Pearl and the babe are doing well and of course it is a wonderful event for me'.

As his letters reveal the years 1920-1929 were the happiest of John's life and his only regret during that period was that he saw Joan only infrequently. 'Though I see little of you, you know that deep down in my heart I have great love for you and shall always do what I can to help you on in life', he said in December 1926, a few weeks before he and Pearl set off for Iraq and Persia. His penultimate and perhaps most touching letter was written on 5 November

1928, the day before he went into hospital for the operation that, although postponed, eventually preceded his death:

> I have tried to do all I can for you for your own dear self and for your mother's sake, whom I loved devotedly and who for 15 years was so much to me in every way. Later on, when I begin to convalesce, you might come down with Jane one day and see me, or with Reggie from whom you can get the latest news. We must hope for the best. I am quite healthy and should get through it all right.
>
> I never forget you, dear, and often think of you and your own problems. I shall always try to help you in all ways and your very dear letter of today has made me realize once more how really closely bound we are, though we see little of each other. God bless you, dear girl.

This was the first occasion on which John had invited Joan to see him at Palace House: their meetings had always taken place at his office at 62 Pall Mall, in tea shops and restaurants and perhaps in the homes of mutual friends. Just as John had had many reasons to keep his *affaire* with Eleanor Thornton a secret, so did he have to conceal the fact that they had had a child. He told Pearl Barrington-Crake about the affair soon after they became engaged but it was not until after their marriage that he told her that Eleanor had had a child and that he was the father. There is no doubt that Pearl would have welcomed Joan into the Montagu family, if that had been John's wish, but he had his own reasons for not issuing such an invitation; above all, he felt that it would have been difficult for him to introduce Joan to Elizabeth Montagu. He may have feared, perhaps without cause, that the two girls might become jealous of one another. So, for various reasons, Joan remained outside the family circle.

Nevertheless, she was no stranger to Beaulieu. The 'Jane' referred to in John's letter was Jane Clowes, who had worked with Eleanor Thornton in Montagu's office and succeeded her as his private secretary in 1916. Jane had a cottage, called By the Mill (now The Mill Race) at Beaulieu and Joan stayed there from time to time. From the cottage's front windows she would watch John and Pearl Montagu's tiny daughters ride up the village street on the family's pony-drawn trap, and from the cottage's secluded garden she would gaze across the mill pond and watch the girls playing on the lawns of Palace House.

Inside the cottage, which is now Elizabeth Montagu's home, there was a painting of a seascape. Eleanor Thornton had once paused to admire it and had been overheard to murmur: 'The sea will be my grave'.

The last letter from John Montagu that Joan Thornton read was the first he had written to her. By the time she opened it 13 years later, much of what John had to say had already been told to her by Rose Thornton, Walter

Barrett, Reginald Ingram and John himself. After reading the letter Joan decided that the fact that John was her father would remain a secret between her and those who already knew. Joan felt that if she introduced herself to the Montagu family, the identity of her father might become generally known and his memory would be tarnished. Joan was unaware that Pearl Montagu had known about her for several years — without necessarily knowing her name or where she lived — and would have made her welcome at Palace House. But Pearl was now responsible for the management of the Beaulieu Manor Estate and was also busy raising four energetic children, whose ages ranged from one year to eight. She had little time or inclination to add to her responsibilities. Then, in May 1936, she married Capt. Edward Pleydell-Bouverie — who like John Montagu had survived a U-boat attack during the First World War. Pearl started a new life, as did Joan three months later, when she married Leslie Moorby, with whom she found the happiness and security that John hoped she would one day enjoy.

Joan Thornton often read the long letter her father had written at the time he feared for his safety during his return voyage to India. The letter now held few mysteries, although his statement that Eleanor Thornton gave up her life for him at the end has never been explained. The 'fine old Spanish blood in her veins' was another puzzle but Eleanor was an imaginative lady; though born plain Nelly Thornton at 18 Cottage Grove, Stockwell, to English parents, she called herself Eleanor Velasco Thornton in adult life and may also have embellished her family background with tales of a Spanish ancestry. Joan acquired many mementoes of the mother she never knew. Among these were photographs of Eleanor at work in John Montagu's office, aboard his yacht and his Rolls-Royce, and in photographers' studios, where she posed in the fashionable gowns and hats of the Edwardian era. Most of these items were given to Joan by Rose Thornton but from John's personal collection of photographs and paintings she received a pastel by Charles Sykes, depicting Martha washing the feet of Christ. Sykes' model for this, she was sure, was Eleanor Thornton. Joan also treasured castings of two sculptures by Sykes — one a bronze head, the other a nude female figurine. Eleanor was certainly the model for the head and perhaps for the figurine too, since this is evidently contemporary with a statuette of Phryne exhibited by Sykes at the Royal Academy in 1909. Eleanor Thornton was the model for Phryne.

An insight into Eleanor's private life was provided by a cartoon that came into Joan's possession. Entitled 'St Eleanor's perpetual prayer', this was drawn by an unknown artist but captioned by Sykes as follows: 'Oh Ye Gods, shower upon this willing mortal everlasting work, that the curse of beauty may be forgotten'.

Joan Thornton was able to keep her secret for 40 years and would have done so for the rest of her life but for a curious sequence of events which, had they not occurred, would have left this story of John Montagu's life incomplete. In 1951, when Edward Montagu inherited Beaulieu and his father's other properties and assets, he read John Montagu's Will in detail, and came across a clause referring to the trust fund that John had set up in 1916 to provide Joan Thornton with an income of £150 a year or a capital sum of £3750. In the Will the beneficiaries of the fund were called 'the relatives of Miss E.V. Thornton' but the clause reminded Edward Montagu that, years earlier, his mother had told him and Elizabeth Montagu that John and Eleanor had had a child, whose name and whereabouts were unknown to her.

It was obvious to Edward Montagu that in actual fact the fund had been created for this child, but he took no further interest in the matter because, by then, the establishment of the motor museum and other ventures demanded all his time. Joan Thornton, now married and living near Tavistock in South Devon with her husband and two sons, remained untraced and, so far as the Montagus were concerned, untraceable.

Fate, destiny, chance, coincidence — call it what you will — began to take a hand 11 years later, when Elizabeth Montagu married Col. Arthur Varley. They went to live at Bere Alston, in South Devon, and Mrs Varley became a regular patron of several shops in Tavistock. Over the years Joan Thornton had kept abreast of events in the lives of members of the Montagu family; she was interested to read of Elizabeth Montagu's marriage and even more interested to learn that she and Col. Varley were living near Tavistock. Nevertheless, Joan decided not to introduce herself to them.

Tavistock is a friendly town whose shoppers invariably strike up casual conversations as they make their purchases or seek rest and refreshment in the local tea-shops. Over a period of about seven years Joan and Elizabeth Montagu passed the time of day on many occasions, although only Joan knew they were half-sisters. So far as Elizabeth was concerned Joan was just another friendly local housewife, always ready to exchange a few words about the weather, or other matters of little consequence, whilst they queued together for fish, groceries or vegetables. And but for 'Mr H.' that would always have been the extent of their relationship.

That Elizabeth Montagu had come to live near Joan Thornton was coincidence enough. What was even more remarkable was that within a few miles there lived a lady by the name of Nan who, during or soon after the First World War, had been a student at the same London art college as the Barretts' two eldest daughters. They often invited her home to tea and she inevitably became friendly with Joan and her husband-to-be, Leslie, another frequent visitor to the Barretts' house. Soon, through an indiscretion on the part of one of the Barrett girls, Nan learned that Joan's father was John Montagu.

This revelation would have been of little consequence but for the fact that both Joan and Nan settled in South Devon after their marriages — Joan's husband, a naval surgeon, was posted to Plymouth, whilst Nan married a Plymouth solicitor. The friendship formed years earlier in Kensington was resumed; later, Nan moved to Bere Alston and events started taking an uncanny turn.

When Elizabeth Montagu settled in Bere Alston, Nan was fascinated by the strong physical resemblance between her new neighbour and Joan. She was even more intrigued when she realized that although Joan knew who Elizabeth was, Elizabeth knew Joan only as a casual acquaintance and had no idea they were half-sisters. Nan's repeated offers to Joan to introduce her to Elizabeth were always politely rejected. Elizabeth Montagu remained totally unaware of the strange way in which the paths followed by three lives had crossed at Bere Alston — until, that is, Mr H., a local jobbing gardener, acquired the crucial role in what was becoming an increasingly bizarre situation.

Mr H. had made a rather good job of laying some crazy paving for Nan; Leslie was one of the first to admire it and sometime in 1969 he asked Mr H. to undertake a similar task for him. Afterwards, Mr H. resumed his routine work around Bere Alston and next time he saw Nan he asked her whether she had noticed how alike Joan and Elizabeth were.

'That's not surprising', replied Nan, 'they're sisters'.

Because of Joan's consistent refusal to allow her identity to be revealed to Elizabeth, Nan was dismayed by her thoughtless response to Mr H.'s observation — a slip of the tongue that was all the more embarrassing because, as Nan knew, Mr H. was also doing some gardening work for Elizabeth at this time and was bound to repeat what Nan had said.

Nan therefore telephoned Elizabeth and told her the whole story — a wise move because, a few days later, during an argument with Elizabeth over some trivial matter, Mr H. blurted out: 'If you knew what I know about your family, you would fall off your chair. I know a thing or two!' Elizabeth insisted upon, and received, a full explanation from Mr H. but by then she had received Nan's embarrassed and apologetic telephone call, and a meeting with Joan had become inevitable.

What could have been an embarrassing situation led to one of the happiest experiences in the lives of Joan Thornton and the Montagu family. Elizabeth and Edward Montagu called on Joan and after 40 years John Montagu's 'lost' daughter became, in Elizabeth Montagu's words, one of the Montagu family. From Joan's memories and the letters she had kept for more than 40 years, the Montagus at last learned the full story of John Montagu's love for Eleanor Thornton and for the child from whom, for reasons that will never be known, she had chosen to remain estranged.

The mourners who crowded into the tiny church of St Mary at Sampford

Spiney, on the edge of Dartmoor, were astonished to notice that one of the front pews was occupied by eight members of the Montagu family, including Lord Montagu; Belinda, Lady Montagu; Pearl Pleydell-Bouverie; Elizabeth Montagu and Anne Chichester. For the last ten years of her life Joan Thornton, her husband, her sons and her grandchildren had enjoyed the friendship and hospitality of the Montagus during numerous visits to Beaulieu, although by now her discretion had become instinctive and most of her friends and neighbours were still unaware that she was related to the Montagu family.

But at 12.30 pm on Saturday 23 June 1979, Joan Thornton had died suddenly at the age of 76 and now the Montagus had come to her parish church to pay their last respects.

After the funeral service Joan Thornton's body was cremated at Plymouth and her ashes were divided, some to be interred in the churchyard at Sampford Spiney, the rest to be taken to Beaulieu for interment in her father's grave. Later, a small group of friends and relations gathered in the Abbey cloisters to witness the unveiling of a memorial plaque and then filed into the parish church for a memorial service.

In the National Motor Museum just a few hundred yards from the Abbey the last visitors of the day were admiring, like thousands before them, the Rolls-Royce Phantom in which John Montagu had enjoyed his last motoring tours. Above its radiator there glinted the Spirit of Ecstasy statuette which Montagu had treasured all his life because it reminded him of his friendship with Charles Rolls and Claude Johnson, his admiration for Rolls-Royce motor cars and his love for Eleanor Thornton.

In Palace House, too, the last visitors would soon depart; but next day more would come to see John Montagu's family heirlooms; his motoring and

Eleanor Thornton's memorial in Beaulieu parish church.

The Montagu family graveyard in the cloisters of Beaulieu Abbey. John's grave is on the extreme left, beside that of his wife Cis, who died in 1919. His parents' grave is on the right. The grave of his brother, James Francis, is in the foreground.

military souvenirs and medals; the German flag that flew over Beaulieu during the Prince Henry Tour in 1911; the controversial illuminated address and other mementoes of his experiences as a railway engine driver; the Gieve waistcoat that saved his life when he went down with SS *Persia*; and the pocket watch he was carrying at the time — its hands pointing to the hour and the minute when the waves engulfed him and all seemed lost.

From Palace House it is only a short walk to the parish church, once the Abbey's refectory. Many of the friends who enriched his life are buried in a private cemetery in a corner of the churchyard, and inside the church can be seen the bronze tablet he installed after his experiences on the *Persia*. Above the tablet there is a portrait of John Montagu in bronze, sculptured against a background representing his work as a pioneer of travel. Beneath this memorial an inscription in gilt and blue letters reads:

In happy remembrance of Brigadier-General John Walter Edward Douglas-Scott-Montagu, who passed to a fuller life on 30 March 1929.

Sources and Acknowledgments

To avoid distracting the reader with annotations in the text and notes on sources I have deposited all my research documents, indexed chronologically, in the National Motor Museum library at Beaulieu. *Bona fide* students and writers wishing to inspect them should apply to Lord Montagu of Beaulieu.

My main sources for documentary information on John Montagu's personal life and his career as a politician, publisher and journalist were the Montagu Papers in the family archives at Palace House, Beaulieu. Certain papers from this collection were lost in a fire that destroyed the home of Laura, Lady Troubridge, soon after she and Archibald Marshall completed a biography of John Montagu in 1930. Their book *John, Lord Montagu of Beaulieu: a Memoir* (Macmillan) was therefore my only source when writing about certain episodes in his life. In other cases I have wherever possible consulted original sources.

The Hon. Mrs E. Pleydell-Bouverie (John Montagu's second wife) and the Hon. Mrs E. Varley (his youngest daughter by his first marriage) granted me several interviews. Mrs Pleydell-Bouverie provided many extracts from her diaries for the years 1919-1929 and Mrs Varley was my guide when I spent a day visiting John Montagu's houses and old haunts on the Beaulieu Manor Estate.

I would like to thank Lord Montagu for his help and encouragement and for allowing me to have unrestricted access to his father's personal papers, so that I could obtain a complete view of John Montagu's life and arrive at what I hope is an objective assessment of his character and personality.

I am indebted to Lord Montagu's personal staff, especially his Secretary, Mrs J. Lindemere, and Mr A. J. Holland, for answering numerous questions and supplying innumerable copies of documents both during and after my many visits to the Muniment Room at Palace House.

For details of John Montagu's motoring achievements and adventures my principal sources were various publications and papers in the National Motor Museum library, where Mr G. N. Georgano, Mr M. E. Ware, Mr P. Brockes and their staff and colleagues gave me active and enthusiastic help at

279

all times. I am also grateful to Mr K. G. Robinson, Managing Director of Montagu Ventures Limited, for administrative assistance.

Most of the photographs came from the National Motor Museum or the Montagu family albums, with the following exceptions: John with fellow oarsmen at Oxford, 1887 (photo by courtesy of the Warden and Fellows of New College); John opening the Rolls-Royce factory (John Fasal); staff of *The Car Illustrated*, June 1914 (Mr D. Hill); John's battalion at Alexandria (Mr R. A. Broomfield); SS *Persia* (P & O Group); the Montagu family graves (author). My thanks to Mr Philip Scott and his staff in the photographic department at Beaulieu for so cheerfully meeting my many demands for copy negatives and prints.

John Montagu's First World War papers, relating to his Army service in India and his political activities between 1914 and 1919, have been deposited by Lord Montagu at the Liddell Hart Centre for Military Archives, King's College, London, where Miss P. Methven (Military Archivist) and her colleagues were patience personified whilst I unravelled my subject's wartime travels and travails.

Whilst writing this biography I have enjoyed the special camaraderie that prevails among authors and journalists and I have benefited enormously from assistance and advice offered by several distinguished writers, whose works I consulted in detail and who subsequently suggested lines of further research. In this context I would especially like to thank Kevin Desmond (*The World Water Speed Record*, Batsford, 1976), John Fasal (*The Rolls-Royce Twenty*, Fasal, 1979), Paul Ferris (*The House of Northcliffe*, Weidenfeld and Nicolson, 1971), Duncan Haws (*Merchant Ships in Profile*, Patrick Stephens, 1978), C. W. Morton (*A History of Rolls-Royce Motor Cars*, Foulis, 1964) and Eric Rosenthal (*Encyclopedia of Southern Africa*, Juta and Company, 1978).

Rolls-Royce motor cars were an essential part of John Montagu's lifestyle and researching his connections with Rolls-Royce proved to be particularly rewarding. My thanks to Mr D. Preston and Mr D. Miller Williams of Rolls-Royce Motors Limited and to Mr M. H. Evans of Rolls-Royce Limited for helping me distinguish between Rolls-Royce fact and folklore.

The staffs of the following libraries and institutions helped me in various ways: the British Library (Reference Division), the Imperial War Museum, Marylebone Public Library, the National Maritime Museum, New York Public Library, the Public Record Office. The Kent County Library at Springfield, Maidstone, obtained, through LASER and other channels, those books that I was unable to find in the library's excellent main and reserve collections. The press cutting librarians at the *Daily Express* and the *Daily Mail* allowed me to inspect and copy newspaper reports of John Montagu's activities. Mr R. Morgan and Mr P.G. Davis of the House of Lords Library supplied copies of John Montagu's parliamentary speeches and other relevant documents.

Without exception, everyone I approached whilst pursuing lines of research responded helpfully and did all they could to answer my sometimes cryptic enquiries. My thanks to the following: Mr P.J. Adams, Allsop & Company, Mrs S. Benfield, Dr G.V. Bennett (New College, Oxford), A. & C. Black Limited, Mr D.S. Booth (British South Africa Company), Mr P.B. Boyden (National Army Museum), Mr R. Brooks, Mr R.A. Broomfield, Mr N.G.T. Brotchie (Foreign and Commonwealth Office), Col. E. Cadogan, CBE, Mr H. Catt (Royal Automobile Club), Mr C.R. Collins, Major L.W. Cox, Miss C. Dalton (New College, Oxford), Lt. Col. C.D. Darroch (The Royal Hampshire Regiment), Cdr. A.E. Fanning, RN (Admiralty Compass Laboratory), Dr R.W. Ferrier (British Petroleum), Mr F. Flower (Royal Air Force Museum), Mr R.J.W. Gieve (Gieves and Hawkes of Savile Row), Mr C. Handford (Property Holding and Investment Trust Limited), Sir Geoffrey Harmsworth, Bt., Mr K.C. Harrison (City of Westminster), Mr G.W. Haysom (Ministry of Defence), Mrs D. Hayter, Mr D. Higgs, Air Vice-Marshal N.E. Hoad, CVO, CBE, AFC (The Air League), Mr C.A. Holland (Scott Polar Research Institute), Miss M. Meaden (India Office Library), Mr D.A. Mildenhall (The Western Gazette Co. Limited), Mr M. Moir (India Office Library), Mr V. Montagu, Sgn. Cdr. A.L. Moorby, RN, Mr W.A. Morris (Institution of Civil Engineers), Mr L.F. Moulton (Union Jack Club), Mr A. Neate (Greater London Council), Mr T. Page (Prudential Assurance Co.), Mr A.W.H. Pearsall (National Maritime Museum), Mrs J. Phillips, Lt. Cdr. J.D. Pugh, RN (Ministry of Defence Hydrography Department), Mr P.Q. Quarrie (Eton College), Mr S. Rabson (P & O), Mr W. Robbins, Mr G. Roberts, Mrs W.A. Robinson, Mr J. Schroder, Mr A. Thorpe (*Shipping World and Shipbuilder*), the Rt. Hon. Lord Tweedsmuir, CBE, Miss M. Wallace (*Motor Boat and Yachting*), Mr F. Whitelaw, Mr D. Whitty, MA (City of Westminster), Mr P.H.J. Whyman and Mr W. Boddy (*Motor Sport*).

My thanks also to the many tenants and former tenants of the Beaulieu Manor Estate who came to Palace House on 27 May 1980 to give me their personal memories of John Montagu.

Sadly, several people who helped me during my research died whilst I was completing the book: Mr A.B. Bartlett, Lord Montagu's Archivist, who helped me find my way through John Montagu's personal papers in the Muniment Room at Palace House; Miss P.A. Harding of New College, Oxford, who located my subject's academic records; Mr M. Sedgwick, who read my first draft and made many helpful corrections and comments; Lady Wardington, whose memories of the Montagu family extended back to the early years of this century; and Captain H. E. R. Widnell, whose varied career as Agent and Steward of Beaulieu Manor Estate, Warden and Archivist at Palace House, and Curator of Lord Montagu's motor museum spanned 55 years. I interviewed Captain Widnell several times and constantly referred to his memoirs, published privately by Lord Montagu in 1973-77.

My work has also benefited from Mrs V. Pollock's editing and from valuable advice and assistance proferred by my publisher's editorial consultant, Mr B. K. Shaw.

I have drawn on many sources, conducted many interviews and corresponded with many companies, institutions and people whilst writing this book, but take all responsibility for any errors of fact or interpretation.

Finally, my thanks to my wife Patricia for allowing the life of John Montagu to become part of our lives for four years; for helping me compile and evaluate my research notes; for reading and constructively criticising my rough drafts; and for typing and retyping numerous drafts and compiling the index.

Paul Tritton
Maidstone, Kent
1985

Bibliography

In addition to the books previously mentioned, the following also provided useful background information:

Andrews, Allen	*The Follies of King Edward VII*, Lexington 1975
Ash, Russell	*The Wright Brothers*, Wayland, 1974
Atkinson, C.T.	*The Royal Hampshire Regiment*, Vol. I, The Hampshire Regiment, 1950
Bentley, Nicolas	*The Victorian Scene 1837-1901*, Spring Books, 1971
Bentley, W.J.	*Motoring Cavalcade*, Odhams, 1953
Bird, Anthony	*Roads and Vehicles*, Longmans, 1969
Bird, Anthony and Hallows, Ian	*The Rolls-Royce Motor Car*, Batsford, 1975
Bishop, James	*Illustrated London News Social History of Edwardian Britain*, Angus & Robertson, 1977
Boddy, W.	*The Story of Brooklands*, Grenville, 1948
Bushby, J.R.	*Air Defence of Great Britain*, Ian Allan, 1973
Buxton, John and Williams, Henry	*New College Oxford 1379-1979*, New College, 1979
Cecil, Robert	*Life in Edwardian England*, Batsford, 1969
Crow, Duncan	*The Edwardian Woman*, Allen & Unwin, 1978
Cunningham, Hugh	*The Volunteer Force*, Croom Helm, 1975
Divine, David	*These Splendid Ships: the Story of the P & O Line*, Muller, 1960
Edwards, A.D. and Bearman, G.W.L. (ed)	*Britain, Europe and the World 1848-1918*, Cambridge University Press, 1971

Eves, Edward — *Rolls-Royce: 75 Years of Motoring Excellence*, Orbis, 1979

Flint, John E. — *Cecil Rhodes*, Hutchinson, 1976

Gray, Edwyn — *The Killing Time*, Seeley Service & Cooper, 1972

Grey, C.G. — *A History of the Air Ministry*, Allen & Unwin, 1940

Harding, Anthony (ed) — *Guinness Book of Car Facts and Feats*, Guinness Superlatives, 1980

Herwig, H.H. — *Luxury Fleet: The Imperial German Navy 1888-1918*, Allen & Unwin, 1980

Hibbert, Christopher — *Edward VII: a Portrait*, Allen Lane, 1976

Higham, Robin — *Britain's Imperial Air Routes 1918-1939*, Foulis, 1960

Hogg, Ian V. — *Anti-Aircraft: a History of Air Defence*, Macdonald & Jane's, 1979

Hook, F.A. — *Merchant Adventurers 1914-1918*, A & C Black, 1920

Howell, John — *Seventy Years of Motor Sport*, Littlebury, 1971

Jackson, Judith — *Man and the Automobile*, McGraw-Hill, 1979

Jones, H.A. — *The War in the Air*, Vol. III, OUP, 1931

Jones, Neville — *The Origins of Strategic Bombing*, Kimber, 1973

Jordan, Gerald (ed) — *Naval Warfare in the Twentieth Century 1900-1945*, Croom Helm, 1977

Joubert, Sir Philip de la Ferte — *The Third Force*, Thames & Hudson, 1973

Lane, Peter — *The Conservative Party*, Batsford, 1974

Lee, Alan J. — *The Origins of the Popular Press in England 1855-1914*, Croom Helm, 1976

Lloyd, Ian — *Rolls-Royce: The Growth of a Firm*, Macmillan, 1978

Longhurst, Henry — *Adventure in Oil: The Story of British Petroleum*, Sidgwick and Jackson, 1959

Mackenzie, Norman and Jeanne — *The Time Traveller: The Life of H.G. Wells*, Weidenfeld and Nicolson, 1973

Marlowe, John   *Cecil Rhodes: The Anatomy of Empire*,
                                        Paul Elek, 1972
Mondey, D., Taylor,   *Guinness Book of Air Facts and Feats*,
M.J.H. and J.W.R.   Guinness Superlatives, 1973
Montagu, Lord and McComb,   *Behind the Wheel*, Paddington Press,
F. Wilson   1971
Montagu, Lord   *The Motoring Montagus*, Cassell, 1959
Montagu, Lord   *The Gordon Bennett Races*, Cassell, 1963
Montagu, Lord   *Rolls of Rolls-Royce*, Cassell, 1966
Moore, J.E. (ed)   *Jane's Pocket Book of Submarine Develop-
                                        ment*, Macdonald, 1975
Munson, Kenneth   *A Pictorial History of BOAC and Imperial
                                        Airways*, Ian Allan, 1970
Oldham, Wilton J.   *The Hyphen in Rolls-Royce*, Foulis,
                                        1967
Oldham, Wilton J.   *The Rolls-Royce 40/50*, Foulis, 1974
Packenham, Elizabeth,   *Jameson's Raid*, Weidenfeld and
Countess of Longford   Nicolson, 1960
Pemberton, Max   *The Life of Henry Royce*, Selwyn &
                                        Blount, n.d.
Petrie, Sir Charles   *Scenes of Edwardian Life*, Eyre &
                                        Spottiswoode, 1965
Plowden, William   *The Motor Car and Politics 1896-1970*,
                                        Bodley Head, 1971
Pound, Reginald and   *Northcliffe*, Cassell, 1959
Harmsworth, Geoffrey
Preston, Antony   *Submarines: The History and Evolution of
                                        Underwater Fighting Vessels*, Octopus,
                                        1975
Preston, Antony   *U-Boats*, Arms & Armour Press, 1978
Priestley, J.B.   *The Edwardians*, Heinemann, 1970
Ranger, T.O.   *Revolt in Southern Rhodesia, 1896-7*,
                                        Heinemann, 1979
Rawlinson, Col. A.   *The Defence of London 1915-1918*,
                                        Melrose, 1923
Roberts, Peter   *The Motoring Edwardians*, Ian Allan,
                                        1978
Robertson, Patrick   *The Shell Book of Firsts*, Ebury Press &
                                        Michael Joseph, 1974
Roskill, Capt. S.W.(ed)   *Publications of the Naval Records Society*
                                        Vol. 113: *The Naval Air Service*
                                        Vol. I 1908-1918

Sheppard, F.H.W.   *London 1808/1870: The Infernal Wen*,
                            Secker & Warburg, 1971
Smith, Brian E.   *Royal Daimlers*, Transport Bookman
                            Publications, 1976
Sproule, Anna   *Port Out, Starboard Home*, Blandford,
                            1978
Thompson, Leonard and   *Oxford History of South Africa*, OUP,
Wilson, Monica (ed)   1971
Villard, H.S.   *The Great Road Races 1894-1914*,
                            Barker, 1972
Webb, Sidney and Beatrice   *The Story of the King's Highway*, Cass,
                            1973

Index

Illustrations are indicated by page numbers in italics. The letter 'n' after a page number indicates a reference to a footnote on that page.

287